MYSTIC HOUR
OR
SPIRITUAL EXPERIENCES

(1859)

The author, a spiritual medium wrote, "Among the thousands who have visited my table, who have affirmed their knowledge of the absurdity of Spiritual Manifestations, I cannot call to mind a score who have not left the apartment more favorably impressed with the truths of Spiritualism than when they entered."

G.A. Redman

ISBN 0-7661-0035-9

MYSTIC HOURS;

OR,

SPIRITUAL EXPERIENCES.

BY

G. A. REDMAN, M.D.

But wake! be glad, ye nations! from the tomb
Is won the victory, and is fled the gloom!
The vale of death, in conquest hath been trod,
Break forth in joy!

New-York:
CHARLES PARTRIDGE, PUBLISHER,
428 Broadway.
BOSTON:—BELA MARSH, 14 BROMFIELD STREET.
1859.

Eng^d by J. C. Buttre.

G. W. Edman M. D.

TO

ADDISON C. FLETCHER,

OF CINCINNATI, OHIO,

TO WHOM I AM JOINED BY TIES OF BROTHERLY LOVE,

This Volume

IS RESPECTFULLY DEDICATED.

PREFACE.

In presenting a work of this kind to the public, I am not unaware of the criticism to which it must be subjected: not only as embodying communications from enfranchised spirits, whose memory is still cherished on earth; but from the facts contained in its pages, which will receive a degree of denunciation, ridicule, and unbelief from a certain class of the public;—neither do I present this work with any claim to literary merit, or finish of style, but as a simple narrative of my experiences as a medium for Spiritual Manifestations. In view, however, of the responsibility I am incurring, I firmly and unflinchingly rely on the support of those, who, from long and intimate acquaintance, know me well, and who have through me receive an impetus (perhaps the first,) toward that new life, to which all Spiritualists look forward.

Since first presenting myself before the public as a Spiritual Medium, I have endeavored to keep a correct diary of the various incidents that have transpired in the presence of investigators, and from the many tests and communications, of which the politeness of my visitors have permitted me to take note, a few are given in the pages before the reader :—in them are comprised various developments, all more or less conclusive of the fact, that we are constantly in the presence of angels, and daily hold communion with them.

Who, that has parted with a father, mother, sister, wife, husband, or child, but inwardly hopes the loved one is near ? Who, that has seen the dear form of some cherished being conveyed forever from his sight, but has yearned to recall it, and in view of the impossibility, has not felt an earnest wish to shake off mortality's habiliments, and accompany the heart's idol to that *hitherto* unknown void ?

Frequently, I may say in almost every instance, the withdrawal of some near and valued friend from the earth sphere, is the first stimulant which impels the inquirer to ask, "If there be truth in the communion with our dear departed ?" Next ensues investigation, resulting in mitigation of sorrow, and a soothing, happy belief. 'Tis hoped that these pages may aid in some degree to lead to more enlightened views of spiritual science.

Each and every one of the facts herein embodied is laid truly and without exaggeration before the reader ; and though many of them may now require an undue amount of credulity to believe, still, I am well satisfied in my own mind, that the future with its unfolding developments will render these even primary lessons in the philosophy connected with the two conditions of life ; as far as regards the signatures appended, they can all be verified.

Among the thousands who have visited my table, (and many have taken a seat thereat, who, on entering the room, have affirmed their knowledge of the absurdity of Spiritual Manifestations,) I cannot call to mind a score who have not left the apartment more favorably impressed with the truths of Spiritualism than when they entered ; and I have carefully observed the convictions pro and con of each investigating party.

A member of a club would be scoffed at for his belief in these things, and would patiently submit to the jokes of his associates, till stung as it were, by their ignorance, he has solicited my aid, and in a number of similar instances, the member has informed me, "He never heard any more of the tirades, to which before he had been subjected ; but that all were convinced there was some unaccountable influence at work." From this arises the conclusion, that it is not in that class, who have investigated Spiritualism, where its denouncers are found ; but among those, who are either completely ignorant of its facts, and have no desire to inform themselves ; or such, as having obtained manifestations through an undeveloped medium, draw hasty conclusions from the results of a few hours.

As regards media, a variety of opinions, both public and private, have been advanced, and a multiplicity of statements have been made. One asserts, that a person to possess mediumistic powers, must be of a highly sanguine temperament ; another, nervous ; a third, phlegmatic, &c. Again, Mr. A. declares, that the best mediums are *females ;* while Mr. B. adjudges the superiority to *males ;* friend C. affirms, all are mediums ; D., however, is positive, he can detect the mediumistic capacity by the expression of the eyes, activity of the pulse, temperature of the extremities, *bruit du cœur*, etc., etc. ; these with many equally frail symptoms, are assigned to the public as infallible for diagnosis. All these, however, by mediums themselves, are known to be positively absurd, for in hardly two instances of developed media will be found the same temperament or disposition. At one time the extremities will be exceedingly warm, the circulation active and full ; at another a general retardation, and a cool surface will be the result. This may as well occur in others as mediums, and hence no discrimination can be observed ; the other so-called indications are alike without foundation. A *medium is a medium*, and what constitutes the individual such, remains still an unsolved problem.

The physical condition of the medium influences in a

great degree the manifestations; if he feel confident, cheerful, full of vigor, as relates to his bodily health, the results of the séance are measurably superior; if his bodily condition be the contrary, an inferior order of manifestations occur, and as far as a medium solicits these conditions, so far may he hope for success. I have attended circles where it required all my strength of will to counteract certain ill conditions of body; and in proportion as I succeeded, so far would be the success or failure of my attendance; again, perfectly well, bodily and mentally, and a feeling of total indifference, would eventuate in most satisfactory demonstrations. As to the direct interference of the medium, he has no more effect on genuine manifestations than other members of the circle, otherwise than placing himself in a passive, willing and receptive condition, he is as ignorant of the mode of Spiritual Manifestations as those whom he attends.

Well-developed media are seldom deceived by pretending or unprogressed spirits. It is well known, that each person lives and moves in an atmosphere peculiar to himself; thus the social surroundings of a man of talent and honesty are totally different from those of a debauché, and so susceptible are many, of these opposite conditions, they easily recognize one from the other without the use of sight. The genial surroundings of the advanced mind render its presence desirable and pleasing, while the coarse and illiterate are seldom flattered by a welcome reception. If we are thus influenced by persons in the form, may not the well-developed medium for Spiritual communion easily distinguish the characteristics of the intelligence out of it, that controls him? This personal attribute is always very perceptible to me, and I can quite readily discover the peculiarities of any spirit who may use my organism. Through this faculty I am rarely deceived or misled by one spirit representing another, and this saves much annoyance and dissatisfaction.

That all are mediums in a greater or less degree, I have no doubt; and very little reflection is required on the part of almost any one to aid them in referring to some *seeming* spiritual interference during their lives, which perhaps they have designated "providential."

To develop and enlarge the capacity as a medium, requires passivity and time, having frequent interviews with advanced mediums, likewise greatly assists spirits in their efforts to control the physical. Next to the aid received from others may be added regular sittings by one's-self, passivity, withdrawing the mind from earthly cares, and (though intent on the object to be attained) throwing the mental powers into space, if I may so express myself, and inwardly beseeching more light, are the essentials for the desired end.

I have known many, who despaired of becoming mediums, pursue this course, and be surprised at their success. A few weeks or months of daily sittings in this manner, for about half an hour at a time, will effect the longed-for object. 'Tis true, it may tax the patience, produce ennui, but will any one earnestly desiring such a result, deem even years of daily sittings uncompensated for, when so glorious an attainment may be the happy reward ?

CONTENTS.

CHAPTER I.

CHAPTER II.

CHAPTER III.

CHAPTER IV.

CHAPTER V.

CHAPTER VI.

CHAPTER VII.

CHAPTER VIII.

CHAPTER IX.

CHAPTER X.

CHAPTER XI.

CHAPTER XII.

MYSTIC HOURS.

CHAPTER I.

EARLY Reminiscences. Susceptibility of Father to spiritual influences and impressions. Spirit visitation. Lizzie's introduction to the second life. Manifestation and prediction by Father of the death of a number of the family. His devotion to his child. "All hands on deck," and fulfillment of his own prophecy. Somnambulism. Visit to the State of New York. Advent of the Rochester Knockings. Removal from Kingsborough to Pleasant Square. First and unsuccessful attempt at forming circles "No room." Return to Boston. Thanksgiving. My first introduction to the mysteries of Spiritualism. Clerk. My first communication. Belief established. Mother's message. "Who is the medium?" Business matters of secondary importance. My first seance. Ground and lofty tumbling. Return to New York.

"Thou! whose thought hast no blest home above,
Captive of earth! And canst thou dare to love?
To nurse such feelings, as delight to rest
Within that hallowed shrine—a parent's breast,
To fix each hope, concentrate every tie,
On one frail idol—destined but to die.
Yet mock the faith, that points to worlds of light,
Where sever'd souls made perfect, reunite."

I WAS ushered into existence January 27th, 1835, in the city of Boston, State of Massachusetts: scarcely was I eighteen months old, when my mother passing into the spirit world, consigned me to the care of an aunt, who well provided for my temporal wants, until I was blessed with a step-mother. I say *blessed*, for (unlike the generality of step-dames) mine was kind and affectionate, and in all things seemed to entertain for me the same maternal feelings she evinced for her own offspring. Thus happily situated in this important domestic relation, my morning of life glided peaceably away with little to relate that can interest my readers, save that as far back as my childish reminiscences extend, memory points to manifestations, similar to those recognized at the present day as *spiritual.* A few of these early experiences of a life, fraught with some of the most extraordinary coincidences of a spiritual character, that have ever marked the pathway of any believer in the beautiful faith of spirit communion, it may not be inappropriate to introduce at this stage of my narrative.

Before entering on a statement of facts and occurrences, it may perhaps be well to mention that father was greatly disposed throughout his life to a credence in omens, warnings, and dreams; he would frequently affirm that he saw disembodied forms passing and repassing about our residence, and with him "coming events seemed to cast their shadows before," for often would he foretell what to others was buried in obscurity, and rarely did the circumstances by him predicted fail to transpire. From this digression I will now turn to some facts which strongly impressed my juvenile mind.

On one occasion, while a young lady in our family lay seriously ill with small-pox, there came *three loud raps* on her bedroom door. Father immediately opened the door, but *no one* was to be seen in its vicinity. Scarcely had he resumed his seat ere a repetition of the raps recalled him, and with the same result ; he then predicted the death of our young friend, and on the same night her spirit bade adieu to the suffering body, and joined her angel friends in their blest abode.

In November, 1846, Lizzie, my youngest sister, was summoned to exchange her temporal for her spiritual home. This was a bitter trial to us all, but especially so to father, and to his grief for this darling of his heart, we mainly attributed his illness and death, which followed closely on our bereavement. Ere removing the loved form of this cherished child to the last dwelling-place of mortality, and while our family were assembled in the room, where lay all that was left of our mourned and lost one, the *latch* of the hall-door was gently raised *three times.* Father opened it—*no one* was there ; he returned to his seat ; the manifestation was repeated ; he rose hastily, and again opened the door, but to find *no clue* to the *cause* of the *effect.* At this moment a young man in father's employment, fell from his chair in a fainting fit ; this increased our already state of nervous excitement. Robert, however, soon revived, but was quite incapable of accounting for the *strange* sensation that produced his insensibility.

On the young man's recovery, we relapsed into silence, which, however, was shortly broken by an exclamation from father, an exclamation which (child as I was) thrilled through my soul at the time, and will remain engraven on memory's page so long as life's fitful fever lasts. "Mother," said he, "there will be another death in this family before the end of two weeks ; God grant it may be I." Our little one was placed in the vault beneath Christ Church, and the ensuing week father was taken ill with typhus fever. During his illness, I was one evening sitting by the fire-place in his room, when suddenly raising himself up in bed, and pointing at the clock that hung over its foot, he exclaimed—"'All hands on deck!' George, where are you?" (I must here remark, that my father was a seafaring person.) As he pointed to the clock, the weight gave way, broke through the bottom of the clock, and fell on the bed, leaving the hands pointing at a quarter to *nine*. From this moment he never uttered another word, but, precisely at the same hour on the following evening, he breathed his last. On the night of father's death, being of a somnambulic tendency, I got up in my sleep, raised a two-story window, and climbing partly out, seated myself on the sill. Mother hearing the noise, inquired who was there, and simultaneously with her voice the window fell, striking me across the thighs, which produced the usual uproar of a boy in such a predicament. I was soon rescued from my perilous situation, and replaced in bed. And what has the falling of a window to do with your spiritual experience? says the reader. To me they are closely connected, for I have no doubt that my spirit friends caused it to fall. Might not that father, who had so recently left his earthly tenement, and whose affections would naturally hover around those from whom he had so lately parted, have seen the danger of the child, whose name was almost the final word he uttered on earth, and have resorted to this physical manifestation to save him from the certain destruction which would have followed his being precipitated into the street? This at all events is my view of it, and to me 'tis far more natural than to suppose that a parent who, when in the earthly form, had ever exerted himself for the welfare of his family, should, on changing his sphere, have suddenly become an inert being, either incapable of assisting or indifferent about helping those whom, but a few days previously, he had so tenderly and watchfully guarded. Father's body was placed by little Lizzie's, and I left an orphan.

Soon after I started for the West in company with Mr. L. D. Nickerson, in whose family I was a resident at the advent of the famous "Rochester Knockings." Mr. Nickerson was a *firm* progressionist, and allowed no opportunity to pass unheeded, in which he could investigate any *new principle*, were it ever so obscure or unpopular. Well do I remember his reading in the New York Tribune the first notice of these manifestations, and the long discussions that ensued on the subject between his brother-in-law and himself. The topic involved Salem witchcraft, what old ladies had seen, heard, and related. The dinner-table was the place of conference, and while we fed the material form with what Mrs. N. declared to be "too good for poor folks," we had every opportunity of learning and digesting whatever of a spiritual nature was advanced by the public press. I must confess that so much discussion upon a subject closely connected as it was with a *dark* room, had no little effect upon me, especially when I was called upon to encounter *night* without *light;* and upon such occasions my mouth would involuntarily pucker itself up and whistle to keep the ghosts away, though in the *day* time I was very eager to hear and know more of these things, for my childish years had been connected in a greater or less degree with phenomena similar to what was transpiring at Rochester.

The Nickerson family now removed from Kingsborough to Pleasant Square, in the immediate neighborhood of the Brown family, who were relatives of Mr. N., and I accompanied them. The Browns being more or less famous for their *independent* way of *thinking*, were (as is usual in sectarian communities,) selected as the subjects of prayer, exhortation, criticism, &c., &c. There was an excellent opportunity for forming circles, and Mr. Brown having become *au fait* at the business in consequence of his perusal of A. J. Davis's works, was chosen as the prime mover in the attempt to establish communication with the spheres. According to Mr. Brown the spirit circle must consist of twelve persons, six males and six females, alternated around the table, with the right hand of each upon the left hand of his neighbor's ; forming a circle like the *above*, the party gathered round a large cherry table, and waited patiently for *hours* in hopes to *hear* a *rap*, or perceive a movement, either mental or physical. *I* was not allowed to join the party —the required number being made up of older heads than myself—but upon condition that I would not breathe a word, I was permitted to sit in one corner of the room, and be a disinterested looker on. Night after night, hour after hour, did these disciples of the new faith strive to produce some sign of intelligence from the inanimate table, the slightest creak of which would bring forth from the grave face of Mr. Brown—"Is there any spirit present?" After which all would again be silent ; the table remaining as taciturn as those around it. After repeatedly unsuccessful efforts, it was unanimously concluded that there was no *medium* in the party, for at no time was *I* allowed to take a seat at the table, because "there was no room." Spiritual publiactions were in general circulation in the neighborhood of Pleasant Square, and the Browns were thus kept in constant excitement on the subject of the Spirit Rappings.

Having made the requisite arrangements with Mr. N.,—I, in the fall of 1850, determined on revisiting my native city, from which I had been absent about three years ; so bidding farewell to friends and associates, I started from Pleasant Square with all the glee and joy that ever accompany youthful anticipations, and in due time reached the old homestead on the eve of New England's great festival, Thanksgiving Day. Kind and affectionate was the greeting I received from my good step-mother ; noisy and jovial the meeting with my younger relatives, which salutations over, we repaired to our snug little parlor, there to partake of that cup, which cheers without inebriating. Of course the various scrapes and adventures that had been mine since launching my bark on the ocean of life were narrated, intermingled with the usual amount of question and reply ; thus sped the hours till that old clock, which had once been the medium for announcing a deep and heavy affliction, notified the hour for retiring, and feign were all to seek in the arms of Morpheus that repose which the excitement of the last few hours had rendered to both old and young.

The following morning, after doing ample justice to a substantial breakfast, I sallied forth to visit former neighbors and acquaintances, which act of duty or politeness, (term it which you like,) was but *partially* accomplished when the hour drew nigh of partaking the *gobbler*, (who but a few hours before had been parading the barn-yard, with all the solemnity of a *dignified turkey*, but who now lay prostrate on a dish, and a subject for dissection,) together with pumpkin pies and the other dainties of a New England Thanksgiving dinner, for you must know, dear reader, that mother's ideas about hours were of the primeval order, one of her maxims being—

> "Early to bed and early to rise,
> Makes one healthy, wealthy and wise."

And in accordance with this idiosyncrasy, the time for dinner was never later than 1 o'clock p. m , where she reigned lady paramount. Thanksgiving Day, however, like all others, must have an end ; so this likewise sank into the lap of eternity. After two weeks devoted to fun, frolic, and hilarity, I began to turn my thoughts to business, and soon succeeded in obtaining the situation of clerk in a mercantile establishment. Subsequent to this, while sitting at home one evening, mother proposed that we should go and witness some of the spirit manifestations, than which no suggestion could have been more acceptable to me. We sallied forth and sought the residence of Mrs. ——— ; after a due introduction, and while in conversation with this lady, there was heard a loud sound overhead, as if some child had fallen. This somewhat startled me ; Mrs. ——, seeing my alarm, assured me "'twas *only the spirits,*" which I was bound to believe only as far as my credulity extended. It was this lady's daughter who was the medium ; she was engaged at the time we called. Making an appointment for nine o'clock, we left and whiled away the intermediate period by strolling through the streets. At the designated hour we returned, and found a young lady, of genteel and prepossessing appearance, awaiting us. On entering, she requested that we would be seated. We complied, and after a silence of about five minutes, the medium propounded something like the following questions :

Are there any spirits present ? (Three raps, signifying "yes," answered.)

Will the spirit spell its name ? (Three raps.)

By the alphabet ? (Three raps.)

The letters of the alphabet were then called over, and the following name spelt, by a rap being given when the correct letter was mentioned.

A L E X A N D E R.

Is that the friend of any person in the circle ? was the next inquiry ; to which an affirmative answer was given, and also was added, "that it was a friend of mine;" upon which I asked the questions which follow:—

Will you give your relationship to me? By the alphabet. FATHER.

Will my father tell his age at the time of his decease? 37 years.

The length of time he has been in the spirit world? Four years.

In what month did you die? I am not dead.

I mean the month of your departure from earth. November.

Will my father write through the medium to me? No, but there are others who will.

Will you give the name? MARY.

What is Mary's relationship to me? MOTHER.

Will you, mother, tell me my age when you left me? 18 months.

Will you, dear mother, write for me through the hands of the medium? Yes.

The following communication was then given, purporting to come from my deceased parent:

MY DEAR MORTAL SON—

A mother leans over thee in love; long have I watched thee in the blossom; with many anxious mortal feelings did I nourish thee when an infant; with a mother's love did I rock the cradle of thine infancy. I am still the same. My parental feelings are growing stronger, as I see thee wandering o'er life's path. A guardian mother's love shall maintain thee in all thy ways, and when duty calls thee to become a laborer in the vineyard, then shall a parent's heart rejoice in forwarding progress to thy soul. In all thy mortal ways, remember that an eye from heaven scans thy actions; fear to do wrong, my son, and thus assist the flow of happiness to a spirit mother's soul. I will be ever near thee, and, as my spirit accompanies thee through life, may I find thee often where thou canst receive the advice and counsel of thy spirit mother. MARY.

Mother, shall I ever be a medium? Yes! yes! yes!

Will you tell me what kind of medium? Rapping, tipping, writing.

How soon? Six weeks, by sitting once a day, ten minutes each day.

Have you any other communication? No!

The above is a correct copy of my first sitting for Spiritual Manifestations. Every iota is correctly stated, and deep was the impression it made on my mind. I had now witnessed for myself that upon which the public print had, since 1849, been lavish in ridicule. 'Tis almost unnecessary to add, that so much was I taken up with this mysterious subject, not only every evening, but one, two, and even three o'clock sometimes in the morning, would find me seated at a small stand listening for raps. One evening, when as usual, I had been sitting at the stand, with my wonted intensity of feeling, I found myself propelled, as it were, towards A—— Place. On arriving there I found that the medium had gone to the museum. What was I to do? "Come," said I at last to Mrs. ——, "let us go up to the table and see what *we* can do." To this proposition she with much kindness acceded; up stairs, therefore, we went, and taking our seats at the table, endeavored to invoke the presence of our angel friends. We had sat silently for about half an hour, when tiny raps, (such as have so frequently sent an electrical thrill through the anxious hearts of investigators) greeted my ears. Great was my delight, for notwithstanding the absence of Miss ——, there was a *possibility* we might have some manifestations; the raps coming louder and louder, I was somewhat suspicious of Mrs. ——, and questioned her on the subject. She plead not guilty to the charge, but said she thought *I* was making them, which having denied, and each of us thus becoming satisfied of the integrity of the other, we proceeded to interrogate the communicating intelligence.

Which of us is the medium through whom these sounds are produced? The alphabet being used, I found to my inexpressible pleasure that *I* was the instrument. This *séance* continued till late in the evening, and I returned home overjoyed at my prospects of mediumship. Even after retiring to bed I could hear tiny raps, and long I lay mentally questioning father on the results of my future in this new cause. I had become a decided spiritualist; every moment some idea connected with this all-absorbing theme was floating through my brain; that my dear father could and would influence me, was a source of ineffable delight. My soul seemed to overflow with love to him, and to do a premeditated wrong was impossible.

While sitting in my employer's store I would often place my hand on the counter, and it would slowly move; so deeply interested was I in this involuntary motion, that customers coming in, and seeing no clerk nor any one to attend to their wants, would pass again into the street. Occasionally I became conscious of their presence ere they had wholly emerged from the store and recalled them. Once, while luxuriating in one of those deep reveries, to which I had become subject, I was surprised by the sonorous voice of Mr. ——, exclaiming in pretty loud notes—"George, are you asleep?" This was to me a startling *material* manifestation, and brought me for a time, at all events, to a full sense of the realities of my surroundings. I was dispatched to the bank, and on coming back to the store, was blessed with a lecture, which, for a few days, effectually checked my propensity for musings and manifestations during business hours, but none the less did I continue my nightly and solitary sittings with patience and perseverance.

Winter was gliding into spring, and as each day rolled on, I could perceive wonderful progress in my mediumship. The raps were louder and louder, and my hand was ever and anon moved with great violence. Having acquaintances in Sun Court Street, I visited them one Sunday morning, and as it had reached their ears, that I was a medium, a circle was formed, and to my utter astonishment the *table began to tip.* Here was a new phase, and my gratification (nay, I should more pertinently term it my *rapture,*) was almost uncontrollable, especially when I saw a large, heavy man, in his attempts to hold the table, thrown violently on the floor. A peal of laughter was elicited from the whole circle at witnessing the overthrow of this ponderous specimen of mortality, in his efforts to contend against spirits. With a merry and thankful heart did I, after the close of this my initiatory circle, walk home to our dwelling ; and after a night of "rosy dreams and slumbers light," awoke the next morning, and with renewed buoyancy of spirit started for my employer's store. After this I held circles once a week in Sun Court Street, but neither being *very* powerful as a medium, nor having much time, my *séances* at public places were few. The day approached when in the fulfillment of promises I must return to Pleasant Square ; on apprising my Boston employer of my intentions, he strenuously urged that I should remain with him ; but, ineffectually, for the spirits had emphatically announced to me that go I must, and after that, all the powers of earth combined in *one great tongue* of persuasion would *not* have moved me ; so once again taking my departure from the city of the Puritan fathers, I was soon whirled away by the Worcester Rail Road towards Pleasant Square.

CHAPTER II.

Return to Western New York. Whence cometh news, have the winds wings? Reception by Mr. Brown. "Might as well keep the winds from blowing." First circle in Pleasant Square. Complimentary concert to Mr. Bissell. Doubts removed. Coadjutor to the Spirits. Facts for the clergy to digest. Miles Brown and the nutmeg. The Rapping Wagon. Mundane manifestations at Gloversville. Rappers discomfited. "Cayadutta House." First seance in Johnstown. Truth outdone. A Pedlar's contribution. Defeat of the vender and his public recantation. Satisfactory termination of our labors. Circles at Orin Brown's. Visit to Amsterdam. Second appearance of Ann Merrick. Skepticism illustrated. John Proper. Mrs. Shepherd in search of a medium. Directions followed and successful issue. Bacheldersville. Return home. Circle at Addison Phelp's. Night of adventures with Ann. Miles's fear and declaration.

"Every soul has partisans above,
And every thought a critic in the skies."

At the close of the day on which I left Boston, I arrived at Western New York, and engaged lodgings at the Cayadutta House; while sitting in the reception room of the hotel, a young man entered, whom I at once recognized as my old friend Thomas Porter. He immediately accosted me thus, "How do you do, George? I understand you have become one of those 'Spirit Rappers,' how is it? anything in it, eh!" "Not much," said I, for I was somewhat fearful least my hitherto established reputation for uprightness and honesty, should be blighted by such a report, so I forthwith turned the conversation to other items of interest ; and he, after entering into an interesting relation of various balls, parties, &c., withdrew to the bar-room to smoke, while I fell into the following reverie—"How came he to know I was a medium ? I have not written a word on the subject to any one ; scarcely any even of my most intimate friends in Boston are aware of it, then how has he found it out ?" After cogitating over this for a considerable time, on my acquaintance re-entering the room, I interrogated him as to the source of his valuable information relative to my mediumship ; his replies were anything but satisfactory—he had learned it from some one who had heard it from another some one, and so on, and so on. Thus despairing of ever reaching the originator of the news, I relinquished my inquiries, and feeling some compunction at my apparent denial, I retracted the equivocation, and candidly admitted that I *was* a medium, but, that my manifestations being for myself alone, it would be useless asking me to have any exhibition of them. "Well !" said he, drawing a long sigh, "*the devil has a mortgage on your soul.*" Not wishing to enter into an argument, I allowed him to enjoy his opinion, without any very particular response. Remaining at Johnstown, two or three days, I resumed my journey in the direction of the original point of destination, and in due course of time found myself at the mansion of Mr. D. Brown. Kindly was I welcomed back by the old lady and her daughter; and not less friendly was my reception by Mr. B. After shaking me heartily by the hand, his first words were, "Then you have become a medium, George. Well, I always said the Lord would not forget this end of the world, and he has now blessed it by developing you as a medium." This remark led to the following dialogue:—

"But how did you know I was a medium?"

"H. A. Parsons told me."

"But *I* have never said I was. But, Mr. B., if you will promise never to speak of me as a Spirit Rapper, I will sit for your family to-night. *I am a medium*, but shall never exercise my powers in a spiritual direction while in Pleasant Square."

"You may as well try to keep the winds from blowing as try to keep these things from the public. Come out manfully and face the music," said he.

"Others," I added, "are more capable of facing the music than I. However, we will have our circle to-night, and it will be the first and the last, depend upon it."

In anticipation of the promised circle, Mr. Brown (with his wonted zeal in the cause) invited a number of friends, and the evening found us sitting round a large dining table in the parlor, and the query was proposed. "Well, Mr. Redman, what shall we do first?" "Keep away excitement," was my reply.

All now sat perfectly mute for about ten minutes; presently a slight ticking was plainly heard upon the table. Each anxious ear was stretched to its utmost capacity, when I told them those were the raps. Questions were asked, and the alphabet was called for by the usual signal. The word "THEDA" was spelt, which was the name of Mr. Brown's mother. This gave rise to great excitement, each person wishing to obtain a communication from the spirit. Altogether, the evening passed off wonderfully well and satisfactorily to all; and here commenced an era in my life. Had my future been then foretold, I should have been as skeptical, with regard to the truth of the prediction, as Thomas was to the belief in the reality of Christ's resurrection.

Circles began to multiply in every direction, and the reverend clergy to stare with wonder at the daring presumption of those who professed to commune with *ghosts*. Every evening was devoted to convincing and converting the heathen; the Brown family all soon became believers, and from them branched out influences of much importance, whereby many were brought into the fold of reason and truth.

During these investigations there occurred an instance of spirit power worth relating, which although it may excite the laughter of my readers, was calculated to produce feelings of a more serious nature in those who were participators in the scene. Mr.

George Bissell, a Jonah among the converted, and a great impediment to the progress of certain individuals, was compelled by the circumstance to change his tone on the subject of manifestations from an exceedingly sharp key note to that of a double flat; but to my story. One evening I went to the house of Mr. Brown, and on entering his parlor found Mr. Bissell seated alone by the stove. On perceiving me, he, with a cold look and in a sarcastic tone, inquired, "How are the spirits?" I made no reply to this inhospitable reception, so he next exclaimed, "Come, George, let us go and see what the *devil* will do for us." Without uttering a word, I took a light and accompanied him into an adjoining room, where, after turning the key in the door to prevent interruption, we seated ourselves at a table. Soon, loud raps were heard, succeeded by a call for the alphabet. Pointing to the letters, the name of Ann Merrick was spelt. This Ann had been, when on earth, an Irish servant at a public institution in Ohio, and had become quite notorious since leaving the form for her noisy manifestations; aware of this, as soon as she announced herself, I cried, "Begone!" but Mr. B. exclaimed, "No, Ann, you're a good girl, go on with your concert, give us something interesting, kick up Jack, and break things." The table instantly rose about four feet from the floor and came down with a sudden crash, bouncing the wick of the lamp into the oil, and leaving our skeptical friend and the writer in total darkness; here was a predicament. The table now began to tip, the chairs to fly, the sofa to dance, and a book was pitched at the cranium of our friend, which caused him to cry out, "hold!" but *no;* every movable article seemed to have wings. Mr. B., in endeavoring to find egress, in the confusion, fell over a chair, and as he suddenly ceased speaking I screamed aloud for some one to open the door. A gentleman in the family, hearing the noise, came to our rescue, but found the door firmly fastened and ingress impossible. He called for us to unlock it. Mr. B. shouted from within, "No, sir, burst it in." The tumult increasing, our rescuing friend pressing with all his weight against the door, the lock was forced off, when he entered with a lamp and the confusion ceased. I arose from a corner of the room, where I had been defending myself with a chair; but my friend was no where visible. In a short time, however, his head was seen emerging from under the sofa, and while he was extricating the remnant of his person, he cried, "My God, let me out of this." Seeking the chair he had occupied when he challenged Ann to the combat, and resting his head on his hand he expressed the utmost satisfaction, giving vent to his feelings in these words: "No power on earth could have made me believe what my eyes have seen and my head felt this night." Never, from this evening, was he heard to utter a distrustful word of our holy cause, but was ever after a zealous vindicator of its facts and truths. Thus was a victory gained over one stubborn soul.

I was counselled by friends, both *in* and *out* of the mortal body, to devote my time entirely to the work of Spiritualism; my spirit guardians promising not only to assist me themselves, but to send some worthy friends to my aid. Shortly after this, as I was sitting alone one evening, Mr. Miles Brown entered my apartment, and proposed to me to accompany him on a "tour of truth," as he designated the contemplated journey; to this, after a consultation with our spirit friends, I agreed, and in consequence took up my abode with him in the character of coadjutor, in the hands of our angel friends for Spiritual Manifestations. The excitement on the subject, in the neighboring towns, was immense; every old woman had some wonderful tale to relate about ghosts and hobgoblins. Humbug, jugglery, electricity, evil spirits, and the witch of Endor, constituted the themes of Sunday discourses. Well, even in this way, Spiritualism was doing a good work, for public preaching had become stale and monotonous, and by scattering among the flock some inklings of truth, it was bidding the dormant shepherds cease slumbering, and "trim their lamps." Even while the condemnations were being fulminated from the pulpits, Mr. Brown continued to investigate, in the most scrutinizing manner, all relating to this mighty wonder. Being a Connecticut Yankee, he was well *calculated* to give a fair trial to this seemingly *new nutmeg.* He was also a confirmed infidel; his only life was the *present;* his only reward the enjoyments of the passing hour. To be convinced of *immortality,* was to him a serious and momentous matter; one may then be well assured every stone was turned under which the shadow of the most trivial doubt could rest of the Spiritual origin of these occurrences. 'Twas not long before Mr. Brown declared his conviction, and came out a noble monument of spirits' erection.

Mr. Brown, perfectly satisfied that these manifestations proceeded from an intelligence no longer clothed in the garb of mortality, bent his every thought to the dissemination of their facts and truths. He possessed a fine horse, and comfortable wagon, that, from the use to which it was now constantly devoted, received the cognomen of the Rapping Wagon. Day after day was he seen, attended by my humble self, traveling over mountains, and through valleys, strenuously endeavoring to impart to others the light which he had received. So conspicuous had we become, that we were frequently saluted by the pedestrians, whom we encountered, with the remark, "There go the Rappers!" If we ventured forth, on this our work of brotherly love, on the Sabbath, it was generally our fate to meet the returning church-goers. Mr. Brown was wont to say on these occasions, "Do they dismiss those Gospel shops on our approach, or do we only happen to meet their contents ?" Whichever of these ideas was the correct one, we continued our diurnal circuit, and each hour the desire to witness the wonderful phenomena seemed to increase, circles were formed in all directions, and mediums were constantly being developed.

One day we journeyed to Gloversville, about two miles from Pleasant Square. The community here being very orthodox, it was somewhat difficult to collect a circle ; ultimately, however, a few persons assembled for the purpose at the house of Mr. Case. Scarcely were we seated at a table when our ears were assailed by some boisterous manifestations from the outside of the house. It had become known that the Rappers were to hold a meeting, in consequence of which, a number of riotous young men, (who, from the serenade they vouchsafed, it was not uncharitable to conclude were more capable of realizing the Pandemonium, about which their clergy preach, than the condition of the heavenly visitors, who, probably, would have spoken through me) had clubbed together, and arming themselves with brickbats, tin horns, clappers, &c., &c., had marched to the house where we were, for the purpose of breaking up the circle, which they effectually did ; for on seeing the state of affairs, my friend and self sought the far-famed wagon, and directed our course homeward. Reports were rife the next day that the Rappers had been discomfited in their efforts to humbug the wise community of Gloversville. Not one was to be found fearless enough to give a correct statement of the case ; so temporarily the cause seemed to wane.

My good friend, Mr. Brown, was not one easily daunted or discouraged, so he resolved to visit Johnstown. Thither, therefore, we proceeded, and took lodgings at the Cayadutta House. The proprietor of this hotel and his family having already investigated, to some extent, were interested in our efforts to sow the seeds of truth. The news of our arrival at the Cayadutta drew crowds of persons there. Towards the close of the day, Mr. Brown succeeded in forming a circle, composed of twelve of the village magnates. After all were seated and in readiness, he informed me that I was about presenting myself before some of the Solons of Johnstown. In no way dismayed at the intelligence, I commenced elbowing my way through the multitude that thronged the hall and stairway ; and having gained the door of the room where the séance was to be held, I entered and became subjected to the scrutinizing gaze of M. D's. and others. Taking my seat, in a few moments a spirit, claiming to be Daniel Webster, communicated ; whether it was really New England's great Literary Colossus or not, was for the circle to determine ; but this much I know, that the communicating intelligence found no difficulty in astonishing and confounding the conclave there assembled. One of the party (Dr. Johnson) was favored by having the name of a recently departed friend selected; he asked for some undoubted test of her presence, to which she responded by writing him a communication, and sketching a human leg, across which was placed a saw. "Surely, there is some truth in this," said the Doctor; "the drawing is as good a test as one could well wish." He then gave the circle an account of what caused the departure from the form of his communicating friend, which was in substance as related below, and which, coupled with the diagram, was as decided a test of genuine spirit presence as could be desired.

"A short time since," said Dr. Johnson, "I was (in company with another surgeon,) called upon to amputate the leg of Mrs. ——. The operation was a severe one, and notwithstanding our utmost care, the patient survived it but a few days." Other incidents connected with the occurrence, which were known to none present, save Dr. J. and the communicating intelligence, were likewise given. These few tests seemed to harmonize the circle, and a unanimous impression, "that there was something in it," to pervade the assembly. Interrogatories became general, and continued so till about ten o'clock, when, feeling fatigued, I withdrew from the table and took a seat on a sofa, in another part of the room; the rest of the party remained in their original places, for the purpose of ascertaining if there were not some medium present exclusive of myself. During this time, raps were frequent on the sofa, but none came on the table. After sitting about half an hour, they were preparing to leave, when their attention was arrested by the desired sounds; instantly reseating themselves, they commenced asking questions, at the same time casting glances at me, as if to say, "You can be dispensed with." The raps seemed to emanate from a friend of Mr. F., but upon questions of identification being put, no satisfaction could be obtained. While this was going on, I understood, from impression, that there was some person or persons who were trying to play the spiritual at the expense of their friends' credulity; no word, however, did I utter, but left them to manage their own affairs as best they could.

The deceiver, having closed his performance, rose from his chair, and in no measured terms denounced *me* as a humbug, and the whole philosophy a palpable fraud upon the public; he declared to his listeners, that the raps were made with the toe of the boot against the table leg, and, hence, that any one with a pair of boots could become a medium. The strong evidence of spirit presence, that had been received through me, was totally disregarded, and the learned harness maker, with the unbridled tongue, was patted on the shoulder, and assured that "he could outdo Redman." As these *savans* descended to the lower sitting-room, they found quite a crowd of persons collected around a pedlar, who had taken lodgings for the night at the Cayadutta. Understanding that there was an exhibition of necromancy or spirit-rapping, (for in his mind, at that time, the terms were synonymous) going forward in the room above, he had volunteered a display of *his* knowledge of the occult science. "Here are your spirits," ejaculated he, flourishing a broom over his own head, and the heads of the bystanders within his reach ; then taking his seat, he began his feats by causing the broom (when commanded by his voice,) to stand erect, or bow to any point of the compass designated by his excited audience. He likewise assured his listeners, that there was as much mystery in that broom as there was in the spirits ; for he had investigated Spiritualism, and had found it as empty as a broken bottle. I gazed at this performance with as much surprise as any one present, and could not avoid thinking that every righteous movement of our angel visitors to enlighten mankind, seemed doomed to be thwarted and overthrown by undeveloped spirits.

Friend Brown and myself, weary with the day's excitement, now sought a place of rest, in hopes that "tired nature's sweet restorer, balmy sleep" would, with downy pinion, light upon our pillows and recuperate our powers for whatsoever the coming day might bring forth. Ere, however, dropping into forgetfulness of the world and its cares we were greeted by loud and frequent raps from our spirit friends, as if to say, "We have strength left," and "Thou hast sown some seed."

The next morning it was my lot to be seated at the breakfast table, directly opposite the pedlar, who had rendered himself so conspicuous the preceding evening; being a talkative individual, he soon commenced a conversation with me, in the course of which he expressed a wish to witness some of the manifestations. I assured him I had no objection to sit for him, but inasmuch as he had asserted the night before, that the manifestations were not only familiar to him, but that he was capable of affording a full explanation of them, it would be rather absurd to expose myself to the ridicule, with which, I presumed, he was prepared to overwhelm me. After this remark he admitted that he had only witnessed manifestations through "Trance Mediums;" but he had never heard the raps, and would like to satisfy himself, as he found in his travels that they formed a theme for general discussion. After this candid admission of his ignorance, friend Brown and myself concluded to afford this itinerant vender of fanciful notions an opportunity of enlightening his darkness. We, therefore, adjourned with him into a small, quiet room, to hold a moment's converse with our friend of the spirit spheres. Soon, loud raps proclaimed their presence, and upon interrogation, the intelligence declared itself a friend of our whilom knight of the broom. He now put several questions, and evinced no little surprise at the promptness and aptness of the replies. He received many powerful tests, and the sitting closed with the declaration of his entire and full belief that Spiritualism was, indeed, a solemn reality, and an explanation to us of his having caused the broom to move, by threads attached to it and to his pantaloons. When about taking his departure, he asked my terms. "They are these," said I: "that you will, on going down stairs, make a full retraction of all you asserted last night, in the presence of as many of your *then* hearers as can be found, and bid them examine and dispassionately judge for themselves." With this requisition he complied, and by the act gave an impetus to the cause, of no trifling moment; an almost universal interest throughout the place was the result. A general desire for investigation arose, which originated with some in mere curiosity, with others in higher motives, and I had the satisfaction of seeing many, who had approached me to scoff and to scorn, leave me with hearts overflowing with thankfulness and conviction.

After a sojourn of about ten days, we directed our wanderings once more homeward, although it was with difficulty we broke away from the anxious multitude, who, but a few days before, thought no insult and contumely too great for the Spirit Rappers. Truly, "a change had come o'er the spirit of their dream!"

On the evening of our return home, I held a circle at the residence of Mr. Orin Brown; here the manifestations were very powerful. One of the party was requested to sit on the table, when it was raised with the greatest ease. He was followed by three others, all large men, and with the four seated on it, it was raised and moved as before. At this séance a lady (Mrs. Green) had it communicated to her, that she would become a medium in two days. During its session, she was shaken violently, and it was plain to be seen that she was being rapidly developed. The news of the manifestations spread far and near; evening after evening were they related by the firesides; day after day heard them repeated in the stores, the lanes, and the meadows. People appeared to have become partially monomaniacs; their eyes must behold those wonders which had reached them through the channel of the ear. In the midst of this state of things at Pleasant Square, I received and accepted an invitation from Judge Belden to visit Amsterdam, situated a few miles from Kingsborough. My first visit here was to the house of Mr. S., a merchant in the village. While engaged in taking tea, the table was moved violently, and tipped to an angle of forty-five degrees, but there seemed to be a suspension of the laws of gravitation, for although observing this angular position, cups, plates, &c., &c., all retained their places, as if held by some invisible power. Upon requesting the name of our visitor, we found it to be Ann Merrick, the undeveloped spirit to whom I have already once alluded. The tea things being removed, and guests, who had been asked to witness the manifestations, having arrived, we formed round the table, and soon found that the spirit Ann was still hovering near. Personal tests were few, and intelligent manifestations unimportant—table tipping, and table moving without mortal contact were the order of the evening; the circle became intensely excited and interested, frequently requesting me to stand up, or sit down, or walk to a distance from the moving object, to show that I had no connection with its performance. Thus, matters went on till the clock told the hours of morn, and I believe would have continued till daylight, had I not excused myself under the plea of weariness. This was my first circle in Amsterdam, which was followed by an excitement similar to that in Johnstown; the knowing and the wise being brought forward to account for what was taking place and failing to afford any satisfactory elucidation.

While holding a séance at a certain editor's residence, one took hold of my hands, another of my feet; lamps were placed in various positions on the floor, to detect if possible some stray wire, which those claiming to be most intelligent declared I carried concealed in my boots. So great was this mental tornado, I deemed it prudent to remain at my host's for the night, lest in the transit to my own lodgings I might be surrounded by a gang of observers, more bound by priestly craft than guided by individual reason. During my residence here innumerable trials were mine; I was regarded by many as a consummate deceiver, and in my daily routine of visitors, was scanned by others as though they wished

A pattern for a humbug.

The greater the obstacles, nevertheless, that were thrown in my way, the more resolute and determined I became that if superstition were to be shaken by my efforts, and my mediumship, it should be made to tremble to its very foundation. Leaving Amsterdam, I felt I had gained a few friends, created many enemies, and carried with me a vast amount of denunciation and holy malediction; but I was cheered by the knowledge that my cause was one of truth and righteousness. On our journey home, we fell in with one Mr. John Proper, from Waterford, New York, a Spiritualist—how he came to introduce himself, or we to stop, (as we were driving quickly in a buggy,) I leave persons susceptible of impression to determine; be this as it may, we enjoyed a long chat with our new-made friend, during which he assured us he could see and converse with spirits, the same as we did with each other. This rencontre relieved the tedium of our travels, and to find a friend in the cause, was as agreeable as unexpected. Mr. Proper had to stop at a relative's on the way, so we separated, with the promise on his part to see us again, and give a more explicit relation of his experiences with the invisibles.

'Tis useless to repeat the occurrences of each day, as their similarity would render them wearisome and monotonous. I will only say, the circles continued interesting; were subject to great vituperation from the occupants of the pulpits, and spat upon by the majority among the high and mighty of the land; but believers increased, and Spiritualism passed from the grosser epithet of "humbug," to the more refined one of "devil."

About this time, (which brings us to the Fall of 1853,) a carriage drove up to Mrs. Green's house, at Riceville, and an elderly lady stepping out of it, inquired if a family by the name of Green resided there: being answered in the affirmative, and asked to walk in, she entered, and forthwith commenced a lively conversation, during which she asked, if there were any Spiritualists in the vicinity, and if Mrs. Green were acquainted with a young man by the name of Redman. The latter question being replied to by an emphatic "Yes," Mrs. Shepherd (the lady visitor,) began narrating the true reason for her calling, which was this,—she had received, while sitting in a circle at Albany, fifty miles distant, a communication from her guardian spirit, requesting her to go in search of a medium, with whose remarkable powers she would be astonished; giving her, simultaneously, the name, place of residence, and every essential particular for discovering the designated individual, all of which was being corroborated to her infinite satisfaction, by what Mrs. Green was relating. Mrs. Shepherd remained with Mrs. G. till a late hour, and at her departure left an urgent request that I would come to Albany, and (making her residence my home,) spend a few weeks there.

Mr. Brown and myself having, previous to Mrs. Shepherd's polite invitation, arranged a different programme for our wanderings, deferred temporarily availing ourselves of her proffered hospitality, and directed our travels to Bachelderville. On arriving there, Mr. Brown having had one of the leading men of the place pointed out to him by the spirits, introduced himself, and from him we received a warm and hearty welcome. After partaking of an exhilarating cup of tea and the usual accompaniments, for the refection of the human body, preparations were made for the spirit circle, and Mr. Brown, with whom "to feel was to be fired, and to believe was to feel," soon had all things arranged in due order. We had sat but a few moments when the raps were heard; upon which the young ladies peered under the table to discover who had the *hammers.* Their efforts not being crowned with success, they concluded to propound questions, and to them ready replies were returned. Becoming intensely interested, they declared "there was a mystery." Mr. Bachelder asked a question, and shortly after being answered, (whether from the heat of the room or spirit influence, I do not presume to say,) but he sank back with a groan into his chair, apparently unconscious. This greatly alarmed the fond mother and her daughters. Mr. Bachelder was taken into the sitting-room, placed on a lounge, and all imaginable restoratives applied, but to no effect.

"Here's a pretty state of things!" said Mr. Brown; "'twill be reported we have come here and set a man crazy." While he was uttering these words, one of the daughters entered the room where we were, and evinced by her looks, that she considered us the authors of all the commotion and fright. Feeling that our welcome had expired, we left the house; our only consolation being, "that it was the portion of reformers to be misapprehended and persecuted." Passed that night at a neighbor's, and at an early hour next morning started for Sacandaga river, there to pass an hour in Isaac Walton's favorite amusement. The fruit of our angling was a fine trout, which served for breakfast. The repast ended, I tendered to our friend a treat with the spirits, which he gladly accepted. His son came, gave his age, date of departure from the mortal life, and various circumstances connected with his career while on earth, which drew tears from his mother's eyes, and caused his father's heart to leap with joy, inasmuch as the child whom he had thought dead was alive ; he who had been lost to him was found. Sincerely gratified was I at the consolation I had been the humble means of affording this worthy couple, and truly did I then feel that such moments compensated in a measure for the mass of misrepresentation and opprobrium it was my lot (as one of the pioneers in this God-bestowed cause) to bear, so with renewed determination to unflinchingly breast all difficulties that might retard the dissemination of its truths, friend Brown and myself, as the sun was nearing its zenith, stepped once more into the good rapping wagon, and soon found ourselves again at Pleasant Square. We reached the house of Mr. Addison Phelps early in the evening, and the news of our return having quickly spread, at the close of the day quite a number of our kind village friends gathered in the wonted manner when disposed

"To scan the mazes of heaven's mystery."

To induce harmony the party sang—

"Joyfully, joyfully onward I move,
Bound to the land of bright spirits above."

Mrs. Phelps spoke, for the first time, under spirit influence. Her utterances were beautiful, and astonished all—cheering us not a little, as it showed that our good spirit friends were actively exerting themselves for the development of Media, and the enlightenment of minds generally. Mr. Miles Phelps was likewise controlled during this *séance*, and through him we received some impressive directions for our future guidance. The evening was spent profitably to all, and when the hour of parting came, we separated with grateful minds for the additional light that had been received. After much persuasion, I was induced to tarry all night with Miles. I had never fancied, since being a medium, rooming with any one ; as the spirits always embraced the opportunity of raising the mischief, and of tormenting both my room-mate and myself. Whether two persons form a battery for the trial of their strength, or it be produced by some other cause, I know not ; but certain it is, that the presence of a second party was not unfrequently attended by great confusion in the surrounding material elements, and the occurrences of this night forms no exception to my past experience.

When the company had all retired, Miles, who was somewhat of a musician, took down his violin and played over a number of pieces which were enlivening, and wore away the influences of the early part of the evening ; when his performances were finished, in the hope that we might obtain a parting blessing ere retiring to rest, the table was drawn up ; soon it began to heave violently to and fro ; the alphabet being called, "ANN" was spelt out. Surmising instantly, that it was the noisy spirit who had, on two former occasions, intruded herself, we politely requested her absence, with which request she refusing to comply, in order to rid ourselves of the obnoxious visitor, we broke the circle ; after the expiration of a few minutes, we resumed our seats, and again and again were we apprised of Ann's presence—so finding she was determined not to leave, we concluded as the only effectual remedy for the evil, to retire for the night. All was dark and still, it was near midnight, and sleep was slowly closing our outward senses, when something, which sounded like an article of clothing, was heard to fall ; thinking it only a pair of our pants, we paid no attention to it ; the noise was repeated, upon which Miles exclaimed, "Well, there can't be many more pair to fall." Again and again were the same sounds made, upon which Miles screamed out for his brother Addison to come up and bring a light ; with which requisition he promptly complying, we beheld our garments all in the centre of the floor. Miles became as pale as the sheet that covered us, and I was in no small degree excited. Bidding Addison retire, at the same time promising that if Ann played any more capers, he should be forthwith summoned, we rose from our beds, and seating ourselves at a small table, we entered into the parley, narrated here with our invisible tormentor.

"Why do you come and disturb us so, Ann?"

"I'm having a little sport."

"Will you let us have some rest if we give you an opportunity to say what you wish?"

"Go to bed, boys! Go to bed! why sit ye here? I'll not trouble you. Go to bed!"

"Will you truly leave us?"

"Try me and see?"

We placed the lamp upon a chair, thinking light under existing circumstances far preferable to darkness, and once more got into bed. I could feel a slight quiver in my bed-fellow's muscles, as if he anticipated at every moment receiving some fearful shock of physical pain; we lay for a short time, when the chair began to move with great velocity round the room with the light upon it. The noise occasioned Miles to turn over, and with a cry of "Addison! Addison! fire! fire!" he leaped from the bed, and with one blow extinguished the light, still, however, screaching "fire! fire!" Such a scene as now ensued beggars all description; I feeling for my pants, Miles frightened to desperation, and sundry articles flying about the room, as though they had wings. Addison now peeped into the room crying, "What's the matter?" "Don't talk about what's the matter," said Miles, "but give us your light," and at the same time, he set vigorously to work to clear the room of our clothing and every other movable article, even to an old funnel that was wedged into the chimney, which accomplished, he cried, "There, we'll try once more, and if she does anything, we'll, we'll, we'll—come let us try once more," so wishing friend Addison again good-night, we locked the door and jumped into bed. Having been told that singing harmonized the mind, and neutralized the efforts of evil spirits, we agreed to favor Ann with a tune, so in true Methodistical style, we chanted thus:

> "We're going home to die no more,
> We're going," &c.

So great was our alarm, we could only remember the first line of the hymn, and had just begun a repetition of it, when our vocalization was stopped by the falling of something heavy on our faces. Such a scream as Miles sent forth had never before escaped mortal lips, which was instantaneously followed by the third appearance of his brother, and the remark, "This is trifling with one's good nature!" A light being procured, we beheld all our clothes and an old coat, which Miles declared he had not seen for months. Considering that the door was locked on its inside, I leave the reader to imagine how the articles came to be in the room.

Excitement had now reached its climax; we could endure no more, at all events that night, so we resolved on leaving the room and the house, as the only means of getting rid of our trouble. Going down stairs, I led, and as my friend followed, a bag of feathers, which was suspended in the stairway, took wings, struck him on the head, and knocked him forward on me. I not having sufficient strength to resist this unexpected weight, we both tumbled into the passage below. Miles, springing up, ran towards the cellar for a lantern to light us in the nocturnal peregrinations we were about prosecuting. As he opened the cellar door, a large stool which, when in quiet mood, was wont to occupy a corner of the room, was pitched with great force against it, the door rebounding, came so violently in contact with my adventurous companion, that had he not seized hold of a shelf which was near him, he would have been prostrated on the ground of the cellar. Ultimately, procuring the lantern, we emerged into the open air, and took our way towards Mr. Nickerson's, which was about three-quarters of a mile distant. Miles wistfully eyed the fences on each side of the road as though he expected, at every moment, to see them used by the persecuting Ann for some destructive purpose. Contrary, however, to his apprehensions, we were permitted to reach our neighbor's dwelling without further molestation. Arousing its inmates, and relating our lamentable story, they not only granted us a night's lodging, but Mr. N. kindly volunteered to sit in the room, while we tried to obtain some rest; his offer being gladly accepted we retired. But even here we were assailed by small articles of the toilet. This attack, however, subsiding, with the wonted elasticity of youth I was soon wrapped in undisturbed repose. But our guardian of the night informed me, the next day, that Miles' eyes continued nervously closing and opening till near morning. Mr. N. retained his post in the centre of the room till almost daylight, but nothing more was heard of Ann at this time, and the sun had reached its meridian, ere Miles and myself unclosed our eyes. After waking, some five minutes elapsed ere either of us spoke: at last, I said, "Are you alive, Miles?"

"Yes," was the response, "but I'll be hanged if I'll ever spend another night with you."

These adventures were generally circulated, and were the themes of many a country school-boy's composition. Had my friend been less frightened, I am convinced Ann would have been less successful in her mischievous performances; but his extreme agitation of mind laid him completely open to undeveloped influences. Many were the offers tendered to me (after this became known) by youngsters, who plumed themselves upon their courage, to share with me my bed; but wishing no repetition of such incidents, and preferring a quiet night's rest to gratifying others curiosity or love for the marvellous, they were all unhesitatingly declined.

CHAPTER III.

First visit to Albany. Temperance Hotel. Mrs. A. D. Shepherd. Faraday non est. Tasso. Circles at Mrs. Shepherd's. Seed sown and the result. Mrs. R. P. Ambler at an angle of 45 degrees. Circle at Mrs. Haight's. "Why don't you go up higher?" Other physical manifestations. Circuit Preacher. Evening at Mr. Chatfield's. Return to Johnstown. Evening with Mr. Mathers. Auld Lang Syne. The Dominis and the Devil. Circle at Mr. Green's. Reception by the table. Ponderous ascent and descent. Doubts and misgivings. Ingenious test. Faith. School of development. Visit from Childe Harold. Glens Falls. Hospitality of Mr. and Mrs. Mc Donald. Manifestations at the Falls.

"Is not Lorenzo; then imposed on thee
This hard alternative; or, to renounce
Thy reason, or thy sense; or, to believe?"

Early in the month of August, notwithstanding the sultriness of the weather, I determined to make my long contemplated visit to Albany; so arranging a few essential articles of clothing in my valise, I once again, attended by friend Brown, ascended the rapping wagon, and turned the head of Waxy (the name of our good steed,) in the direction of Fonda. On reaching Fonda, after taking an amiable leave of my traveling companion, stepped into the cars, and in about two hours more was in Albany quietly ensconced at the Temperance Hotel, where I remained for the night.

The next day I sought and found Mrs. Shepherd, by whom I was cordially welcomed ; a mutual recapitulation next ensued of various experiences since her visit to Pleasant Square ; then we seated ourselves at a table, and Mrs. Shepherd was favored with a communication from a little spirit daughter, named Frances, who sent many cheering words to different members of the family. Afterwards I strolled forth to view the city, and amuse myself as best I could ; but when the shades of evening gathered o'er me, I once more seated myself at a table to pursue my accustomed vocation. The friends having harmonized, the manifestations by table tipping were very strong, all hands were withdrawn, and I stood at a distance from it, but this produced no change. Such independent motion was especially gratifying to all just now, as an article had been published by Faraday, asserting "that tables moved only by an involuntary muscular motion of the medium's hands."

Mrs. Shepherd was next influenced by the Sorrentine Poet, Torquato Tasso ; not understanding the language, I could not pretend to offer any comment ; but those who were conversant with it, assured me that the lady's pronunciation was perfect, and the sentiments most beautiful. Our séance continued till near one o'clock in the morning—the party then separated with the usual amount of amazement, incredulity and incomprehensibility of the subject, as usual with the novices in investigation—and thus closed my first evening in Albany.

Continued sittings at Mrs. Shepherd's; converts were daily multiplying, and the dormant faculties of the Albanians arousing from lethargy and supineness. I must not omit mentioning here, that, at one of the circles at the above mentioned residence, a small music stand, full of books, was taken up and placed upon the table, and to crown that evening's demonstration, Mrs. Shepherd herself was raised, chair and all from the floor, and deposited likewise upon the table, and while occupying her elevated position was entranced and addressed the circle in her usual eloquent manner.

These things did not pass away with the fleeting moment, but left seed, which now blooms and spreads the fragrance of its consolation over very many souls. Circles were held twice each day at the residence of some one of the friends, for the purpose of ascertaining to what extent the influencing power would go, and to them the most intelligent and enlightened of the community were invited.

One evening we met at the house of Benj. Lodge, Esq., where were present about fifteen persons, among whom were Mr. and Mrs. R. P. Ambler; soon after harmonizing, and winding up a musical box, which had been brought for the purpose of contributing its quota to the evening's entertainment, the table slowly tipped to an angle of 45 degrees, and then kept time by its undulatory motions to a tune played by the box. The alphabet was next called for, and Mrs. Ambler was told to "sit on the table." In obedience to the wishes of the invisibles she placed a chair, as she was enjoined, and seated herself in it. The table began moving and tipping in perfect time to the sounds of the musical box. A light was then placed on the floor, and all drew back from the table; the only contact with it being Mrs. A. and the chair. It still, however, continued its fantastic exhibition. This was another nut for the learned Faraday to crack.

Circles were next arranged to be held at the house of Mrs. Haight. Here much that was surprising resulted, and a few out of the many wonders I will relate. We gathered around the table, selections from the Spirit Minstrel were sung, and a very subdued light kept in the room; the influence that pervaded the circle was calm and beautiful, giving evidence that high and progressed spirits were present. So perfectly harmonious were we, it seemed as though actual converse might be held with our loved ones. I was raised in a half stupified state from the chair, conveyed to the ceiling of the room, which was some ten feet from the floor, and I floated alone in the air for a few moments. I was then joined by Mrs. Shepherd, and soon after by her daughter. Here were three of us, all suspended in the atmosphere, in no contact with any material object, but upheld by an unseen power, and wafted by it over the heads of some dozen individuals all wide awake, and in the perfect possession of their reasoning faculties.—"Why don't you go higher?" "Why don't you go higher?" was loudly vociferated by Miss Shepherd; but this was impossible, unless we could have passed through the ceiling. We were kept in this aerial locality, as near as I could judge, some few minutes, when the two ladies were gradually lowered to their seats, and I very unceremoniously brought down invertedly. I soon, however, resumed that upright position, which through life I ever maintain, and reseated myself.

The spirits' next amusement was that of stopping the musical box in the midst of a tune. Mrs Haight thought it had worked down, but on trying to wind it up found this was not the case. Loud raps were given, and we were told that our celestial visitants would stop the music and then resume it whenever we expressed a wish to that effect, which they actually did.

Ere closing my account of this night's marvels, I will relate one more occurrence, which is too ludicrous to be passed over in silence. The lights were lowered by spiritual command; a slight rustling noise was heard, after which, by celestial behest, they were made to spread their rays on us again, when, lo! *I* was found seated on the table, with my coat turned inside out and buttoned down my back.

Of course this elicited peals of laughter. Whence the use of this ? I think I hear some caviler say. It consisted in the *conviction* it carried to the minds of those among us, who were yet doubters, of the super-mundane origin of the act, for all present knew that no individual could have performed this feat without the assistance of a second party, and they were fully satisfied that no human being had approached me. The coat was righted, after which four raps, as the appropriate letters were named, indicated the word "Done" and "Good Night" being spelt out by the table tipping, we reciprocated the politeness to our kind companions of the spirit spheres, and repeating it severally to each other, adjourned.

During the following week I performed the office of circuit preacher or demonstrator, in various families, in all of which there were the usual manifestations.

One evening took tea at the house of Mr. Chatfield, whose wife and some other members of the family, were partially developed as mediums. We had been seated at the tea-table but a few minutes, when a tremulous motion was apparent all over it. Mr. Chatfield asked, "If I raise my side of the table, will our spirit friends raise the other ? Three sounds announced their compliance. Mr. C. elevated the side nearest to him, and a corresponding movement took place on the opposite side ; the table was next lifted to a level with our heads. Mr. C. then said, "Come, let us put it on Mr. Redman's head," which was no sooner uttered than done, and my cranium was made the axle for the tea-table, laden with dishes, lamps, cups filled with tea, &c., all of which retained their places; and the table itself, while resting on my head, seemed as light as a common shingle. It was after a little while raised sufficiently high to allow me to extricate myself, and then it slowly sank to the floor, when the spirits expressed their joy by rapping long and loudly, to which we responded, "Thank you a thousand times." An account of the above was published in an Albany journal by Mr. Chatfield.

Tea was scarcely over when we were joined by invited guests, among whom were some literary gentlemen. The editor of the State Register was the first selected, and received a written communication from a spirit purporting to be his father; after questions and responses having passed between these parties, Mrs. Toby's mother presented herself, communicating on past troubles, and although the expression, "*Pooh! my mother!*" had been uttered, when the spirit first came, so peculiarly characteristic was that which was given and signed with the spirit's name, that Mrs. Toby wept and exclaimed, "That that communication could have emanated from no other except her maternal parent." A few questions put by Mr. and Mrs. Toby were next answered by the table tipping, when suddenly all manifestations ceased. "What does this mean?" inquired Mr. Shepherd. "It is certainly very singular," remarked Mr. Toby. We remained in our seats *trying* to be patient; at last we once more heard the raps and a call for the alphabet, and we received the following: "We do not wish to lift thy legs and the table too, Mr. Hammond." Silence ensued, which was broken by Mr. Hammond saying, "That is pretty good; I have been trying to keep the table down with my legs; when it tried to tip I put my weight on it, and endeavored to retain it in its place; this caused the cessation of the manifestations. I am confident none knew it, and the communication is an undisputed test." The laughter produced by this admission having ceased, all went on smoothly and satisfactorily till a late hour, when we parted; and here terminated my visit to the Capital of the Empire State. It had been attended with beneficial results to the public at large as well as to myself, for I had gained much in development. Truly grateful was I to my spirit guardians for my advancement, and fully determined to yield implicitly to their guidance and instruction.

On my journey homeward, I stopped at Johnstown, and was induced through the importunity of friends to remain and gratify them with an evening circle at the residence of Mr. Mathers; the séance was numerously attended, and made up principally of men disposed to be guided by reason in the weight they would attach to any evidence that might be received or judgment they might pass. From this general rule, however, I should except Squire Frothingham, a short, dark-eyed philosopher of an exceedingly nervous organization ; but I will let him portray himself by relating some of his antics. On the first annunciation of a spirit's presence, he would push his chair back from the table, draw it up again, run behind me, then back to his chair, and when the table rose suddenly, we would jump as quickly as thought, first to one side of the room, then to the other. After the gentleman somewhat controlled his excitability and conditions thus being rendered more harmonious, the spirit of Margaret Ossoli Fuller visited us. She replied to the various interrogatories of her decease, life, position in and out of the form ; and to more fully identify herself, wrote a long poem, which I have unfortunately lost. Many other excellent tests were given, which 'tis useless to recapitulate. We separated after sitting a couple of hours, and I had the pleasure of carrying with me pressing invitations to visit Johnstown soon again, and many kindly expressed wishes from the friends for prosperity to myself, and success to our glorious and holy cause.

The morning succeeding my Johnstown séance found me seeking the cars that would conduct me back to my old home with its pleasant remembrances.

As in all small villages, each person knows his neighbor's affairs, the news of the arrival of the devil, (the sobriquet generously bestowed by the pious on me) was quickly circulated; the Dominis were thus furnished with a rich theme for the edification of their flocks on the ensuing Sunday, and could there have been a subject presented for their consideration, on which, according to their own showing, they were so capable of dilating and commenting fluently! Giving myself no concern about the commotion I was occasioning, after a little cozy home chat, Mr. Brown and myself sallied forth to call on old acquaintances, which labor of love we terminated at the house of Mr. and Mrs. Green.

Soon after taking my seat in our friend's comfortable parlor, the old table, as if conscious of our needs, came sliding into the room, no one touching it, and all present, nothing loath, assembled round it. Mr. Green (lest any requisition should be made upon his musical talents) took out his violin, and his contribution towards the harmonization of the evening was soon claimed. Simultaneously with the sound of his skilfully wielded bow, the table commenced pirouetting like some votary of Terpsichore. It would balance itself, first on one of its legs, then on one of its leaves, then wheel round again, till it ultimately reached the parlor door, against which it then began thumping as if to say, "Let me out." We opened the door, and great was our surprise to see the inanimate fellow, without any delay, walk up stairs: when the turning was reached, the passage-way being too narrow for it to proceed with open leaves, it very quietly folded them up, turned the projection in the balusters, ascended the remaining steps, and entered the upper hall. While this was going on, the circle was almost in hysterics from laughter, and our violinist nearly incapable of continuing his part in the evening's entertainment. All, nevertheless, went up to tender congratulations on the successful ascension, when, lo! Mrs. Green being lifted by the spirits from the floor, and placed on the bed-piece of the table, it started down stairs, not stopping till it regained the lower hall, when Mrs. G. stepped off, to the no small amusement of those who had thus had an opportunity of testing the reliability of Professor Faraday's expositions. During this manifestation, a full blaze of light was brought to bear on every movement of the table, so that collusion or mortal interference in any way was utterly impossible.

I was now perpetually receiving test after test, and manifestation upon manifestation, yet, in the midst of all, a dark cloud of mistrust and doubt would, ever and anon, overshadow my mind, as to the *source* whence emanated these marvels and mysteries. I would ponder and meditate and reason and ask myself, whether the writings that were given through my hand, did not, unknown to myself, originate within my own brain: true, there were things written which seemed totally foreign to my spirit; circumstances told through me, of which I had not the slightest knowledge, still I was beset by lurking misgivings, which harassed my very soul. My wretched feelings, at this time, would oft vent themselves in words, which outbursts were invariably followed by gentle chidings and rebukes from my guardian spirit-mother. About this time, I was holding a circle at Mrs. Green's, when the guardian spirit of Miles Brown came, and expressed a desire to write a small volume, entitled, "The Philosophy of Man's Physical and Spiritual Nature." The first chapter was written that evening, and we were told that I was the chosen instrument for the conveyance of his ideas: that we were to sit one hour every morning, immediately on rising from our beds, and that he would communicate a chapter at each sitting. In accordance with this arrangement, Mr. Brown and myself met every morning. Punctually did our spirit attend, and transmit his ideas on the proposed subject.

While this work was being communicated, my former doubts and perplexities reassumed their sway over me; so haunted was I by them, that one morning, I threw down the pencil and refused to continue writing, at the same time declaring it to be my conviction, that the whole was the involuntary action of my own mind. Isaac, (the name of the communicating intelligence,) having no intention of being thus cheated out of his work, instantaneously seized my hand with superhuman force, and impelled it from *right to left*, till about three sheets of paper were covered with writing; he then quietly controlled my hand to turn the blank side of the paper towards myself, and thus holding it up to the light, to peruse the mysterious production. This was certainly interesting to me at such a skeptical crisis; I immediately exhibited the strange scrawl to the friends, who were not a little amused at the method adopted by the celestial being to bring my mind into harmony with *truth*. Time passed on, and every communication was written in the same manner; becoming quite wearied with transcribing every document given, I remonstrated with the spirits, but unavailingly. I plead, they remained unmoved; they were resolved I should never again ascribe their productions to my own brain, and from that all communications of any character or length have been given in *reversed* writing. Annoyed as I was at first at having to copy off the communications, I soon became reconciled; by degrees I instructed my sitters how to read what they received, and *now* I am *truly thankful*, as it excludes all possibility of collusion, and destroys the supposition, that the ideas flow from my own mind.

More enlightened views of the new faith were now distinctly perceptible throughout the villages in which I spent my time. Atheists, infidels, and professed Christians became alike convinced, that the manifestations were not humbug, nor electricity, nor more terrible yet, the work of that great bugbear of Christianity, the devil. Thrown among none but the most *inveterate* skeptics, who would be satisfied with *nothing* save *indubitable* tests, and their spirit friends being as anxious to afford them every possible evidence as *they* were to obtain it, I had an excellent opportunity for development as a "*test medium*," and indeed not only was I conscious myself of great accession of strength in my mediatorial capacity at this time, but I had the gratification of being complimented upon it, by friends both in and out of the form.

Converts were numerous, the proofs admitted not of cavil; saint and sinner were compelled to admit that there was truth, immortal truth, in our yclept heterodox faith.

One day about this period, after returning from a very delightful morning's ramble, during which I had greatly enjoyed the beauties of the surrounding scenery, I was seated alone in my room, when a most exquisite sensation seemed to pervade my whole system. My hand was seized, and he, who sank to sleep at Missolonghi, and whom Erin's bard calls

> The noblest star of Fame,
> That e'er in life's young glory set!

communicated the following :—

A mortal well may worship on such morns as these,
For with his outward everything in nature blends.
Had he a soul of adamant, could he resist awhile
The glow of nature's beauties? No! the bird notes,
Like chisels, each would clip away the jagged
Surface of his idolatry.
Not idolized to God, but to himself; and woe be he
For *self* idolatry. External objects fail to please,
And damming up his soul's flood, drowns himself.
E'en though he drowns, methinks these godlike beauties,
Were he mortal, might act as straws, to catch at;
And grasping even these perchance might find support,
And save himself.
But such as this, thou art not! but rather view
These gems, like strings of an Æolian, each one distinct;
Yet all by blending gratify the soul's ear,
And bid the springs of inspiration rise,
And water whate'er of virtue is within thyself.
Not like dew within the crystal to be gazed at merely,
Are these to thee; but fresh from weeping clouds,
That hang thy gardens o'er;
Bidding the maiden violet and virtuous butter-cup
Lift their heads, and smile beneath their blushing beauty—
A fitting type of Heaven, or Spirit Spheres, as you may wish,
Are nature's pictures, a *type* alone, however,
For while one is lovely, the other is divine;
One, beautiful; the other God-like;
One yields the fragrance, the other, flower and fragrance both.
A Fair is holden now within the spheres,
This very instant. Nobles, Sages, Peers,
And all the rest and residue of immensity,
With hurried step and tread, haste to contribute.
If dormant thou'lt become, and leave the clay,
I'll promise thee, this very day, to take thee thither.
"What a sight!" I hear thee say—
A fancied dream alone 'twould be to thee,
Ne'er tinged with slight reality.

However, remain awhile; hang thy eternal on a pin,
Perchance its loveliness may stimulate thy generous nature,
To multiply to others that we give to thee.
But of the Fair; each angel brings donations of its own;
The man of *grey* brings joyful tidings of success.
Quoth he, "I've been to Earth to-day,
And those I love have learned to pray,
Therefore, I do propose a gift. My victory—full worthy."
Husband and Kiddie arm in arm emerge,
From space, laying the lover and the wife before the fair tribunal,
And a blessing get as recompense.
"Lover and wife," you say; "those are *too* fair at Fairs to throw away."
But stop! 'tis not at avenues of *Fancy Goods* you take these diadems,
'Tis to the "Fair of Progress," where their names,
Freedom from *Gospel Faith*, (which when disrobed of fact,
Sinks like a stone,) proclaims
Thy own name, long since entered there.
'Twas tendered by thy father.
More worthy objects could we ne'er behold,
Than curiosities like these, numbers untold.
One from a *Deist* is transformed, another from a beast,
A third was plucked from a sectarian Hell.
A fourth from infidelity's deep chasm,
Where death unceasingly her knell begets;
And I might multiply to thee these contributions,
But enough! Seek thou the "Golden Bowl,"
And while you quaff its limpid life,
Put not thy foot in, like the viler beast;
But let thy neighbor his parched bill insert,
And animate the powers of life inert.—BYRON.

Towards the close of the year 1853, an invitation was extended to me by Wm. McDonald, Esq., to visit Glens Falls. Having met Mr. McDonald while in Albany, I was gratified by his politeness, and prepared without delay to accede to his request, and Mr. Brown being desirous of accompanying me, we were soon en route. As we neared Saratoga, an accident occurred, which caused the detention of the cars, and while we were stopping, loud raps were heard throughout the one we occupied; this made me restless. Mr. Brown, however, became much elated: he entered, mentally, into conversation with the spirit, but was interrupted by a religious discussion, that was being held at the farther extremity of the car. Mr. B., with his wonted zeal, insisted on moving towards the scene of debate: so going forward, he took a seat, and remarked, "Some spirit has been round here." I made no response, but silently listened to the conversation of the disputants; it ranged from one tenet to another, till it finally merged into Spiritualism, on which, Mr. B. took his part in the controversy, not alone, however, for soon after he commenced, a voice was heard issuing from the assemblage confirming all that my friend asserted. Victory ultimated with us, and Mr. Brown, after gathering his laurels, introduced himself to the friend who had come so opportunely to his assistance, when we found, much to our gratification, that it was Mr. Harris, a resident of Glens Falls, who was even then journeying thither. On reaching the village, we took up our quarters for the night at the Public House; and at an early hour next day, sought out Mr. McDonald, by whom I was most cordially welcomed, and the hospitalities of his house extended to me during my sojourn at the Falls. I unhesitatingly availed myself of his kindness, as I greatly preferred the quiet of a private residence, to the noise and confusion of an inn. And here let me say, that never can the kindnesses I experienced from his family and self, be obliterated from my memory. Extensive have been my wanderings since that time, and to many have I to acknowledge my thanks for attentions conferred, but none will ever be remembered with more lively sentiments of gratitude, than those I received from this true specimen of one of nature's noblemen, and his very amiable family. Dear reader, pardon this apparent dilation from my theme. I say *apparent*, for is it not in reality a manifestation, if, "out of the abundance of the heart the mouth speaketh," mine would take this opportunity to manifest its lively appreciation and remembrance of all, of which I was then a recipient, and now *revenons à nos moutons*.

One lovely evening, while a circle was holding sweet commune with their angel friends, at the house of Mr. McDonald, a request was made by a spirit to open the door, in order to allow another spirit to enter. We complied, and were immediately greeted by the announced visitor, who gave the information that an additional spirit guest was on his way and would join us in about ten minutes. We asked if we should (at the expiration of that time) open the door. The spirit answered,

"No. When he comes, he will cause the dog, that is lying on the steps, to bark."

We here opened the door, and found the dog (a noble-looking animal) stretched at his ease, on the spot designated. Returning to the table, we were favored by some physical manifestations, in the midst of which, our canine watch gave three or four quick barks. We instantly looked at our time-pieces and found that the ten minutes had just expired: the expected visitant saluted us and gave his name. Here was an instance in which the question, Can spirits influence animals? was as clearly demonstrated, as in the good old story of Balaam and his ass. Various other manifestations were given during this séance, remarkable enough in their nature to tax general credulity, yet given under circumstances that admitted not the possibility of human intervention: one only of these will I select for present relation.

We had been told that, in the course of that evening, we should have a strong test of spirit power; curiosity was on the *qui vive,* as we could not imagine that any more forcible evidences could be adduced than had been already received. It was said that a token was to be given to a member of the circle, that Mr. Harris was to be the recipient of this additional favor, and that he must *place his hat upon the table.* This was done, and shortly something was heard to drop into it; upon inspection, a small round piece of metal, something in the shape of a common saucer, and about the size of a shirt button, was found; in this curious article was a lock of hair, which was bound in its place by what seemed to be an excessively delicate golden bar. Upon applying a magnifying glass to this diminutive wonder, strange characters were distinctly discerned upon it—what they were, or what their significance, I have never yet learned. After examining the hair, we remarked that it was very small, and asked the friends if they would favor us with a *larger lock.* To this they immediately signified their assent, and bade us *take up the carpet and we would find one directly under the table.* Hammers were procured, the tacks in the carpet taken out, the piano and other ponderable articles drawn aside, and the carpet raised, when to the astonishment of all, was found a *flat square piece of paper, curiously folded, containing a larger lock of the identical hair,* that had been previously given. This was almost beyond all credence; some thought that a hole had been made in the carpet. Well do I remember entering the parlor the next morning, and finding a person holding the carpet to the light to see if some rent had not been made in it. But no; the fine Brussels was perfect in all its parts, there was no cavity for the admission of the hair, and thus the mystery was dropped as inexplicable. Had I been charlatan enough to wish to impose upon the credulity of these good people, the necessity of taking up the carpet and removing the heavy furniture, ere I could have deposited the hair where it was placed, would have exposed me to certain detection, and I was not dupe enough to risk my future reputation on any such ephemeral adventures. 'Tis true, this little incident did not prove satisfactory to all, for plainly did the eyes of at least one, if not more of the party, seem to proclaim, "Others may believe this, but I do not; there is some collusion, and I am not deceived." They could not believe, because they were unprepared for it, and the manifestation was too wonderful. The result, however, was not changed, and though it carried not its due weight, it left its mark, which was probably all that the unseen intelligences contemplated.

On another occasion, when Mr. and Mrs. McDonald were seated at dinner, each more or less intent on allaying the necessities of the physical body, the table, at which we were sitting, moved slowly to the side of the room it occupied, when not being used for meals, leaving us knife and fork in hand, minus our dinner. "Well," said my hostess, "don't you wish us to eat any more?" Three raps was the reply. "Then please give us back our dinner;" the table was slowly returned to the spot whence it had been removed, and we were left to finish our meal without further interruption, save an occasional tip or rap. Our repast ended, Mr. McDonald entered into correspondence with the spirit of Daniel Webster, which was both entertaining and agreeable, and according to his own testimony very convincing.

Yet, one more incident connected with this individual family, for although the number of the occurrences might occupy much more space were I to relate them all, yet as 'tis said "enough in an egg shell is sufficient," I will enter no further into detail.

Returning home one night quite early, and withal somewhat fatigued, I went immediately to my bedroom, and was beset on all sides by raps, and the moving of the furniture. I got into bed, when the bedstead was rolled to and fro with the motion of a railroad car. Mr. McDonald hearing the noise, came up stairs, and was greeted by a perfect shower of raps; he asked questions which were answered; he crossed to the side of the room opposite to where the bedstead stood, when it immediately followed him, I lying quietly in it; he pushed it back, it then moved to the centre of the apartment. Mr. McDonald thinking it useless to interfere, again put some questions, and turned to leave the chamber, when a chair which stood in a corner of the room, was thrown at him with full force, struck the door, and had the back broken off. This manifestation rather displeasing Mr. McDonald, he remonstrated, saying "he wished nothing to do with such unruly characters." As soon as this was uttered there was continual rapping. The alphabet was called for. "Pray, excuse us, we did not mean to break the chair," was spelt out. The apology was accepted, and my host returned down stairs, quite satisfied with the origin of the noise and the object thereof.

My residence at Glens Falls extended over some three months, far beyond the time indeed that I had proposed on leaving home, but, finding much uncultivated soil, the reflection came, "Why may I not be the gardener?" So taking for my motto, "Whatever your hands find to do, that do with all your might," I did truly labor, (regardless of the overwhelming sneers and scoffs poured on me and my cause,) with all my might in that village for a full quarter of a year.

CHAPTER IV.

RETURN from Glens Falls. Second visit to Albany. Business Matters. Suspense. Father's Communication. Swanee. Tests. "Quicker than shot." Anathemas of the church. Visit to Johnstown. Circles. Interest and Believers. Discord in the churches. Assistance of Mattison required. He is invited to instruct himself. "Sufficiently wise." His invitation accepted. How they investigate. Opposition Lecture. The Elder's confusion. The "Quarter production." Result of the Giant's visit. Circle at Mr. Wells's. Taken at his word. Return to Boston. Father's Prophecy. Monthly meeting at Mrs. Leeds's. Circles. Second edition of Glens Falls. Rooms at No. 45 Carver Street. A Spiritual Household. "Big thunder." Remarks.

"Know all; know infidels, unapt to know,
'Tis immortality your nature solves,
'Tis immortality deciphers man."

Returned home from the Falls; my stay, however, was transient, as Mr. Brown and myself were ordered by our spirit guides to Albany; found some difficulty in procuring rooms there, but when once located we received a fair amount of patronage. There is a great lack of curiosity and interest in spiritual truth in the old Dutch city. Long established prejudice is too deeply rooted to be removed, without much difficulty; hence Albany will be one of the *rear* cars in this long life train; but, perhaps, for all that, it will arrive well filled. The seed sown there will be planted in the mud of bigotry and ignorance; but as the slow growing tree is sturdy and strong, and unflinchingly meets that storm, by which the towering but puny sapling is prostrated, so may our holy faith, when it penetrates the minds of the Albanians, become more enduring, more firm, in breasting the tempest of public opinion, than where it has met with more precociousness, and from the sandiness of the soil into which it has dropped, has withered and died from want of stability.

I continued in Albany about four weeks, and then went back to Kingsborough. Here father desired me to discontinue my séances, and seek other occupation in order to recruit my bodily vitality for some future day.

I entered into copartnership with Norman B. Dodge, than whom, I very much doubt, if there exist a man more totally void of every principle of honor and integrity. But as this episode in my life is unconnected with my spiritual experiences, and is not one of the green spots on memory's page, I only allude to it, in order to say that at this time scarcely a communication or manifestation could I obtain from my spirit friends. Morning succeeding morning found me sitting at my little table in the hope of witnessing some movement in that hand which had been so long a ready instrument for the conveyance of truth to the inquiring mind, and of consolation to the bruised and almost broken heart. I began to despair of ever again holding sweet converse with my angel visitors, when, after a lapse of about four months, while seated at my usual post, striving by patience and perseverance to recall vanished favors, a slight quivering was perceptible through my arm, and my hand wrote the following:

MY CHILD:

Use thy powers with wisdom; destroy *not* thy gift by vain and foolish efforts; but when to thy soul is presented a *hungry* traveler on life's pathway, *open* thou the doors of thy gifted temple, and welcome him; feed him with the manna of life, and thy abundance shall show thy benevolence, and thy *future* joy shall picture to thee those that have enjoyed *real* life at thy hands. We are now to send thee forth from thy own hearthstone, and thou shalt have as thy duty the watering of the feeble plants by the way, that have been wilted by superstition, and blasted by bigotry. Each soul that gains wisdom by thy aid, shall be as a sparkling gem, a glowing ruby, a precious treasure to thy house in the future. Henceforth thy power shall receive no check, but smoothly shalt thou glide, undisturbed by influences detrimental, and uninfluenced by those that would place discord at the gate of thy prosperity.

Thy Spirit Guardian and Father,

ALEXANDER.

Swanee (an Indian spirit, and, *en passant*, one in whom we had great confidence, and who had identified himself in every possible manner,) became, after this second advent of my mediatorial powers, a constant attendant and communicator at the circles I held. As an original character drives away long faces, and gives a more natural and passive tendency to the mind, his presence seemed absolutely indispensable; his rap could always be distinguished from that of other spirits, it being a loud, heavy, mallet-like sound, at some distance from the table. He was frequently seen by Mrs. Green, who described him as a stalwart, noble-looking person, possessing all the endowments of moral and physical superiority. He evinced much partiality for Clark Dye, a hunter, and would accompany him to the woods, often apprise him of the game's locality, and give an unerring aim to the rifle. That he should be a great favorite with those whose fastidiousness did not lead them to conclude that spirits should eternally chant Te Deums, and converse of naught but heaven and beatification, is not astonishing; truly, a jolly boon companion, and a merry, welcome guest was our friend Swanee. One out of the many tests received from our friend of the merry green wood, may be neither inappropriate nor uninteresting in this place.

On an excursion with Mr. Dye, for the purpose of disturbing the haunts of the partridge and woodcock, I realized peculiar tests of the presence and knowledge of this Indian spirit. We were crossing a low marshy piece of ground, and being somewhat fatigued, sat down by a spring to partake of some refreshments; after the repast was ended, the jerking of my hand warned us that Swanee was near by; Mr. Dye, taking a blank book from his pocket, gave it to me, and my hand wrote something of the following import;

"Go east to a field of brakes, there you will find *three* birds, you will get *two*," at the same time pointing out the direction and the means of obtaining them. Although this seemed a somewhat novel performance, still there was but little doubt in our minds as to the superior knowledge of our spirit companion; oft repeated proofs of a similar nature had confirmed our faith in his accuracy to an incredible degree. Taking guns and dogs, we proceeded to the spot indicated by Swanee. Scarcely had we climbed the unusually high rail fence, when the dogs started one of the birds; Clark, who was noted for his excellent aim, brought the feathered unfortunate to the ground, and bagged him, remarking at the same time, "Well, there's one of the two." "Yes, and the other two will have to be quicker than shot to escape," said I. How one was to evade our combined shots, we could not conjecture. We separated in the centre of the field, Clark taking one side, I the other. Soon a report from my friend's gun gave evidence of *one* of the remaining two, and almost simultaneously, a bird took wing close by my side. I fired and fired, but its wings refused to fold, and, unharmed, it lit some few rods from where I stood. I followed, and again discharged my fowling-piece, but with the same effect. Clark now joined me, inquiring how many I had shot; but my answer was "ne'er a one." We both gave chase to the bird I had missed; we got him up once more, and fired four successive loads at him; but all in vain; we saw the nimble wings bearing the small body and long bill far, far away above the trees of a wood near us. "Gone," said Clark, "and we may as well evacuate these premises, for Swanee is even now chuckling over the fulfillment of his prophecy." Thus ended this day's ramble, and with it (had it been needed), confirmation strong of the perceptive powers and truthfulness of our invisible friend.

Visitors from Mayfield, Gloversville, and Johnstown, thronged Pleasant Square to hold converse with those after whom their souls yearned; and on Sundays, it was difficult to tell whether Mr. Brown's house or the church contained the larger congregation.

Mr. S. Ripton, a member of the Johnstown Methodist church, and one in good standing, both religiously and materially, was so full of interest in this truth, that it was no unusual thing for him to drive eight or ten miles two or three times a week, attended by friends, for the purpose of satisfying those who sneered at him, for making what they called "a fool of himself." This sage commentary upon what they deemed their friend's weakness, was generally dismissed after seeing and receiving the overwhelmingly convincing tests that were usually theirs on such occasions. Thus it is with the world (or rather with the narrow minds in the world), they call their neighbor *fool*, and laugh him to scorn for knowing *more* than they do, but after gaining some insight, and tasting of this same tree of knowledge, are fain to exclaim:

> "This tree is not, as we are told, a tree
> Of danger, tasted; nor to evil unknown
> Opening the way, but of *divine* effect
> To *open eyes*."

How frequently, in my journeyings, have I been stopped with the salutation, "Well, Redman, do you still believe in necromancy and Devilism?" "Certainly I do," would be the response. "Have you ever witnessed what you term Devilism?" "No! nor have I any desire." "Then show your wisdom by studying that, of which you declare your ignorance, ere venturing an opinion. A *fool* can pooh! at simple addition: wise men often do the same at *simpler truths*." A few such retorts generally silence those who view this subject through the dense veil of their own folly and superstition.

Seasons for prayer, periods for exhortation and condemnation, were almost innumerable at this time. The clergy of Johnstown, in an especial manner, thundered forth their anathemas, which caused that part of the community still in leading strings to quail and loudly pray. But their darts of vengeance fell pointless on those at whom they were principally aimed, for from Mr. Shuler, and other Spiritualists of that place, I received an earnest solicitation to once again take up my residence there. Mr. Shuler had many times visited me at Pleasant

Square, and had become sufficiently interested to wish me to make his home temporarily mine, and to try the experiment of holding regular investigating circles. Having acceded to his proffered arrangement, the Fall of 1854 found me at Mr. Shuler's mansion, prepared to beard the frantic bishops and priests, and to convince them how futile were their endeavors to uproot such a God-given reality. To them I felt might not be inaptly applied the words, "Paul ! Paul ! 'tis hard for thee to kick against the pricks."

Our first circle, which consisted of Mr. and Mrs. Shuler, T. Ripton, R. H. Johnson, G. Perkins, and myself, was not very satisfactory, for shortly after being seated, quite a number of full-grown boys and girls, each furnished with a respectably sized stick, began amusing themselves with performing initiatory lessons in drumming, on different parts of the house, and although Mr. Shuler's presence caused an immediate retreat, yet passivity was scarcely restored, ere our ears were again assailed by their noisy uproar ; so with the exception of a few raps, nothing was obtained.

Our second effort was more successful. Mr. Shuler's grandfather announced his presence, and entrancing me, spoke long and fondly to his child. This interview was deeply affecting, and many that listened, shed tears. Mrs. Shuler was influenced to write, and strong physical manifestations were given.

At the conclusion much satisfaction was expressed. Mr. Shuler and myself accompanied Mr. Johnson to the hotel, and gave a statement, to the guests there assembled, of the evening's occurrences. The usual terms of humbug, &c., &c., were forthwith currently applied. But some, claiming to have more brains than the rest, entered into what they termed a philosophical explanation: but the exemplifications involving more that was inexplicable than the facts, and not edified or enlightened by the abstruse problems advanced, I withdrew about midnight; but understood, on the following day, that the excitement was continued far into the morning hours, without any nearer climax to the bona fide truth.

Mediums multiplied in all directions. A musical spirit took possession of Mr. S. Wemple, when he (although not knowing one note of music from another) played on the violin with surprising accuracy. This manifestation attracted large and wondering audiences.

A few evenings after my arrival in the Council seat of the Mohawks, I held a sèance at Mr. T. Ripton's, composed chiefly of members of the old Methodist Church, who with long faces, (and I *suppose, sanctified* souls,) propounded their ecclesiastical questions, and often received answers adverse to their preconceived notions. One member especially, Mr. H., seemed keenly alive to such discussions; he would become excited, shake his silvered locks, and I am forced *feelingly* to relate, that in one of his antics of rage, brought down his crutch (he was lame,) with no gentle raps on my pedal extremity. Notwithstanding these sanctimonious contentions, we managed to have a part of the time devoted to tests, and thereby convinced some of the righteous, that the operating powers were unconnected with diabolism, necromancy, or trick. In view of the accumulated proofs one by one let fall their preconceived ideas, and supported by reason and philosophy, came with gladdened hearts and rejoicing souls into the spiritual faith.

In view of the sparse attendance at the Methodist meeting house, and the failure of prayer and exhortation to recall the wandering sheep, Mr. Mattison, the author of a work, entitled "Spiritual Manifestations explained and exposed," was summoned to lend his aid in leading back those who were verging on the confines of Satan's habitation. The learned expositor of his own ignorance speedily came to the assistance of the brother in tribulation, and his presence was intimated by large placards posted in the most conspicuous parts of the town, proclaiming the arrival of a "Lion," and the recommendation to all "wolves in sheeps' clothing" to evacuate the place, at the same time announcing that a lecture on Spiritualism would be delivered at the Methodist church on the ensuing evening. A meeting of Spiritualists was immediately called, when it was voted to send and ask Mr. Mattison and the Reverend Mr. Dudley to attend a séance at Mr. Shuler's, previous to the delivery of the lecture; in accordance with the resolution, a messenger was dispatched to the Reverend's abode with the invitation, and the following was the reply returned: "Dear Sirs, Mr. Mattison having fully investigated the subject, seeks no further opportunity—but, should it please you to call at 3 P. M. we shall be at home."

Not wishing to be laid aside in this manner, a committee was selected to visit the sanctum sanctorum; two mediums were to attend, Mr. Edward Cooper and myself, and at the designated hour we all pursued our muddy way, (it had rained the preceding night,) to the Reverend's domicile; having reached which in safety, an introduction of the party by Mr. Miles Brown, gone through, and a table (after some demur) obtained, we seated ourselves around it, expecting to see the other persons present join; but such was none of their intent. Mr. Dudley started up stairs like one deranged, and shortly after came down in fever heat, with an arm full of books that looked as if they had been saved from destruction, "yet so as by fire." "There, translate *that* passage, and *that*, and *that*," said he, pointing to different places in the volume before him. Mr. Brown assured the learned theologian that spirits did not come for the purpose of translating Hebrew, Greek and Latin, but simply to convince mortals of their presence and power ; he then requested him to take a chair at the table. "Sit up to the table," said Mr. Mattison. "No ! no ! Go on with your humbug, *we* stand aside to *detect*, not to *join* with you," at the same time stretching himself up like an enraged gobbler. Notwithstanding his denunciations, he was requested again and again to join, but in vain ; he persisted in refusing, and in declaring his superior knowledge of the manifestations, at the same time showering on us a succession of epithets, which although in perfect keeping with the blusterer's entire deportment, were rather too unrefined for ears polite. Messrs. Brown and Shuler, becoming rather excited at the ungentlemanly behavior, denounced those who *feared truth* and its investigation, and we took our departure.

The evening drew nigh when Spiritualism and Spiritualists were to be annihilated. The sidewalks were lined with multitudes all eager to attend the immolation. Mr. Brown, Mr. Shuler, and myself, three of the principal victims, presented our doomed persons at the door of the sacrificial temple, and having dropped the required dimes (there was an entrance fee of ten or twelve cents per head) into the hand of the attendant acolyte, proceeded to take our places and collect our thoughts preparatory to the awful moment of total demolition. The Great High Priest of the night arose, and called orally on the Lord to bless the cause of the meeting ; internally, I dare say, he was praying for the sale of certain books piled up by his side, which he declared he would dispose of at cost price.

Having delivered his ejaculatory invocation, he began quoting from Judge Edmonds, A. J. Davis, Ambler and others, animadverting with sarcastic insolence on all points opposed to the rusty dogmas and creeds of which he was the advocate, and intermingling his comments with ridiculous anecdotes, originating, in all human probability in his own brain, for the purpose of eliciting laughter from those in the audience, who were only less despicable than himself, because less maliciously ignorant. He adduced some Greek characters written by Fowler, pronouncing them plagiarisms ; related his detections of mediums, and gave the programme of our afternoon's performances, intermixed with euphonious epithets similar to those I have already alluded.

One of the elders of the church was next introduced : he remarked "that he had a few words to say previous to the dismissal of this important meeting ; but ere laying before the assembly his views, he would suggest an intermission of fifteen minutes, during which Mr. Mattison would offer for sale his valuable work, entitled "Spiritual Manifestations, explained and exposed." A general rush was made for the speaker's desk, and for about half an hour quarter dollars accumulated around him, during which the Professor's face dilated with an acquisitive grin, and he favored his listeners with the accompanying history of his *quarter* production.

Friends and Brothers:—

This work contains a large number of plates, engraved expressly for it at my own expense; one of which is a representation of a writing medium, who sits perfectly passive at his table, while the devil in the opposite corner is impressing him. Another represents a trance medium; his own spirit stands some feet from his body, shivering in a cloud, while another is seeking entrance into his form, the feet of which may be perceptible in the cranium. Another diagram exhibits physical manifestations—the medium stands on one side giving orders, while in the background may be seen a table and an unlucky visitor flying in the air, thus violating all the known laws of gravitation, &c., &c.

The above is a synopsis of the ridiculous harangue of this Reverend Mr. Mattison. I do not wish it understood that I have, throughout, given his exact words, because all his frivolous puerile vociferations my memory could not retain, but it is the substance of what he said, and partially the exact language.

The time allotted for vending and intermission concluded, the elder once more became the cynosure of all eyes, and opened his valedictory with a relation of an occurrence said to have taken place in a saw mill upon Mayfield mountain. "The Reverend Mr. Yale, a devout teacher, had been represented as communicating with a parcel of Sabbath breakers in a saw mill," was the tenor of the speech, which was closed by denouncing me as the medium. Truly, when the Reverend was so scandalized and thought it degrading to have his co-laborer present himself in a *saw mill* on the Sabbath, for the purpose of either finishing the work he had left incomplete, or of correcting erroneous teachings he had inculcated while in the form, and thus trying to feed those he had left starving; He must sadly have forgotten the lowly cradle of the Great Medium, and the sanction that that same pure being gave to his disciples breaking the ears of corn on the Sabbath, when they were a hungered. But to my theme; scarcely had the orthodox gentleman closed his strain of eloquence, when an influence seized and lifted me upon the bench, on which I sat, and involuntarily, on my part, I pronounced his remarks to be false and without foundation. This produced some excitement, which was quieted by his observing, "I will leave the audience to use their own judgment, whether to believe a minister of the gospel or a spirit rapper." The ceremonies were then closed amidst hissings, cheerings and stampings of feet.

"And when the tumult dwindled to a calm,
We left *them* to practice the hundredth psalm!"

Shortly after this renowned exposé, Mr. Dudley, as I learned, renounced his Methodist faith and became a proselyte to some other creed; and the success of Professor Mattison's lecture was evident, in circles becoming more numerous, the credence given to the manifestations witnessed, stronger; and the subject being generally debated.

My services, the evening after this lecture, were engaged at Mr. Wells's, there were present including

Miss Wells, who presided at the piano, nine persons. The circle, after having been favored with various well executed pieces of music, became restless in consequence of delay in the manifestations, when Mr. W's. son expressed a desire for a specified spiritual performance, which, if gratified, would convince him beyond all doubt. "If," said he, "the spirits will move a tangible object disconnected with the medium, I will doubt no more: if they will move the piano at which M—— is sitting, I will believe; *break* it, *smash it in pieces*, do anything with it. I am going to New York next week, and if they break it, I will buy another." No sooner were the words uttered than the piano (a heavy rosewood instrument,) turned a complete summersault in the air, and fell upon the floor, jarring the *whole house.*

A rush was made for the instrument, to ascertain if it were broken, and at the same moment, the attention of a part of the company was directed to Mrs. W., who had fainted, and fallen. The lady was taken into an adjoining room, and then the instrument examined to see how far the injuries extended. While four strong men were raising it, Miss W. exclaimed, "Oh! my poor piano! 'tis broken all to pieces." But no, it was unharmed, except the breaking of a hinge, and was not even out of tune. "Well!" said one of the party, "what do you think of that, John? You were taken at your word, and it came near costing you some five hundred dollars." John's conclusion was to ask no more decisive demonstrations. The company now adjourned to pay attention to Mrs. W., who had been completely overpowered. This closed that evening's circle, and all meetings of a spiritual character, for some time; the conclusion being, that the manifestations were injurious to nervous, sensitive persons. The good Book says, "Seek and ye shall find, knock and it shall be opened." But, when we are seeking and knocking, we should be careful neither to *seek* nor *ask* for that, which, upon mature reflection, we would rather not possess: and those of nervous temperaments should not seek to be present at demonstrations, which, when witnessed, are overpowering to their keen susceptibilities. Had the request to the spirits *not* been complied with, the cry would have been "humbug:" being *acceded* to, it was, "the manifestations are injurious."

In accordance with instructions received from father, I, about this time, turned my wandering steps towards Boston; on reaching which city, I, through the same parental guidance, located myself in the house of Mr. Gates, whose family were all Spiritualists. While here, my room was perpetually crowded by anxious investigators—scarcely had I one leisure moment. Hour after hour, day succeeding day, were passed in the same (to me) monotonous occupation; but to my visitors, there was a perpetual influx of light, joy, and satisfaction. To encourage and cheer me through the dull routine of every day duty, I at this period received a communication from my guardian (father,) in which he briefly sketched an outline of my future: a copy of which I herewith subjoin.

Beloved Son—

Ever near you, I behold each act. My spirit's love for you, bids me also *direct* each act: if then, with persevering fortitude, you continue to be advised and directed by me, how can you stray?

I would not take from you the identity that God hath given you; neither would I bar from thee certain privileges, that you are permitted to enjoy. In short, I would make thee dependent on thyself, and, at the same time, dependent upon angels for directions, when their superior wisdom shall overreach the boundary of thy personal vision. At all times use thy judgment, and in no instance allow thyself to swerve from its promptings. If I advise, I will also appeal to thy better sense as to the philosophy of that advice, and bring thy mortal to know the reasons of our immortal.

I would, at this time, plant a seed in the soil of thy soul, and follow me, as I trace its growth for a time.

You are to remain here, in this house, but a short time. You will be urged to remain. You will attend a meeting of harmonial friends, and in that assembly you will receive a new impetus, which shall not only lay open a wider field to thy influences, but associate thee with all that shall tend to develope, purify, and make thee more perfect as a teacher, as an instrument; and one of the few who are to bear the *cross* in a holy cause.

My child, thy developments are to become even stronger than thy most sanguine hopes. Physical things shall move at thy approach, and thy name shall be first among those who move in these ranks of truthful philosophy—from north to south, from east to west, thy name shall be spoken, connected with manifestations given by us through thee. But not to thyself be the praise, my child, for thou art but an orbit wherein the mighty wheel of progress shall roll and mark its immortal career. Thou art but a simple earthen jar, wherein the plant of life shall grow, mature, and blossom for the world.

Work on, then, my son; tire not at this early stage of thy career; but lend cheerfully thy hand, wherever the wheel of spiritual truth needs an additional revolution: the great future contains thy reward. From time to time, I will prop up thy branches and make thee strong.

Thy loving parent and guardian,

ALEXANDER.

My séances at Mr. Gates's continued throughout the winter, during which time my development became gradually stronger, and not wanting in tests of identity. During my residence here, through the polite invitation of Mr. A. Adams, I made my débût at the monthly spiritual reunion, held at the residence of Mrs. J. B. Leeds, 45 Carver Street. On the evening of my introduction, found the large parlor at Mrs. Leeds' filled with a goodly company, all anxiously desirous of receiving spiritual communications: prominent among the mediums present was Mrs. Leeds, who, for spiritual fervor, amiability, pureness of motive, and internal spiritual principle, has no superior. A circle of mediums was formed in the centre of the room, and after some singing by the company, an Indian spirit, purporting to be that of Red Jacket, controlled Mrs. Leeds, and gave eloquent evidences of a superior mind having command of her organs. The remarks of this spirit were followed by those of others, all of which contributed to the pleasures and profits of the evening. No manifestations of any moment were given through me, save a few revolutions of a centre-table, which might have been accounted for on the principle of mechanical pressure. This evening passed off most agreeably, and, *spiritually* speaking, the benefit to me was great; I could perceive new influences taking possession of my system, and though months had elapsed since father's communication, I could at this moment plainly see the first step towards the corroboration of his statements. At a subsequent meeting of a few friends at Mrs. Leeds's house, a large centre-table, at which the company were sitting, was taken entirely from the floor, carried over the heads of all present, and placed at a distance of some feet from the circle. So lightly and prettily was this manifestation performed, that scarcely a sound above our voices was perceptible.

Subsequently to the above, and in the presence of the same party, a manifestation similar to that which took place at Glens Falls in the house of Mr. McDonald, occurred.

After interchanges of salutations with our spirit friends, we were desired to repair to an upper room, which was quieter and more retired than the one we usually occupied ; we complied, and took our seats as usual. On the table before us lay a lead pencil and paper, these we were directed to place on the floor, and to commence singing ; we obeyed the injunctions, and after the lapse of a few minutes, we were notified to take up the pencil ; but lo ! it had disappeared—a search was immediately instituted, but it could no where be seen ; we reseated ourselves, when we were told to look underneath the carpet—we did so, and the missing pencil was found, placed directly under the table and beneath the spot in the carpet on which it had been previously laid ; with it was a note, purporting to come from the spirit son of Mr. A. B. Hall. It was signed with his name, the writing was in printed capitals, and was very distinct. Other manifestations of a similar or equally convincing character, all tending to carry conviction of supermundane agency, and to show that "change makes not death, except to clay," were received by all present.

Towards the close of the winter, I was requested by spirits through both Mrs. Leeds and myself to change my location and establish myself at 45 Carver Street. Thus actuated by this and the additional counsel of friends still in the earthly body, I became a resident in the family of Mrs. Leeds.

Behold now an interesting spiritual household—my apartments on the first floor, where the manifestations, being principally of a physical character, were calculated to awaken interest and inquiry ; Mrs. Leeds occupying those above, where the teachings uttered through her tended to instruct in the divine philosophy of our faith after the *ice* of doubt had been broken ; 'twas a spiritual volume, in which the facts that were perused below were substantiated by the philosophy above. Many who entered the portals of that dwelling, adverse to every thing connected with our belief, were compelled ere leaving it to admit :

> " C'est en vain qu 'on se met en défense
> Le bon Dieu touche les cœurs lorsque moins on y pense."

Among the earliest and not the least prominent of my spiritual visitors, after my removal to Carver Street, was an Indian spirit, who gave his name as "Big Thunder." He always announced himself by a loud sonorous rap in one corner, and usually made his appearance with Mr. Adams, of whom he purported to be the guardian spirit. Were my eyes closed on the entrance of this gentleman, I could detect his presence by the peculiar rap of his red attendant. Not alone, however, in *raps* did our forest friend excel, but in all manifestations where great physical force was requisite ; indeed, he seemed to take delight in such exhibitions ; and did we at any time need an independent performance, we had only to dispatch a messenger for him, and, without any delay, he would wait upon us. I would not have it understood that we regarded him as subservient to our will, but that he was a fine spirit, who, being ever anxious to do good, was willing to comply with our requests, when, from his knowledge of the results, he felt that his assistance could be beneficial. Here I would say, that throughout my mediatorial life, there have always been spirits, remarkable for great power, upon whom I could call when a manifestation of a physical character was necessary, and whom I have always found willing to do all in their power, even if what they did was not exactly that which, at the time, I desired.

The person, who rejects a physical demonstration of spiritual power, on the plea that it is low, or proceeds from a low class of intelligences, should, in my opinion, *cast* from him *all* that grows *beneath* the soil, and partake only of that which matures in the *uppermost* part of the tree—or *idolize* the *majestic* oak, and repudiate the acorn whence it springs. I view the physical phenomena of Spiritualism as the foundation of the whole philosophy; *without them* we *sink* back on *faith alone*, deprived of a *tangible basis.*

Is it low, degrading, or useless to study the minor grades of development in *any* condition of life? Is there not a volume of perfection, beauty and wisdom to be found in the billow-tossed sea-weed, or earthly shrub? Does not the perfume of the lowly violet speak as plainly of its divine origin, as that exhaled by the queenly rose? Do not the cowslip, and wild flower of the prairie display the perfection of the Almighty constructor, equally with the choice exotic of the hot-house ?

In almost every spiritual community are found mediums and Spiritualists, who express disgust for the more tangible manifestations of spirit presence, and loudly proclaim the trance speaker, and clairvoyant as superior orders of development. That trance speakers more freely express ideas, is *true ;* and it those ideas, purporting to be spiritual, are so altogether, then truly is the abnormal condition a superior mediumistic development : but this it is not. Every idea expressed through such channels, is tainted, more or less, with the characteristics of the brain through which it comes ; and without doubt we may take seven-tenths of such matter at a discount. The only perfect mode of spirit communion *free* from mortal interference is, where the communication given, is *wholly* mechanical, and disconnected entirely from the mind of the medium, which can be obtained in various ways,—by rapping, tipping, or writing in such a manner, that the medium cannot read it at the time.

I am well aware that there are believers in Spiritualism who contend, that all communications given, in whatever possible manner, are more or less connected with the minds of those present, or more particularly with that of the *medium. I deny this in toto ;* and the sooner persons upholding this doctrine disabuse themselves of their error, and learn to the contrary, the better. Another erroneous idea advanced by many, possessed of more zeal than knowledge, is, that the *extremities* of mediums *must* become comparatively *frigid*, or the pupil of the eye be *abnormally dilated* (when they are influenced by spirits) is likewise without foundation ; and certainly those who devote their life and time to practical mediumistic experiences, should be deemed prior authority, and more competent judges, than persons who merely theorize.

CHAPTER V.

William Lovett's Interview. Communication. Mr. Allen Putnam's Seance. Mr. Hart's Letter. W. A. Fogg's Manuscript. Poem. Mr. Charles Bruce's astounding Experiences. Shelley.

"Thou, *thou* hast rent the heavy chain that bound thee;
And this shall be my strength—the joy to think
That thou mayst wander, with heaven's love around thee,
And all the laughing sky!"

In the early part of the spring, while still a resident in Boston, I was called on by Mr. W. Lovett, who came, he said, not so much for the purpose of testing the matter, as to have certain questions, that were already written, and which he held in his hand, answered. This much explained, Mr. L. propounded his questions as follows :—

Will the spirit of my father answer question No. 1? No response.

Is father present? No.

Will the spirit present, if a friend of mine, give its name? Yes—accompanied with a call for the alphabet. Edward D. Lovett, the name spelt.

Here the inquirer paused, and seemed much affected. He then told me that the spirit claiming to be present was a brother, who had been absent from home for many years, and as he had never been heard from, was generally supposed, by his friends, to be dead. Continued rapping, during this explanation, showing a desire on the part of the spirit to converse. Mr. Lovett then addressed him thus:—

Dear Brother, do you see father, and the rest of our loved ones?

"Yes, William, I am with father and sister; we live and progress together; though we are *not* in the same circle, still we see and know each other's acts, and our spheres not being distant, we can sympathise."

What is your condition in your spirit home?

"'Tis difficult for me to express in *mortal* words my condition; but it is *far* different from the earth state. I find we can dispense with many of the necessities of *earth*, and there is added to us much that we had *not* while mortal; I find an equality in every thing—temperature, health, appetite, &c.; at the same time, there is a constant desire to diligently study, that I may reach a higher grade of development."

You say "you have a constant desire to study." Study *what?*

"Cause and effect, dear brother. *Effect*, we know, is a child of *Cause;* and to determine the character of that cause is our study. The same principle governs alike the moth, and more beautiful of the insect world; if we understand *how* the *one* is developed—the spiritual principle that first expands its tiny wings—we can apply the same divine law to the unfolding of *every* living thing, for in every thing there is life. 'Tis an eternal study, William, and one, of which man can know but little ; he may judge of effect and admire it ; he may criticise, and ecstacise—'tis well ; but he cannot go *before* himself, for the *cause* of his existence was prior to *him ;* in himself, he sees the *effect.* This was one of the questions you were to have asked father. I have answered it as well."

Will father be here with you at this time ?

"He will not ; his spirit was cognizant of your engagement, but he was unable to attend ; he will, however, meet you at your next interview with this medium."

Can you tell me, dear brother, when and where you died, or left the earth ?

"One question at a time."

When did you leave earth ?

"November, 1843."

Can you tell me the day of the month ?

"No."

Where did you leave the earth from ?

"New Orleans."*

Here this interesting séance ended.

A few days subsequent to the above, I was called

* The communications or manifestations marked thus * have been already published by the Spiritual Press.

on by Mr. Allen Putnam, accompanied by two ladies. After the party assembled around the table, names were written on ballots, as is customary; this is done, I would here observe, not so much to procure tests, as an invitation to those with whom we are desirous of communicating: in this instance, some five minutes elapsed after the pellets being written, when one was selected and handed to one of the ladies; on it was the word, Benjamin, a name which she had placed among her invitations. The remaining pellets were all gathered into my hand, then placed in that of the other lady, and afterwards all withdrawn, save one, when Catherine was written, purporting to be the name on the paper left; this was also correct, both as regards the name and the writer of the ballot. Mr. Putnam, likewise received a pellet, which was attended with an equally satisfactory indication of his spirit friend's presence. The table was made to manifest tokens of pleasure, by being turned upon its side and end, and perform other feats. A communication was then written, in which the unseen intelligence expressed a desire to fulfill a certain promise made to one of the ladies previous to her leaving home. The promise was, "that she should receive a communication written under the table, without human hands." A card, with a sheet of blank paper, was placed under the table, and the following was written legibly:

* My Dear Mortal Friends—

I am very near you, though you cannot appreciate my presence. Faithfully, your spirit friend,

Benjamin.

Much was received at this session that was interesting, but the *writing* was noted as being strikingly characteristic of the spirit, while in the form:

"O! that the tide of the world was pure enough for us to give the glorious truths, which are now waiting in the spheres! But be patient. Slowly and steadily come the waters from the mighty ocean upon the mind of the natural world: 'tis now but a little rivulet, running round a few truth-seeking hearts; 'tis not yet sufficiently strong to carry all bigotry before it; but it swells, as each morning sun rises, and will swell and strengthen, until those walking tabernacles of sin shall be overwhelmed and drowned."

At the same sitting, another spirit wrote:

"Each flower, each plant, each stem that grows
But to the heart perfection shows;
And each doth some sweet anthem sing,
In honor of these days of Spring.

The *Spring* of *Truth*, we mean, that sends warm rays of wisdom (while it blends harmonious chords from nature's bower,) on hearts, to paint the purest flower."

The following highly interesting letter, containing an account of Mr. Hart's introduction to Spiritualism, has been kindly tendered by that gentleman.

Doctor Redman :—

Dear Sir:—The facts connected with my first sitting with you are simply these.

You requested me to write on different slips of paper the names of my friends who were in the spirit world. I wrote ten, rolled (not folded) each one separately into little pellets, and then mixed them thoroughly together on the table before me.

You then, pointing at each pellet with your pencil, asked, if there were any of my spirit friends present, and if they would pick out their names. Three raps answered "yes," and two of the ten were pushed towards me, the names in which were spelt by the alphabet being called, previous to opening, and in each case correctly.

One of the names was that of my *Father*. I then asked if the intelligence (for I did not *then* believe in spirit communion) could give me any proof, by which it could be identified. The answer, "I will try," came ; and I commenced asking questions, all of which were answered in accordance with facts then in my possession, and correctly, with one exception. The question was, "How many were with you at the time of your death ?" and the answer received was *seven*. This I believed to be erroneous, for previous to calling on you, I had written the names of (as I believed) all, who sailed with my father, and there were *six only*. I varied the question, insisting that there was a mistake ; but was as positively told that I was wrong ; and at last it was written through your hand, "there were eight of us in the boat." Here I was forced to let the matter rest, and although in after sittings I received ample proof, by which I could, and did identify the spirit as that of my father ; still I could not get any other answer to the disputed question than the one first given.

For three months that answer was inexplicable to me ; but, at the end of that time, I visited my home and learned from my mother and brother that, in fact, *I was wrong*, for seven persons did sail with my father.

You can judge of the strength or force with which this test struck me. "*Od force* and *mind reading*" were wholly inadequate to explain it away, and if I had had no other proof of my father's presence, that would of itself been sufficient to,

Yours, very truly, SAMUEL C. HART.

At one of the regular public circles, which I held weekly, while residing at Mrs. Leeds', Mr. W. A. Fogg, who was a constant attendant, received a communication written without mortal hands. The hands of all present were at the time on the table, and the room lighted by two gas burners. The communication reads thus:

"O! try to be good, I am ever with you."—JULIA.

Another, at the same circle, and addressed to the same gentleman, was given through my hands. In consequence of the singular manner in which it was written, Mr. Fogg preserved it as a curiosity. While writing, my attention was directed to different persons in the circle, as they were asking questions in order to draw my mind from what I was doing. The first and second lines of this singular production were written backwards and inverted. Of the fourth line, *each word was spelt backwards;* the next line backwards and inverted, the next the usual way, the last inverted and backward with a signature thus:

"NNA."

The communication reads in this manner:

* My Dear Brother:

I am near you trying to make known to you my guardian presence. If you knew the many anxious feelings of the spirit friends who have gone before, you would see the many endeavors which they make for thy spiritual welfare. O! try to fill well thy destination in this life, and bright angels will soon crown thee with rejoicings from the spirit world. I am ever near and will constantly watch thy progress. Thy spirit sister,

Ann.

The time occupied in writing the above, Mr. Fogg says, was not over a minute, and all the while I was conversing with some member of the circle

The ensuing poem was written through my hand, and purported to come from one, who while in this rudimental sphere declared, that

"Matter cannot
Comprehend spirit wholly—but 'tis something
To know there are spirit realms."

'Tis passing kind for nature's God to smile
In laws, that bid the mortal soul beguile
His hours in busy learning:
'Tis passing strange, that man from fact should stand
Like Eastern Mummies in their mounds of sand,
No page of progress turning.

And stranger still, since man was born of God,
Desires, like plants, to rise above the sod
And breathe the freedom given:
That he *content* should lie as planted, still
Refusing with the germ his shell to fill
And blossom in pure heaven.

These truths were not forgotten in the past,
Can they with olden miracles contrast
And *separate* by-ways trace?
No! for one's twin sister of the other,
Born by the same Eternal Father
In heaven's high resting place.

Amphictyon, like priests, did weak the wine,
That Greeks imbibing might not be divine,
And rob him of his plunder:
Ye Gospel saints with Chameleon skin,
Would also chaff the barley in the bin,
Compelling dupes to hunger.

But day by day, these famish'd souls awake,
And with a strong convulsive tremor shake
These fetters off their feet;
Then rising to a sense of holy trust,
Will celebrate the hour, their chains had burst
And made them men complete.

At this period of my mediumship, I was frequently visited by Mr. Charles Bruce, of Cambridgeport, Massachusetts. His séances were weekly, and the manifestations received by him were of as extraordinary a nature as any I ever witnessed; so wonderful, indeed, that I expect but few, save those who were witnesses of the facts, will be disposed to give them much credence. I am satisfied, however, that all manifestations, occurring at the present day, will be corroborated by the future; and when greater works than these shall come to pass, then will doubts of what are now deemed marvels, settle into belief.

The greater part of the manifestations I am about recording, were published at the time of their occurrence, by Mr. Bruce, in the New England Spiritualist. Although they took place at different intervals, I have collected and embraced them all under one head.

MR. BRUCE'S MANIFESTATIONS.

The circle consisted of Messrs. Bruce and Andrews, and a lady friend of the former.

1. The spirit of Julia Bruce, the spirit wife of the first named gentleman, announced her presence, and wrote a short communication, in which she greeted her companion, and declared the pleasure she experienced at finding him still seeking for evidences of mortality, not through *faith* but by *works.*

A message was written under the table to Mr. B, of the following import,—"I will do all I can for you, to-night;" here the pencil dropped, and the sentence was left unfinished. The same test was repeated, when, "I am very near you. Julia," was added. The above papers are now in Mr. Andrews' possession.

*2 Mr. Andrews placed a watch under the table on the floor; after waiting a few minutes, the lady present felt the watch touch her clothing; we looked under the table, and it had disappeared; a short time after, we looked again, when the watch was found with its case open, in the place it had been first laid. The table was next raised, and remained balanced without contact for some minutes. This interesting séance was closed, the time appointed for its duration having expired ; great anxiety was, however, manifested by the invisibles to have it prolonged, promising us *much*, if we would only allow them time, but, quite time enough (and that in broad day light,) had already been given, during which, astonishment had been created that would serve as food for meditation, at all events, for a little while.

*3. At the request of my spirit wife, "Julia," I carried an accordeon to a sitting with Mr. Redman, 45 Carver Street, Boston, Julia having promised if I would do so, she would play upon it. We had not been long at the table before she called for the instrument. At her request, I put it on the floor under the table—it soon began to play without visible agency, and was played well, as I thought ; after a while, she wrote through his hand, "You may take up the accordeon now." On looking under the table, I found it in two parts, the top having been drawn out, an operation requiring the exercise of some force ; I took it up, put it together, and laid it again under the table. She then said to me, "Put your hand under the table, and I will hand it to you." I did so, and the instrument was immediately placed in my hand. At the request of Redman, the same was done for him. The accordeon was again placed under the table, and she said to me, "Tell Redman to look for his ring." (This ring had been given to Mr. R. some time before, and he wore it securely fastened to his watch chain, (it has cut some queer antics, and more may be expected of it.) Mr. R. searched for the ring, but, without being able to find it, he said, "Julia, what have you done with it?" she replied, "Take up the accordeon and look in that ;" we did so, and found the ring *within* the instrument.—CHARLES BRUCE.

While sitting alone with Mr. Redman I was requested by the spirit of my wife to put a newspaper (which I had brought with me,) under the table, I did so, and while Mr. R. and myself were bending over the table listening for sounds which were being produced, we smelt smoke; hastily springing up, we found the paper under the table in a blaze. There were no matches in the room, and the spirits claimed to have produced the fire by a chemical process.

Why may not this fact account for some instances of spontaneous combustion?

*5. At a subsequent meeting I was requested to lay my watch under the table; in a few moments after doing so, on looking for it, the chain, (a heavy gold one,) had been unfastened and had disappeared; both cases were open and the minute hand was taken off. Putting on the hand and closing it, I laid it on the table, when it suddenly disappeared. The spirit said she had taken it, but would return it before I left. As I was about to leave the room, I was directed to look beneath the table, and, behold, there was the watch, but no chain. On inquiring, I was told, the spirits would keep the chain till my next interview, which they did, and returned it, by placing it in my hand under the table.

*6. At a sitting with Mr. Redman, the manifestations this time eclipsed all previous ones.

A hand resembling a human one came up on one side of the table, and remained long enough for us to see that it was a perfectly formed female hand, and one of the most beautiful I ever saw. This was repeated several times; it occurred when no one else was in the room, and *in the light*. I then put a tambourine under the table, and the invisibles played on it for some time. I then held it with one hand under the table, and requested them to take hold of the other side; they did so, and gave me a specimen of their strength by taking it away from me. I next requested the spirit to take hold of my hand under the table ; I immediately felt a hand grasp mine, and I held it long enough to satisfy myself that, in all respects, it resembled a human hand. It had finger nails and was warm like the human hand. I could discern no difference. After this, to show us how they could use their hands, they untied our shoes, took off both *shoes and stockings*, and left us barefoot. The above are only a part of what was done, but a fair sample. I think such things are some proof of the agency of disembodied spirits. President Mahan to the contrary notwithstanding.

The editor of the New England Spiritualist makes the ensuing comment.

Incredible as the above might seem, were there no corroborative testimony; yet, it is but an item in the volume of evidence, which is accumulating on every hand.

We know Mr. Bruce, and his testimony on any other subject would be taken without hesitation.

The following manifestations with Mr. Bruce, have not before been published ; they will, no doubt, tax the credulity of many ; but, as the object of these pages is to set forth *facts*, as they *actually* occurred, I feel, that *withholding* anything, from the probability of its not being credited, is both weak and unnecessary, for there is a future, in which we may have presented to us a philosophy for occurrences, even more remarkable and incomprehensible.

Mr. Bruce is the possessor of many of this world's luxuries, some of them are certain fruit trees, which grow in his garden, among which is the delicious Bartlett pear. On one of his visits, Mr. B. brought with him several pears ; he presented me with two, which I laid away carefully, in the drawer of a closet in the room; when he exhibited the pears, on entering, loud raps were heard, and Julia expressed herself well pleased with her husband's present; according to his own statement, he had actually intended some of the pears for her. After sitting a few minutes, Julia commenced touching her husband, and Mr. Bruce's daughter likewise manifested her presence, by tipping the table into her father's lap. Mr. B., as usual, put his hand beneath the table, when Julia seized it, and there followed some powerful grasping and shaking of hands. Mr. B. next requested the spirit of an Indian chief, with whose manifestations he was familiar, to take him by the hand. "Almost immediately," says Mr. B., "a strong, rough, powerful hand grasped mine." He described the grasp, as altogether different from the gentle, delicate touch of his wife and daughter. At my request, the same manifestation was extended to me, but in a more forcible manner, if possible, than that given to friend B.

Mr. Bruce took one of the *pears*, and holding it in his open hand, invited Julia to take it; he held it a few minutes, when he assured me it had been taken from him, and he withdrew his empty hand from beneath the table. Again, he was touched on the knee, and putting his hand under again, to our surprise, he withdrew it with the *core* and *peelings* of the *pear*, which he had previously given Julia; prints of teeth were visible on the core, and the residue was in a mangled condition, as if fresh from the mouth of an epicure. We searched the room, but not a particle of the fruit could be found any where; hence, it was evident, that the *substance* of the pear had disappeared. Another pear was held in the same manner, for his daughter, and with a like *result,* except that a little *more* than the core was left. On going to the drawer, where I had placed the two given me by Mr. B., I found that both of them had been partly eaten, and there were unmistakable prints of teeth on what remained.

No one was in the apartment save Mr. Bruce and myself; the closet where my two pears had been placed was (as I have before said) in the room—its door was open, but the drawer closed.

The only way in which my reason can account for this extraordinary manifestation is, that by the aid of their hands, (and hands they have, for have we not felt and handled them?) they may so disfigure an article as to cause it to assume the appearance of having been bitten. Again, "if they have hands," says one, "why not a mouth, teeth, &c., &c.?" That they form the hand from the elements surrounding the medium is to my mind conclusive, and to form a mouth, teeth, &c., may be accounted for in the same manner. The precise philosophy for these formations is as yet not understood; we know the fact, and rest with it. The various philosophers in our spiritual ranks have all some theory of their own, and each tenaciously clings to his own idea; but according to my conception a more perfect condition of mental culture will have to be attained ere such things can be satisfactorily explained. All spirits that I have questioned on this point agree that the precise philosophy of touch, as given by them, remains for us a future study.

At another time, after an interchange of our usual manifestations, such as shaking hands, and other tangible demonstrations, we suddenly felt a dampness in the atmosphere of the room. Scarcely had we commented on this change of temperature to each other, when a *light shower of rain* descending upon us, completely wet the table at which we were sitting, and caused us to wipe the water from our face and hands. This being out of the customary mode of things, caused us some little astonishment; but we, at last, concluded, if spirits could produce *fire*, why not *water* also—a combination of chemical elements might produce the one as well as the other. Whether spirits would allow us to turn such experiments to a practical account is a matter that rests with themselves. I have often heard it said, "If spirits can move tables, why cannot we have them propel railroad cars?" Undoubtedly they could if it were necessary, and they chose to gratify mere vulgar curiosity; but while they might be willing to give such a test of their *power* and *resources* where they saw that an effort of the kind would eventuate in some benefit or use, they might not be equally ready to leave their bright abodes and pass their unlimited future in a repetition of the same, when by such a generating of steam the only progression produced would be an increased, gassy, vaporish vociferation of *humbug* and its sister epithets.

But to return to Mr. Bruce, who writes thus:

Before leaving Cambridgeport this afternoon, the spirits informed me, that if I would bring some eatable thing to my sitting with Mr. Redman, they would experiment with it—the spirit so promising purported to be an Indian Chief, whose mortal name was "White Cloud." Accordingly on my way to Boston, I purchased a pie, as I had some curiosity (inasmuch as the pears had been demolished) to see what my friends would do with that. I so wrapped my pie in paper that no suspicion should arise in the medium's mind as to its contents. On sitting at the table, I was as usual greeted with loud raps, and almost simultaneously with them my knee was touched. After enjoying these manifestations some little time, I held the pie beneath the table and uncovered it; almost instantly the pie was taken from me, and I withdrew my arm. A communication was now written to me by my wife, which I was directed to put in my pocket, and read after I returned home. My foot was next seized and raised so as to touch the under side of the table. I placed my hand once more beneath it, and as I did so, the pie was returned to me; on taking it from under the table, I found it had been cut in quarters; two pieces of it were missing and could no where be found. The pie had the appearance of having been cut with a sharp knife. The invisibles assured me, that they had performed the feat and had taken the portion that was missing. Not one crumb could be found on the floor of the room, and the hands of both Mr.

Redman and myself were on the table in full sight during the process, so that as far as we were concerned there was no possible human agency in the matter.

This will, no doubt, appear quite ridiculous to those who look at the *thing* and not the *philosophy*, but to me it shows a power more minute and delicate than that required to lift a table or produce raps. CHARLES BRUCE.

The communication here annexed, was given one day, about this time, on the departure of a member of Congress, with whom I had had a circle.

"I'll speak a word with thee, my friend. I, by chance, was passing, and a moment with one like thyself, seems like carrying a spring of water on one's back and spilling it here: perchance some *hungry* statesman may wet his feet therein, and, taking cold, have time for sweet reflection.

What think thee, has this bell* of many tongues a tinkling as of *brass;* or has it sides of gold so much, that it emits *no sound?* I hardly think the first, for brassy metals ring sonorous; nor more the next, since *pride* seems uppermost, and stands on ore like that. Can it be *Clay?* Oh, no! for *he* has long since passed beneath the arch of deeds, and treads on Memory's field alone. I have it: its *base*, *ambition* is; its *tower*, *pride;* its *metal*, *treachery* to *truth.* Three million *tongues* it has, and *they* are *slaves;* its welkin ring is not to call a church-hold, but to drag forth into the sunny fields thirty million fingers, all so black, that mortal *worth* and *dignity* sit like a sickened cuckoo—not too weak to sing, but, alas! has no notes. Who fed this vulture of the East, and bade it strut from hill to hollow? Not God! too wise is He to *cast* a form like this. Apollyon 'twas, who bade this biped *wallow*, thievishly hiding from man his *sack*: not that he is *white*, but *black.* The white man colored is; the dark, no shade at all. Then let *us* turn the *belfry*, and *freemen* term them all." SHELLY.

* Congress.

CHAPTER VI.

"A Visit to Worcester." Bolts drawn by spirits. "Affectionate Meeting." Mr. Lovett's second interview. Mr. Curtis from his Spirit Wife. "Fools not all dead yet." Mr. Farquhar and his odic Snuff Box. Call to Washington. Mr. Brooks. Doctor Gardner's letter. Communication from Sir John Carmichael. Vision.

"The Dead! Whom call we so?
They that breathe purer air, that feel, that know
Things wrapt from us!"

THE manifestations I am about relating, took place in Worcester, Mass., in the latter part of 1855. I give them as they were transmitted to me in writing by the lady, in whose presence and at whose house they occurred.

The lady, to whom I am indebted for the preservation of these facts, is one, whose known intelligence, and acuteness of perception, render it *impossible* for fraud to be practised on her without detection, and her well established reputation for veracity, places it altogether out of the question, that she would countenance trickery. These considerations, coupled with the position she holds in society, should place the occurrences (strange though they be) beyond the range of any possible deception, and divest them of cavil on the ground of human production.

The manifestations occurred in the presence of a number of the first citizens of Worcester, among whom were

Dr. Benjamin F. Heywood,	Perley Hammond,
Samuel Davis,	George W. Paine.

Also several ladies.

DR. REDMAN'S VISIT TO WORCESTER.

The manifestations commenced about eight o'clock by the rolling of a bell from the mantle-piece to the floor, as we stood at the fire waiting for breakfast. When we were seated at the table, I heard raps, and turned to my writing table for an alphabet I had a moment before put there for the use of a circle; it had disappeared, nor could we find it. The same alphabet, I may remark here, came and went twice during the day, in a manner that rendered the idea of interference on the part of the medium out of the question.

When we resumed our seats at breakfast, I found a salt spoon in my cup of coffee, and Dr. Redman an extra tea-spoon in his egg cup. The table was in frequent motion, and when he had finished his breakfast he was unceremoniously taken away from it.

About nine, A.M., a circle was formed, and many unexplainable things took place. I will mention but one, although there were many others, that might controvert the doctrine, that mental action in the circle, is the source of all apparent intelligence. Each person was requested to write several names on slips of paper, one name on each, to roll them into separate balls, and then throw them together on the table. These little pellets, the medium took in his hands, and rolling them over, flung them promiscuously upon the table ; then pointing with his pencil to the one which seemed to be attracted, he drew it out, and giving it to some one to hold, proceeded to write the name before opening it : in every case, he was correct, both as to the person, to whom he apparently at random gave it, and the name it contained. Where did he learn what even the owner of the paper could not tell, until he had examined ? Dr. —— had engaged him for an hour, commencing at eleven ; at this period, the power was very strong ; the table was raised several times from the floor, more than a foot, and held suspended horizontally for some seconds ; it was made *light*, so that you might raise it with your little finger, or *heavy*, requiring exertion to lift it : it rapped, and tipped, and tossed to and fro, and did other things expected of tables under the hand of a medium. The doctor wrote questions on one side of it, while the medium wrote answers on the other—sometimes simultaneously ; and I have the doctor's word for it, that the replies were appropriate.

This over, the medium went into the parlor, and sat at the piano; he said he could not play, but that the little music he could make, quieted his nerves, when he was weary, as he often appeared to be, after long-continued manifestations, while here. I sat down by the piano myself, and soon heard distinctly a tinkling guitar sound from within the instrument; it was evidently produced by vibration of the strings, but was occasionally as loud as a tiny bell, and would cease or sound at our request; and we should be grateful to an investigator of natural laws, who will give the law that can produce this.

On returning to the dining-room, we found an ornament from the corner of a picture frame, lying on the corner of the writing-desk. The picture thus despoiled, was at least thirty-five feet from where we found the fragment, and no one at that time had been in the room during the day, though I ought to add, the doors were open, and it must have been passed within a few feet of me, as I went through. I may as well state here, so as not to interrupt the subsequent account, with which these trivial things have no connection, that all day we were having similar occurrences.

A small Swiss box was opened, and its contents strewn over my desk; pencils were in perpetual motion, being taken from the table, and dropped in a distant part of the room; or, after we had hunted awhile, they would be quietly laid on the paper before us. My penknife was carried off just after I had pointed a pencil, and paper-cutters were never in their places; even now, one is missing, and another, in the first thirty hours after Dr. Redman left, came twice into an adjoining room. He lay on a sofa to rest himself, when a large apple, which stood on the mantle, rolled off, and bounding through space, we do not know how, fell at least seventeen feet from the chimney. A few cents were on the desk, they fell around him on the sofa and floor in a shower of copper, and several of them were tossed about at a later hour.

When dinner was brought in, I stood at the table a moment before calling Dr. Redman: hearing a rattling among some spoons, I looked and found a small key of a work-box that had been tied to the clapper of a bell to please a child; and hunting for the bell, it was found in the writing-desk at one end of the room, the chain was wrenched out with such force as to straighten a link, and was left on the table in the centre, from which it rose to fall on the floor.

We had not more than taken our seats at the dinner table, when a lady's glove fell noiselessly into a goblet, and the table began to rock and heave, and at last was raised at least a foot from the floor on one side, and some inches on the other; it was an old fashioned mahogany table, five feet square, and one of the heaviest I ever saw, but it tossed like a pine board. Twice or more, I thought we should have to leave our dinner; but we got safely through, and after it, Dr. Redman had another private circle, when writing was done under the table without hands, and other curious things occurred, but as it was among friends, I make no record.

Our table was even more unruly at tea time than it had been at dinner; it jarred our cups, spilt our tea, and threatened such havoc, that we hurried through as fast as possible from fear of accident.

Soon after tea, our evening circle began to collect. One of the ladies was startled at having the window by her side open of itself: the room had been warm through the day; and during the morning, I had been directed to open the window, which I had done, but had shut it again as evening approached; it now opened without human agency.

I had been promised early in the day that the strings of an Æolian harp should be played upon, accordingly we put it under the table around which we seated ourselves; soon we heard the clumsy frame knocking about, striking several of us, while trying to get a right position; that effected, the strings were swept again and again by the invisibles, for no current of air could have produced the sounds we heard; there could be no music on such an instrument, but the sounds were soft and sweet.

Suddenly we were ordered to go into the parlor. Redman declined, saying, "he could not play and it would be no use." Again we were ordered to "go into the parlor, and to the piano." He still objected, but I rose and said, "the order was too imperative to be disobeyed, we ought to go." As I insisted upon it, my guests could do no less than follow me, and we formed a circle of eleven persons, including the medium around the piano. We rolled the instrument from the wall, so as to admit a number of persons behind it; the piano was not, however, satisfied with that, but pushed forward, till it got room for its subsequent labors. Dr. Redman played a simple tune, and again was heard the guitar-like sound, but not as loud as previously. Mr. —— asked him to play "Buy a broom." He said he could not; but as he spoke his hands were seized by invisible influence, and he was controlled to play whether he would or not. Portions of "Buy a broom" were very distinct, and a march called for by Mr. —— was played so as to be recognized. We were now ordered to extinguish the lights, shut the doors and window shutters, open wide the piano, and keep in the circle. I held one of Dr. Redman's hands, Mr. —— the other. Singing being called for, "Old Hundred" and some other tunes were sung, and with the singing a series of manifestations commenced, that require an abler pen than mine.

As we sung, the piano struck into an accompaniment, frequently playing a whole line without stopping. Some thought there was additional music, but to my ear, it was more like an echo or vibration of the air within the strings than any thing distinct from it. The string seemed at times to snap, as if they were broken, and I said so; but, the instrument somehow gave me to understand that I was mistaken. It beat time with its legs, it beat time with its lid; it rocked and swayed about to and fro. Its weight appeared as nothing; in fact when the singing ceased it was like a living thing, emitting sounds so appalling they filled us with awe and wonder. Suddenly some one exclaimed: "I am touched." I know not how many were so favored: the touch received is so common to me, that I was less surprised than my friends; but I, too, had a new experience; *three* times I felt distinctly a living hand touch mine: first, a small hand apparently of a delicate skin, whose fingers ran rapidly over mine as one runs over the keys of a piano before commencing to play. It was not cold, but of a clammy, disagreeable softness, and I was saying to Dr. Redman that the effect of the touch was less pleasing than that on the dress, when a larger, firmer hand was laid on me, the palm on the back of mine. One cannot measure time very accurately under such circumstances, but I judge as I review the thoughts I had while it lay on mine, that it was with me some seconds.

Next I felt a cold air sweep across my face, and I asked, "Is that you, Redman?" "No, indeed, but I feel it *too*," was his reply. I rose from my seat so as to be above him, exclaiming, "If it come again, I will know the truth;" as if in answer to my doubt, a colder, stronger current rushed over me, my face, head, throat, and shoulders feeling its influence. At times I saw and felt a living presence about me, while my hand was clasped by one fully developed and perfectly human to my sense of feeling. It pressed mine as a human hand would do, long enough for me to reason with myself, and be sure there was no delusion. I looked for distinctness in this shadow, but it assumed none. I can only say with the Temanite, "When a spirit passed before my face it stood still, but I could not discern the form thereof." I cannot add that, "my hair stood up;" my thought (if it can be called a thought) was a longing to see the face as well as feel the hands; perhaps they were not connected. Both manifestations were unmistakably present to me, yet they were not necessarily connected in their origin.

In the midst of this excitement, before one of us had moved, and while we were in perfect stillness, the entry door was opened without hands. I stepped out of the circle and shut it, but was ordered to open it "wide—wide—wider," till I got it as wide as possible, and the light from the entry lamp was fully admitted.

Let philosophy and folly laugh at this if they choose, for so far as *Spiritualism* is concerned, they stand in the same category. The arguments and assertions of the one are equally valuable with the levity of the other: *facts* stand before both.

—— ——.

During this visit to Worcester, I attended a circle, in the family of a Spiritualist, whose residence was in a different direction of the town from that at which I was stopping. On leaving, I informed my hostess, that I expected to be back about nine or ten o'clock. The circle, however, being of unusual interest, and the manifestations of a startling character, I was (forgetting the promised hour of my return) induced to prolong the séance far beyond what I had anticipated. On leaving the party, I sauntered towards my resting place, (the distance of about half a mile); reaching the door, a strange feeling came over me,—I felt dizzy and seemed to be pushed forward. I could not account for this singular sensation, but arousing to my usual consciousness of surrounding objects, I found myself in the *hall*, in the act of taking off my overshoes. I was aware of being in the hall (which was perfectly dark) but a few moments, when I heard a voice, asking, "Who's there? who's there?" and at the same time, a head, accompanied by a lighted candle, appeared over the balusters. "Why, Redman, is that you?" said the voice, which I immediately recognized to be that of the lady of the mansion.— "How did you get in?" "At the door, I suppose," was my reply. "But," said the lady, "my son locked the door before retiring, as we thought you were not coming, it was so late." I related the singular feeling I had experienced. No doubt this was a temporary trance, during which the spirits had let me into the house. Here was as direct a spirit manifestation, as was that which opened the doors for the egress of Peter. A strict inquiry was instituted the next day, which ended in all being convinced, that the door had positively been unlocked by the invisibles for my accommodation.

This is one out of the numerous instances of a similar nature, that have transpired in my presence. Another opposite occurrence, was where a party, of which I was a member, had walked quite a considerable distance, and arriving at home, it was ascertained that the key of admission to the house had been left where the circle had been held; but by request, we were admitted without trouble. The medium present at that time, besides myself, was Mrs. Frances Green, of Mayfield, New York. Truly these things are unaccountable, and all that can be said is, *Ce sont les dons du ciel, et non de la raison.*

"Le bienheureux moment ('pour quils soient compris') n'est pas encor venu;
Il viendra, mais le temps ne nous en est past connu.'

Shortly after returning to Boston, from my Worcester visit, the following affectionate greeting was received by Mr. Whiting, at one of his weekly interviews with me, from a little spirit daughter. When the rapidity with which such productions are written is remembered, added to its being the effusion of a very young spirit, I think it more than interesting.

* As time swiftly flies, each moment brings nearer the meeting between my father and me. Long have I watched thy bark, father; long have I filled its sails, and helped on thy progress. I now stand on the shores of spirit-life, and hold out to thy view the beauties of that land, where mortality accepteth immortalilty. I will, instead of teaching thee of mortal things, unfold to thee spiritual realities; for man's days are as grass, he falleth beneath the scythe of Time: therefore, will my spirit open to thee spiritual blessings, and exhibit to thee pearls upon the gateway to the entrance of the sphéres.

Then over the waters, over the sea,
Thou'lt glide on, and yield thy mortality;
With hopes high and noble, still glide on in love,
I'll steer thy frail bark to those bright realms above.

Over life's waters,—yes, over life's sea,
I will draw nearer, still nearer to thee;
Gently the zephyrs shall waft thee along,
While the echo repeateth the notes of my song.

Over life's waters,—yes, over life's sea,
Angels will follow wherever you be;
Guardian's will watch thee, and cherish thee more,
As nearer thy frail bark-approacheth the shore.

Over life's waters,—yes, over life's sea,
Annie, thy dearest, clings nearest to thee;
Watching with spirit-love each rippling wave,
And guarding thy spirit, its virtue to save.

Upward and onward still, that is my song,
And angels my verses with raptures prolong,
As upward I pass, to spheres high and true,
I am but preparing the pathway for you.

ANNIE.

SECOND SÉANCE WITH MR. WM. LOVETT.

As on a former visit, this gentleman brought his questions prepared: after sitting at the table for a few moments, manifestations of spirit presence were given by raps, and the alphabet called for by the usual signal. The letters being repeated, we obtained the name,

PINGREE JOHNSON LOVETT.

Mr. Lovett put oral questions, and the responses to them were made in raps. They are as follows:

What relative is the intelligence to me?

"Father."

How did you know I was here to-day, father?

"*Edward* told me you appointed this hour to meet me, and I have come with pleasure."

If this be you, tell me the disease that carried you to spirit life?

"My disease was *not* complicated."

Here a bridge and cars were sketched, the *bridge* falling through, evidently intimating an accident; and beneath the sketch, the word *Norwalk* was written. The recognition on the part of Mr. Lovett was immediate, and in his joy, he almost pressed the priceless paper to his lips.

I should not ask more evidence from you, father, but let me trouble you with only two more interrogatories, for the sake of brother Pingree.

What car were you in at the time of the disaster?

"The one that separated; *I* being on the *front half.*"

Did you die from wounds?

"I cannot tell: I did not stop to examine my form, *after* its spirit was *free.*"

Who were in the cars with you that you knew?

"Mr. Knight, Mr. Daniel Fellows, Mr. Winsted."

Any more?

"I do not *remember* the names of the others."

I am perfectly satisfied, dear father, that this is truly your spirit. Did Edward come with you?

"Yes."

Will you answer me by writing, through Mr. Redman, the few questions I desire to ask?

"Yes."

Do you take the same *form* in heaven, that you do on earth?

"Does the insect differ in form, when it escapes from its covering? Does the *seed*, when sprouted, yet remain a *seed;* or does it unfold more divinely into forms majestic? Compare thyself, my son, to the encased germ placed in the *soil:* remember, that what is left *behind* when you blossom is the *covering.* Then tell me, how differs the *leaf* from that which was first planted?

"Many of the grosser incumbrances of the earth form, we can easily dispense with, and surely there is nothing in the Divine creation superfluous. I cannot exactly describe my form to you; but, truly, were I to appear bodily, as it *were*, you would not recognize me. We are known, *not* by *form external*, but by the identity of the spirit internal. Does it *need* the *eye* to *select* the rose? Does it require external perception to pick from the garden-bed, the orange bud—the mignonette? No; identity in the *one* is by its spirit essence, so also is it truly with the other."

Where do you live?—have you a city—a home—a destined locality?

"The local heaven is imaginary, my child: the true Eternal City is *within*, not without. 'Tis God's kingdom, where we can find happiness in following *out* a *law* of self-improvement; and that law can be no better developed than in the culture of the divine principle of purity in those we love. There are grades of development, and these are named spheres, circles, &c.: but *all space* is our *home*, and we enjoy earth beauties *even* more than earth's children, for our higher development opens the avenue of appreciation, and the object that you would ruthlessly and unmindfully tread upon, *we* would lay aside, as a volume in itself, where principles of the unfoldings of the Divine flower would be gloriously manifest."

Shall I continue to keep my position in church?

"If it afford you happiness. The church, William, is *not* the type of what one *should* be, but rather what he should *not* be; if you adhere to its *fellowship, practise* its *principles; not follow* its *practice;* for if *you nurture* the *principle*, you can do *no* better; if you encourage its practice, you can be on *no* better road to damnation."

I think I understand *you*, the *Christ doctrine* is the true one.

"Yes."

Was *he* God?

"What matters it, my child, whether he be *God* or *man;* he did *not* live to teach what *he* himself *was, but what* his *Father was*, and *what* man *should be.* To enjoy the *beauty* of a *truth*, 'tis well to isolate the author."

Are you happy ?

"No ! I am *not arguing* my own position, my son, but am laying down truths to you, that I daily pray to enjoy myself; you know full well, that my earthly nature was too *impulsive* to merit immediate content, and those moments, in which I *cursed* myself and family, still *act* as *barriers*, to expel me from a *more* rapid progression. I cannot remain *longer*, but shall be with you from time to time ; and as I pass upward myself, those I love shall be participators in my happiness."

Have you any word to send any of the family ?

"No."

When shall we meet again ?

"Any time you wish, I will be near. Adieu.

PINGREE J. LOVETT."

As the sitting closed, Mr. Lovett assured me that every word uttered by his father as to the *manner* of his *death* was *strictly* true ; that he had thought, at his first sitting, he had given leading questions, and had been determined this time to make no opening, whereby an answer could be evident ; he had adhered to this resolution and the result is before us.

Circle with Mr. S. S. Curtis, one who had weekly sittings—his son had been suddenly taken from him and had met his mother in spirit life. On this occasion, Mr. C. received the following from his spirit wife, Mary ; her influences were as pure as the divine sphere in which she moved.

"Dust to dust," the Prophet said,
Shall follow in the path of man,
Look happily then upon the dead,
And there thy own reflections scan.

Look not mournfully on him, my dear,
  A mother holds him to her breast;
And with her spirit voice doth cheer
  A father's soul, by death oppressed.

His spirit now is standing here,
  He smiles to see thy passions still,
Yes, Efy's spirit sheds no tear
  That it hath passed, through death's cold chill.

We'll hie away, and in some bower
  Of heaven, we'll wait for thee,
And waiting there we'll drop the flower
  Of our eternity.

On the day after that usually devoted by children to the examination of the supposed presents from the good old Dutch Saint, I was visited by an individual, the complete opposite of saint Nick; he was tall of figure, had dark complexion, black hair and lengthy side appendages occupying the place in his gaunt body, where arms do usually hang; indeed his *tout ensemble* did involuntarily give rise to the idea in my mind, that in him it had been,

"Nature's mistaken largess to bestow
  The gifts, which are of others, upon man,"

nor was the impression created by his fair proportions immediately eradicated when in a coarse croaking voice, he inquired,

"Is this the place where the spirits rap and perform?"

"They communicate to their friends here," said I.

Oh! to their friends, hey! let us see them act?

I bade my questioner sit opposite me, which he did with astonishing nonchalance, and then he asked how they performed.

The spirits began to rap under his chair in no very easy manner, and I informed him, that that was a manifestation probably from some of his spirit friends.

"I haven't got any," was his abrupt reply.

"Well then, some one that knew you in the form," I answered.

Whether the man was afraid that he would meet some one that did know him, or whether he supposed I was humbugging him, I know not; but he immediately rose from his seat, and stepping back to the door, he raised his long, bony, cadaverous finger and gave vent to the following:

"Go on, young man, you'll stop by-and-bye; the fools ain't all dead yet. You've got a girl down stairs, pounding for you."

"Will you go down and see?" said I.

"No! she'll get into or under a barrel before I get down there; and woe be to her and yourself—the judgment of time awaits you; fools are not all dead yet."

With the last sentence on his lips, his shadow disappeared from the door. Perhaps he was wiser, perhaps he thought I was. At all events, I felt the force of his last remarks, that "fools were *not all* dead," for had *he* not come to represent the fraternity?

Not long after this partly farcical, partly insolent visit, a more agreeable séance awaited me with Mr. John Farquhar. This gentleman received a communication from a spirit claiming to be Peter Ferris, whom Mr. Farquhar had known on the Grampian Hills of bonnie Scotland. During the interview with his friend Peter, Mr. Farquhar drew out his snuff-box to take a pinch of its odoriferous contents, when the spirit immediately signified his disposition to take some also. "What! you take snuff?" said John to Peter. "Place the box under the table and you shall see," was the answer.

The box was placed as desired, and we continued our séance. On looking to see if Peter had fulfilled his declaration, neither snuff box nor snuff could be found; search was instituted everywhere, even to our pockets, but the box and its contents were "non est." The invisibles stated that they had taken the box, and would return it on the following week at the time Mr. Farquhar usually sat. While searching for the snuff-box, I found the miniature of a friend that had been taken from me at a meeting some weeks previous. The miniature was in a gold case, and was returned to me perfect.

A week later Mr. Farquhar called as usual, and while we were engaged at the table, no other person being in the room, the snuff-box, which had been taken the previous week, fell with great force on the table, bounded to the floor, sprang open, and a small piece of paper rolled out, on which were these words, written in capital letters :

"I have done with the box. Please take no more of the filthy weed, and oblige thy spirit friend, PETER."

We distinctly saw the box as it descended, and our hands were upon the table at the time. It occurred in the middle of the afternoon, so that no darkness obstructed our vision.

In the spring of 1856, by special invitation from persons of distinction in the National Council, Dr. H. F. Gardner and myself proceeded to Washington. On reaching here, we were kindly and hospitably welcomed by brother Laurie, at whose house I occupied rooms during my sojourn in the capital of the Union. I was favored with quite an influx of visitors, especially members of the House, who seemed to take a deep interest in the tests they received. Prominent among these

"Upon whom the public gaze,
Is fixed for ever to detract or praise,"

was the Hon. Preston Brooks. The manifestations received by this gentleman were of an unusually powerful character. I was not made acquainted with the particular spirits who claimed to be present, but as one of his séances made a lively impression on my mind, I will here relate it.

Mr. Brooks came to my room between the hours of four and five in the afternoon. After receiving answers to various questions, the table rose slowly from the floor about three feet, giving Mr. B. sufficient time to pass his hands under each leg to ascertain that there was nothing lifting it from below. While he was performing this manipulation, a chair, which occupied one corner of the apartment, moved deliberately across the room, and took a position by his side; immediately, as if seized with some wild influence, he caught the chair up and holding it at arm's length, exclaimed: "Is this God, Man, or Devil?" then placing his dollar on the table, he bid me good day, with the ejaculation, "I'll see you again."

Doctor Gardner, in a letter to the New England Spiritualist, gives one of our nights with the spirits at this time. He says·

* While in Washington, Dr. R. and myself occupied the same bed, and he informed me, that under such circumstances, it is not uncommon for the spirits to take advantage of the favorable conditions thus furnished, to display their power. The first night, after retiring and extinguishing the light, we were startled by some solid substance being thrown on the bed; which upon examination proved to be an earthern brush-dish which had, but a moment before, occupied its place on the stand about twenty feet from the bed; the room being sufficiently lighted by burning brands on the hearth to enable us to see figures of the paper on the walls of the room, at a distance of about twenty feet. This article was replaced, and instantly the cover of the same was thrown across the room, striking the wall back of the bed, and falling gently upon the floor without being broken. Again, after I had awoke in the

morning, the room being literally as light as day, Dr. R. being in rather a drowsy mood, and occupying the front portion of the bed, and I endeavoring to rouse him, when he was seized by some unforeseen force and taken entirely out of bed, taking all the clothes with him!

This ended our first night's experience. On the next, however, as the sequel will show, we were to have a still more tangible evidence of their power.

We had but just retired, when we noticed considerable agitation of the bed under us, accompanied by a creaking of the slats upon which the bed rested. We were wondering what the unseen ones were endeavoring to do, when Dr. R. was again seized, and so far pulled from the bed, against his utmost effort and my whole strength, as to nearly relieve the slats of his weight. Almost in an instant, after regaining his position in bed, some four or five of the middle slats were removed, and both Dr. R. and myself with the beds and all, dropped on the floor; and one of the slats thus removed was placed on the top of the bed, and us. This was certainly very "odd," be the force what it might. I recollect a case on record, where, in presence of an ancient medium, a sick man took up his bed and walked; but do not recollect of ever hearing or reading, either in ancient or modern times, of *a bed taking up two men*—for we must have been taken up before we could have been lowered upon the floor. We, of course, had nothing to do but arise, repair damages, and again retire; after having obtained a promise, through concussions or *raps* from the invisibles, not to disturb us more, as it was late and we were weary—which promise was faithfully kept.

The following communication was received while sitting alone one day in musing mood, on far different thoughts intent.

My Kind Mortal Friend,

Permit me, though to thee an unknown one, to open a correspondence for my own good, and perchance, for thine also. Many, I have *no doubt,* ask this same privilege, and if thy hand were the continual medium for such application, thy *body* would weigh less day by day.

I have been in the spirit world long years, yet of time wot not *how* long. I would learn myself; *but* as a *day* to us is but as a sleeping *hour* to those on *earth,* we cannot divide them into years and centuries.

Since my entrance into this timeless world, where the *formalities* and intricacies of mortal existence are banished, it has been my continual study to find a small *avenue,* through which I might communicate with one like *thyself,* and perhaps from you to those I love, on the gude old hills of my Scotland home: but, time effaces even the *wrinkles* from the old man's face, and *memory,* from those we have served and loved; and were I to send a carrier-dove to those vine-clad cottage windows, they would hardly think my message else than a tempter's missile: then, let me content myself with looking on the progress and development of a germ, which in time will be a *savior* to mankind, and a *conqueror* going forth to vanquish.

In comparative prime of physical strength, I was coolly *murdered* by a party of Borderers at Raesknows, near Lochmaben: I was at the time proceeding to court to try the case of one *Baldwin,* and his confederates were among the party, who deprived me of a living *germ* that was necessary for the growth of the immortal spirit. I was *also* at the execution of Scott, one of the party, and, had it been in my power, I would have severed the cord that strangled him, and have bid him live to *repent* of the past, for e'en the soul of steel may find fire of conscience hot enough to make it liquid. But, I come not here to tell of *myself,* nor to rehearse the matter of my mortal life, that is so well known to many e'en now on earth, but I come that I might, by this privilege, be enabled perhaps to hie away to my earth-home and influence them even as I now do *thee*.

'Tis *not my* angel Marie, that I would go to meet, for she is even *now* supporting *herself* on my arm, yet she was mortal; when I was forced away, and in my painful moments of separation from earth, one kiss from her would have antidoted all bodily suffering, and given me a grand reception into the *world* of *space:* yes, even in that last gasp, the still sparkling tear sat motionless on my blood-stained brow, and imagination helped my fancy, that *she* was wiping it with her lily fingers; but I soon met the good old dame, who sang me Scottish airs, when I was a child, and who, in my prattling infancy, I called mother; yes, she knelt by me, and said, " Come John, my son, awake, thy pain is gone, and I am here to greet thy spirit;" then taking me, for I was bewildered and could na' take myself, I was introduced into a new springtime, and the physical incapabilities, which vexed me sore, had given place to activity like the rills that flow through the heather.

My little *idol*, for she was such, and I watered her garden of virtue ten thousand times a day, soon fell weary of earth-life, and as I saw the leaves on her gentle stalk, one by one, hang their heads, I wept not; but when the bud fell, I held my arms and caught it, to transplant it only into an arbor, where the principle of death is unknown and *decay* is a forbidden guest.

Many changes have passed o'er earth's mantle since then; where she had once a patched and tattered raiment, she now wears seamless garments of progress, and her path seems less disturbed by the impediments of injustice and lawlessness. 'Tis for us to watch and aid this development toward a general and world wide perfection; and as races and cross-races fall into the lap of time, the children shall recognize God's first and holiest law of complete and unstained progression.

I must leave thee now, and ere I leave, accept my vow of servitude; whene'er I can bestow *one* smile of pleasure, or one gift to make thy future *more successful*, at that moment it is *done*, and though I now am but a stranger I pray to be a friend.

With a grateful acknowledgment of this favor, I am thy sincere friend,

JOHN CARMICHAEL.

VISION DURING MY SOJOURN IN WASHINGTON.

One lovely morning, when all nature was clothed in the beautiful inflorescence of Spring, and the sweet notes of the feathered warblers gave additional charm to the surrounding scenery, I felt an irrepressible desire to stroll into the Capitol grounds; so taking my diary I started out, and picking my way between the blocks of marble that were being prepared for the extension of this national edifice, I merged into the park, in the rear of the noble pile.

I had continued my rambles for some time, now turning this path, then that; when I saw in the distance what seemed to be three persons approaching. At first they looked like mere *dwarfs*, and as they drew nearer, I was surprised at their peculiar appearance.

The elder of the trio resembled a lady, dressed in a long, flowing robe of brown fabric; she wore a large, homely, white bonnet, the strings to which were of the same material as itself, and might have served as penants of truce to a flag ship; a string of beads, about the size of an acorn, hung from her neck, to her waist; attached to this was a cross studded, apparently, with garnets; her visage was pale and sunken, and, as she was engaged in conversation, seemed unnaturally attenuated. In her right-hand she held an open book, and with the fore-finger of her left, she pointed to some passage, upon which, if I judged correctly, she was dilating.

Her companions were of the opposite sex. The one on her right, was a tall, dignified man, clad in Revolutionary habiliments, who, as he approached, stooped and picked up a rod that lay in the pathway. The individual on her left, was a small, humpbacked personage, supported by a staff somewhat more lilliputian than himself. The latter character was the most engaged with our Charity sister, and nodded his assent to her commentaries, at the same time bringing his staff with a nervous thump upon the walk. The mind of the right-hand companion seemed little attracted to the subject of discussion between the other two; as they came near to me, I stepped aside and let them pass.

When in the distance, I had thought them mortals; but, on a closer proximity, their influence was sufficient to indicate their spiritual character. I gazed in silence, wondering who they were, what the object of their visit, and what the subject that so deeply absorbed the attention of two of the party.

As they passed, I stopped and watched their movements: they went towards the statue of Washington, which was some fifty yards distant, and on reaching it, they turned round, and facing the tribute to the Great Patriot, seated themselves with their backs towards the Capitol. I immediately approached, and took a seat about ten feet distant, to contemplate their motions.

They sat perfectly motionless for about a quarter of an hour, when the Charity sister (as I have designated the female) came to the base of granite, and, without the least apparent effort, raised herself by the side of Washington. After leaning upon his chair for a few moments, she took the scroll from his hand, and passed it to her little humpbacked associate; then, placing a mark in the book she had held in her hand, she laid it open into the lap of our illustrious chief; at the same time, grasping the finger of stone, that points to heaven, she placed it upon the page that lay open before the statue; then putting her pale, bony finger to her lips, she came down as easily as she had ascended. The trio, scroll in hand, seemed to glide noiselessly from the spot, and, with a gentle adieu in the shape of a bow, vanished into thin air.

What can this mean! thought I; and the more I reflected on it the stronger grew my desire to have some explanation. I opened my diary to note the occurrence, when my hand was seized, and wrote:

SIR,

Each Sabbath morn, my giant casement receives these visits—not from promiscuous parties, but from these *same three.* The name of *one* is *Law*, the other, *Prudence*, the third, *Union*. It may seem strange to thee; but stranger than *all* is the *eternity* through which these same visits continue. The trio seen by thee are censors, and as the weekly hours note events of progress in our race, by these condensed, they come into the lap of stone, that a nation gave me, and this same matter, thus condensed, is seen by myriads, who live in spheres immortal. Go read the substance beneath the finger.

I approached the statue, and as I did so, the book seemed turned to me, and I read :—

The gem is rough—yet valued more
For nature's garments, that it wore.
But when they fall—beware! lest God
Doth dam the spring that makes the flood.

I asked the meaning of the stanza, but received only the ensuing :

"Its purport is plain enough to the student, and lest you forget it, become a student, that you may learn it; but at some future time—a day to us, perchance years to thee—its import shall be made known, not through thyself, but through one similarly gifted.

"I watch with eyes of love and care o'er each breath that echoes here, to give law to our infant world. *World* in itself; for by its revolution it may magnetize the mental powers of all around it. Greenough hath well portrayed the mortal; I thank him for it. There's such a thing as forgetting one's self. I have my earth form before me, though when it rains, I cannot cover my head, neither can I shake the dust from those cold chiseled brows. I cannot smile on those who nobly shake virtue by the hand, nor frown on deeds that, like the smaller beast, may gnaw an opening in our pipe of principles, and let the liquid power out. Yet, in their hearts they know me, and I am pleased. Adieu.

WASHINGTON."

I cannot say that my preconceived ideas of our national capital were at all realized by my visit to it: the spiritual was all, and even *more,* than I had anticipated, and as far as success in the good work of man's redemption was concerned, there was every thing to encourage and urge on to a faithful, and energetic discharge of my portion of the labor in the vineyard. Although aware that Washington was far from being extensive in dimensions, I had indulged in such day dreams of what it *must* be, that when I came to view it as it *was,* I was forced to admit that imagination had far outstripped reality, the only truly imposing object that I beheld, being the Capitol and its surrounding grounds. Disappointment, then, was mine in inanimate nature; not so, however, in the welcome and cordiality that awaited my arrival from the intelligent part of God's creation: indeed, the Spiritualists here, though *few* in number, yet, for devotion to this much abused infant in swaddling clothes, contrast favorably with those of our northern cities, where, in numerical strength, if not in faith, they are far exceeded.

I might indite a prolonged account of many interesting circles during my stay, but as nothing more remarkable, than what has been already related as taking place with others, occurred, I give a few, least such repetition should become tedious and monotonous.

Our enjoyment at Brother Lauries was greatly enhanced by the presence of Miss Emma Frances Jay (now Mrs. Bullene), who discoursed the philosophy of Spiritualism nightly, to numerous and appreciating audiences.

My stay at the Capitol was not long, in consequence of engagements elsewhere; but the two weeks I remained were profitably spent, and I can now refer with gratification to the product of seed planted at that time.

CHAPTER VII.

ARRIVAL in Baltimore. Mr. Lanning. Circle with the Editors. Rooms in Liberty street. Mr. Lanning's Letter to Dr. Gardner. Visitors. F. Wharton Pierce. Unsolicited spiritual perception. Incidents. Mr. Lanning's second letter. Boarding-house gossip. Chivalry below par. Remarks.

" Even to the disposition that I owe,
When now I think, you can behold such sights
And keep the natural ruby of your cheeks,
When mine are bleached with fear."

IN company with Miss E. Jay (Mrs. Bullene) went by railroad to Baltimore, where my good friend the Doctor had preceded me, to make arrangements for our location, and reception of visitors ; arriving at the Monumental City, we proceeded to the residence of Mr. Wm. M. Lanning, 11 Eutaw street, where we were received with that courteous hospitality for which Mr. L. and his lady are distinguished ; the customary salutations and friendly greetings over, arrangements were made for holding a circle in the evening, to which the editors of the Baltimore *Patriot*, Messrs. Wells and Carpenter, were to be invited.

The press, wielding as it does so powerful an influence over public sentiment, we have deemed it advisable and prudent in all cases to afford its votaries every opportunity and facility for obtaining an insight into the *truths* of Spiritualism, that they might be enabled the more effectually to bear witness to the genuineness of the manifestations, and be the better prepared to judge how much weight to attach to the voluntary contributions that are tendered to the public print by the ignorant, the disappointed, and the presumptuous ; the crafty *would be* Solomons, who, from prejudice, want of due investigation, or, worse yet, to gratify some private pique, would feign persuade the world they know *more* than those who are absolutely informed. In all stages of society have been found a number of such weak brained philosophers, ever on the alert to extinguish any flame of progress, by which their own darkness might be illuminated ; or some aspirant for fame, who, Erostratus like, rather than be forgotten by posterity, would ignite the match that should consume *our* great temple, were it not from cupola to foundation stone, the erection of an All-merciful and Divine mind.

But to return to my subject, from which I have made this desultory flight ; the proposed evening séance was attended by the invited editors, and passed off with remarkable activity ; there was no coaxing for physical manifestations, and a spirit friend of Mr. Carpenter gave evidence of its continued existence and knowledge of his *daily* acts.

The ensuing morning we procured suitable rooms for the reception of friends, at No. 15 South Liberty street, and notices of location having duly appeared in the secular journals, among the first of the visitors were the gentlemen who had favored us with their presence on the night of our arrival, Messrs. Wells and Carpenter; a notice of their séance appeared in the *Patriot* the following morning, and I give it below.

SPIRITUALISM—MR. G. REDMAN.—Those who desire to know something of what are called spiritual manifestations, may have their curiosity excited, and their taste for the marvellous gratified, by a visit to the rooms of the famous test medium, Mr. G. Redman, No. 15 South Liberty street. We are not prepared to say that these singular and unaccountable developments and manifestations proceed from the spirit-world; but by whatever power they are produced, their extraordinary character certainly renders them well worthy of close investigation. A number of gentlemen who were present at these rooms yesterday—and in whose perfect truthfulness we have every reason to believe—declare that, though not believers in Spiritualism, they yet witnessed phenomena so marvellous, and of a nature so perfectly beyond anything they had previously considered possible, that, notwithstanding their most rigid scrutinies, they were compelled to acknowledge the existence of some intelligence, or seeming intelligence, unknown to modern science.

The names of departed friends were given with an accuracy truly astonishing, their relationship, where they resided at the period of their decease, and the age at which they died were distinctly indicated, and in a manner which seemed to neither admit of any possible deception or collusion. After this, while standing around the table, removed from it, but with their hands about six inches above it, the table rocked from side to side violently. These are alleged to be facts which any one may verify for himself who thinks proper, and as they come to us from a source entitled to credence, we would suggest that others would undertake, by investigation, either to disprove them or to establish their correctness. Spiritualism, so called, is gaining ground among us, and if there are unknown truths connected with it, they should be promulgated; if it is wholly a delusion, it should be denounced.

My friend Lanning having heard of the midnight manifestations that occurred with Doctor Gardner and myself, determined, if possible, to witness and experience some such effects himself. I therefore consented to lose one or two nights' rest on his account, and his version of the results may be found in the letters from him to the Doctor, given below.

LETTERS OF MR. LANNING TO DR. GARDNER.

* Some years ago, before I became a believer in the New Philosophy, I invited a Mr. Savage, a medium for physical manifestations, and Goodall, at that time a very promising actor, whom I had known from boyhood, to spend the night with me, for the purpose of witnessing the strange phenomena, said to be produced at night, in Mr. S's. presence. Nothing of any importance, however, occurred at that time, except, that a few sounds were heard upon the walls, floor, &c., upon retiring.

In the morning, I arose, and while dressing, the idea occurred to me to play Goodall a trick: he and S. being sound asleep at this time. For this purpose, I crawled under the bed, and commenced to rap upon the floor, posts and sides of the bedstead. The noises soon awoke Goodall, who rose up in bed, and commenced interrogating the spirit (as he believed it to be); and after requesting the sounds to be made in various places,—which

I with great difficulty accomplished, to his entire satisfaction it seems—he expressed his gratitude to the invisibles, by saying very emphatically, "Thank you :" to which I as emphatically responded, (at the same time putting out my head from under the bed) "You are welcome." This was enough! With an ejaculation expressive of disappointment and chagrin, he sprung from the bed, but I had the start of him, and for that time escaped: but now for the sequel.

Upon entering the chamber with Redman, on the night in question, I was careful to lock the door, and try it afterwards, to satisfy myself that all was right, and that we were alone in the room. We had hardly extinguished the light and got into bed, when muffled sounds were heard upon the opposite wall. They gradually grew louder, and approached nearer; and I raised my head to endeavor to ascertain from which quarter they proceeded, when a book was thrown upon the bed. This I picked up and opened: it being a moonlight night, I could almost see to read the title page. Five raps were now given in quick succession (a call for the alphabet) and, "We are going to have a good time of it" was spelt out. Another book came flying through the room and struck the Venetian blind; at the same time, our friend Redman called to me to hold on to him, as they were pulling him out of bed. I took hold of him, and endeavored in vain to keep him in; a powerful force seemed to be exerted, and he was drawn off, and then pulled under the bed. We had scarcely got comfortably in bed again, before another book was thrown with violence against the Venetian blind, and fell upon the bed, which made us draw the cover over our heads. This was hardly done, when we were pretty severely cudgelled with a small cane, which stood in one corner of the room, when we retired. Redman, in his efforts to protect his head with the clothing, exposed his feet, and was struck upon a corn, and cried out most lustily.

Believing that these things would not occur if I sat up in bed, I determined to watch more closely, and see, if possible, how they were done. Accordingly I arose to a sitting posture; distinctly saw the cane raised over me, and was struck several times with it, while it was in full view. Redman, at this time, had his head well under cover, and although I could see the cane clearly, I could see nothing at either end to control it. The blows coming heavier and heavier, I deemed it advisable to protect myself, by interposing the covering between the cane and my head; and got down in the bed again, when it seemed as if some one was trampling upon me. The lamp was also thrown on the bed, and the alphabet again called for, and, "*You are welcome,*" was spelt out. I asked if it were my old friend Goodall, and was answered in the affirmative; while sounds expressive of merriment were being made about the room.

Redman appeared to be quite alarmed and anticipated some mischief, as the pitcher and other vessels were being disturbed in the room, and there seemed to be a determination to drive us out. In vain we remonstrated and begged them to permit us to sleep, but they seemed incorrigible.

Once more we got under cover, when we were both pulled out of bed, clinging to each other, and while we were on the floor the cane was again employed rather actively upon our shoulders and backs. I made a clutch at the stick and succeeded in disarming the invisible assailant, and retained possession of the weapon. Again we adjusted the bed and got in, when the alphabet was called for, and "You are welcome," spelt out once more. The strangest noises were now heard, and fearing injury to the furniture, we concluded it would be best to retire and seek for other lodgings. As there were no matches in the room we were obliged to dress without a light, and while so doing, my pocket handkerchief was drawn around R's. neck, and books and newspapers were thrown at him, and around the room. We succeeded at length in getting out, and while going down stairs, R. was struck over the back with some matting. The table in the hall raised up while passing it, and a book struck Redman upon the head while opening the front door. We, at last, emerged into the open air, and congratulated ourselves upon our escape. Proceeding homeward, as we passed under a sign next door, raps were made upon it, and after entering the house, something was thrown at us while in the entry. The sounds were continued after we had again retired; but we were soon permitted to sleep unmolestedly.

Thus ended these *striking* manifestations. I can now understand why Redman cared so little about spending the night with me; for myself I felt no fear, whatever, but heartily enjoyed the sport, and would have braved it out, but some threats were made by the spirits, which caused our friend R. to believe they would repeat an experiment they had performed once before, and he was unwilling to remain.

It was a quarter past one when we got home, and in the morning the entry and stairway, as well as room, were strewn with books and other articles, which the servants gathered up.

WM. M. LANNING.

My rooms now received a certain class of persons, who, from love of the marvelous, are always ready to grasp at any thing apparently *new*. Prominent among these were old ladies, whose minds being unoccupied with ought save obtaining favors from Dame Fortune, would seek lucky numbers in the lottery; others, whose aim was to ascertain the whereabouts of stolen goods, fathom the doings of wicked house-maids, or dive into the secret amours of unscrupulous husbands. None but those who have served the public in a mediatorial capacity can comprehend the various ridiculous scenes, absurd comments, and (but for the ennui, attending repetition) the farcical associations, which 'tis the lot of those so situated to realize. One or two of this nature I will relate.

The door bell rings, and you are met by a forty-five year old female, with eyes, ears, and all her senses agog. You ask her into the spiritual tabernacle. She stands with a mystic air; you scarcely know whether to break the silence yourself, or permit her that privilege. Finally, with a determined effort, and an air of sanctified dignity, she opens her elocutionary powers.

"Are you the man that is a spiritual mejum, and calls up husbands, and tells about one's affairs?"

"Well, madam, I suppose I am the person you *seek;* but you will need, perhaps, a little instruction in this matter, before you understand its bearings, or its beauties."

"But you tells lucky numbers, and so on, don't ye?"

"The spirits of departed friends purport to *communicate* with those they love on earth, my good woman, but not to lead us to fortune or fame."

"Oh! that's it, *hey.* Then you're one of them sperit rappers, as writes communications. Will the sperit of my mother, that died about ten years ago, at Wilmington, with the bilious fever, come and tell me what I ought to do, and how to live?"

"You can try, madam, and see if she will speak with you. I have no doubt if she loved you, and you also had the natural affection of a daughter, you may receive some advice from her."

"Well, what do you ask for the infurmation ?"

"One dollar, madam."

"Then I'll take a dollar's worth, and if I get anything as does me good, or such as I want, then I will bring others."

The sharp visaged visitor now takes a seat at the table, and we patiently wait for some evidence of spiritual presence. While attending the pleasure of the invisibles, the communicative lady enlightens me on all the various characteristics and peculiarities of her family and self, which are not over and above interesting, especially from one more gifted with loquacity than personal attractions.

The good old rap comes at last, which causes our visitor to start and with nervous tremor inquire if "Them is the sperits ?" I assure her in the affirmative, and she begins a written correspondence with her son David and her husband Samuel. After mutual questions and replies, she looks up, and with a broad grin informs me, that the old gent is "*just* what he used to be, and he loves her more, but thinks she is not in the right path to happiness."

After a prolonged, prosy interview, during which she again and again reiterates the declaration that "it's quite remarkable, it's very singular ;" she resumes the control of the organs of motion, and wishes me a "good morning." Such is one specimen of numerous calls of a similar kind received by me, and I have no doubt mediums who sit in public may recognise in this true picture, an old tormentor, a not unfamiliar friend.

Another comes, self-possessed, intelligent, and apparently comprehending the *why* and *wherefore* of his visit, and taking a seat at the table, *tout à son aise,* commences a series of questions as to the manner of my development, and the nature and different phases of the manifestations given through me; at the same time, expressing his anxiety for tests of supermundane intelligence communicating with friends on earth: such a character was Mr. Warren Pierce, whose interview, though not as extraordinary as some, may be interesting. He objected to writing ballots, on the ground that they would afford some clue to his desires, and give me the opportunity to ascertain the names of his absent friends, with whom he wished to correspond.

After a silence of some minutes, he inquired if I had touched him with my foot; I assured him that it was quite impossible for me to take any such liberty, as the distance between us precluded all possibility of it, at the same time demonstrating the truth of my assertion by extending my leg. He affirmed that he was touched by something, that seemed to him very much like a dog's nose. Raps reverberated in various parts of the room, which caused Mr. P. to scrutinize rather closely the *table* and myself, but failing to discover the intelligent *wires,* he propounded the following questions—

"If a spirit be present, will he or she announce its name?"

Immediately the name of Frederick Wharton Pierce was given, and the muscles on the investigator's face might have been seen to quiver; a short communication was written, in which was the following:

MY BELOVED WARREN,

Though apparently dead to you I am invisibly *present*; though unconscious, as you suppose me to be, of *your life* from day to day, still I am as thy very self, traveling with you; and, in the silence of thy hours of reflection, penetrating thy soul, and separating the accumulated chaff, the quantity of which would astonish and confound you when compared with the more refined matter, *which should*, and, in some degree *does*, fill thy being.

Catherine is not in the *spirit* world, but is very low; if you write to her, tell her she *will* recover—it will give her hope, for her time is not yet.

Thy immortal parent,

F. WHARTON PIERCE.

In the signature of this letter, Mr. Pierce immediately recognized the handwriting of his father, and declared it could not be counterfeited.

The table made certain evolutions, which caused my guest to move back, in order to give more room, and in so doing he fell over in his chair, the table at the same time pursuing him, till he lay directly beneath it; loud raps, indicative of merriment, were given on the table, as if to evince the entire satisfaction of the intelligence, and Mr. Pierce rose from his recumbent posture. A few minor points being discussed, he left the room more enlightened than when he entered it, and asserted, that the ideas of trick, with which his intimate friends had deeply imbued his mind, were fallacious in the extreme.

Whether there was any peculiarity in the influences of Baltimore, or that the harmonious surroundings of brother Lanning affected me in any way, I cannot say; but I know that the power of discerning spirits, was more clearly given me, while in the monumental city, than at any time before or since; in fact, hardly an hour passed in which I did not mistake a spirit for a mortal, or vice versa; and the confusion created by this mingling of mortal and immortal, was a source of no small amusement to many, but to myself 'twas one of much annoyance. I could scarcely walk the streets without coming in contact with one or more of my spirit tormentors: I say *tormentors*, for while no doubt they entertained themselves, developing my interior sight, still it was at the expense of my peace of mind. While promenading, I would frequently see a form coming pell-mell from an opposite direction, and would involuntarily step aside, to allow the hasty pedestrian to pass unobstructedly. Then, as a natural consequence, I would turn to witness the headlong progress of the person, when lo! he would have disappeared: amused at myself, I would continue on, determined to scan more closely the next time. On turning a corner, I was unexpectedly confronted by a female with vermilion complexion, and dimensions that might contrast favorably with Falstaff. Looking me directly in the eyes, she turned to the right, but I, unfortunately, at the same moment wheeled round to the left, which evolution brought us again vis-à-vis: a pause ensued. I now dashed to the right, when, with the same apparent desire of progressing, the portly personage pirouetted to the left; behold us then, again in statu quo. It is said, "when man meets man, and the pass is contended, then comes the tug of war;" but nothing is related of when man meets woman. A natural perceptiveness, however, determined me, in this dilemma, to give the corpulent form an opportunity of choosing her own path, so I assumed an immovable attitude. As if enjoying a knowledge of my intentions, and acting under a resolution to thwart my plans and test my patience, our lady adopted a "stand at ease" position likewise. I could endure this interruption to my wanderings no longer, so to terminate the point of opposition, and rid myself of my unsightly opponent, I jumped into the street, and thus succeeded in eluding this enemy to my wonted equanimity. Congratulating myself on my ultimate success, I turned to observe the lady from another point of view, and she had vanished. I now felt convinced that some spirit had been tampering with my amiability: but the ridiculous idea of my thus facing open space with feelings bordering on pugnacity, forced from me a laugh, which did not dwindle to a smile till I reached home.

When walking with Mr. Lanning, I would often turn aside to let these passers-by have more sea-way, and my politeness would be met by that gentleman's inquiring, "why I crowded so."

"Why," my reply would be, "to let that gentleman pass."

"What gentleman?" Mr. L. would ask.

"Didn't you see him?" would follow from me.

"No! indeed!" came the response.

And true enough, once more had I been *victimized.* But the sight of such apparently human forms coming, as they always did, under high pressure propulsion, generally created in me a desire to avoid them if possible.

Returning home, one evening, from holding a circle at a private dwelling, on going up stairs to my bed-room, I fell over a little girl. "Why, sis," said I, "I didn't mean to hurt you; but you should not sit on the stairs in the evening, especially when the hall is so dimly lighted as this:" and compassionately reaching down to take up the youthful unfortunate, my hands locked with nothing to intervene, but thin air. I was compelled to laugh, and in consequence fell up stairs.

So common did these manifestations become, I at last learned to disregard them, and the swift-footed perambulator passed unheeded by me. I soon, however, found that this would not do; this similarity of treatment to spirit in the form, and spirit divested of its mortal encumbrances, I was soon sensibly enlightened would not answer in the rudimental sphere, as in consequence of my disregard of man in his fleshy habiliments, a biped, of some 200 lbs. weight, one morning coolly knocked me over a bale of cotton, ejaculating as he passed—"Impudent!!" with an adjective affixed, more expressive of anger than elegance. Ere I had recovered from my involuntary gymnastic feat, the mighty man of valor was some distance from me, and thus prevented any *striking* demonstration on my part.

A short time after, as I was returning from a morning walk, and was coming through Monument Square, I actually fell over a veritable little boy with earthly integuments, and a wheelbarrow.—Whether I injured the child I know not, I did not stop to consider, but I blessed him, and pitied the wheelbarrow, for I had fractured one of its legs. So presenting the lad with a douceur, which could be converted into candy, and thereby, render his notes in alto more round and mellifluous, I continued my route, biting my tongue to check more declamatory expressions of pain, occasioned by a bruise on the patella. I saw the stripling before I reached him, but the vision of the little girl came so vividly before me, I did not diverge from the direct line I was pursuing at the time of perceiving him.

Many incidents of a laughable character, but similar to what I have related, happened about this time, the recital of which might amuse my readers; but as the same class of developments were resumed after my location in New York, I will defer their relation, until giving my experiences in that city.

Below is a second letter from brother Lanning, and the manifestations there recorded, he affirms, eclipsed those in the one addressed to Dr. Gardner. Possibly if a third had been given, the record would have surpassed all: but two sleepless nights sufficed. We had no ambition for a renewal of such pleasure, nor for an increase of the hippocratic countenance, which was so plainly indicative of both mental and bodily excitement. In Mr. Lanning I found a companion, differing essentially from many others, with whom it has been my lot to pass a night. As a general thing, my friend in tribulation becomes "distilled almost to a jelly with the act of fear, stands dumb, and speaks not;" or has his organ of combativeness excited—he goes in for breakers, and comes out broken. But our Baltimorean takes it smilingly, and good-naturedly cries out—"Hold, enough!"

MR. LANNING'S SECOND LETTER.

The occurrences of my preceding night with Mr. Redman, were thrown into the shade by the experiences of the night of the 27th of April.

As Brother Redman had determined to leave for the north on Monday, he accepted an invitation to spend the last day and night with me; but before retiring, we were careful to remove every thing from the room, which could receive injury, and I was particular to see that all the *canes* were safely disposed of, as I felt but little relish for such *striking demonstrations* as I had experienced before.

As soon as we had extinguished the light, a bottle was thrown on the bed, and then a large rocking chair was lifted from the floor, and turned first over Redman, and then over me, and pressed down upon our stomachs with such power, that, with all our efforts, we could not remove it. We cried out lustily for help, and two of the family came in with a light; and with our united force, we could not get the chair off. To satisfy all, that there was no deception practised, I caught hold of Redman's hands, and held on to them, calling upon those who had come to our assistance, to pull the chair away; but after several ineffectual attempts, they were obliged to abandon it, when the alphabet was called for, by five loud raps, and "*Now you may have it*," was given; when the chair was raised, and taken off without difficulty.

The light was put out, and the door, opening into the entry, where a gas-light was burning, was closed, when a band-box was plied vigorously over our heads and backs; then bonnets were thrown upon the bed, and the empty band-box placed over my head, and then over Redman's, and held there, so that we could not remove it for a time. We were then beaten with a hair brush, and while I was hunting for the matches to make a light, Redman was drawn out of bed, the bed and mattress thrown over him; and at the same instant, the bedstead (a heavy mahogany one, French style) was moved out from the wall, and turned on its side. While we were endeavoring to get the bedstead down, a vessel, containing about a pint of water, was emptied upon us, which made it necessary to change our night clothes; after this, we toiled for about fifteen minutes, in a fruitless endeavor to right the bedstead, but it would not move; becoming desperate, at length we essayed once more; but now it moved almost without aid.

Some time elapsed before we could adjust all right, when the light was once more extinguished, and we snug in bed again. Raps were now made upon the head-board with an earthenware lid, and the alphabet called for, when "Thank you," was given; to which I replied, "You are welcome." The lid was thrown upon the bed, when it seemed as if a score or more of spirits were rapping at the same time, in unison with our peals of laughter. Once more, Redman was pulled out of bed, over me, taking me with him upon the floor, and before we could recover, we were assailed with a gum (rubber) shoe, which I tried to get possession of, but could not. In the intervals between these demonstrations, we could see small stars, and bright points, and lines of light, through the darkness. Again we got into bed, and now hoped to escape farther molestation, concluding they had exhausted all their resources. But not so; we soon found they were fertile in expedients, for heavy blows descended upon us, and reaching out to discover the character of this new weapon, we caught hold of a strip of stair carpeting twisted, which we endeavored to retain. An irresistible power would pull it out of our hands, and strike us several times, before we could seize it again, when their hold upon it would seem to relax for an instant, and then it would be forced away from us, despite all our efforts. The alphabet was then called for, and "You are welcome" given, letter by letter.

The bedstead was again moved from the wall. Redman was pulled out of bed, and whilst lying on the floor, his traveling trunk was heard moving towards him by jumps. Whilst I was getting a light, I was struck over the back with a blank book (folio) which was thrown at me, as I lit the lamp. I found Redman in the corner, behind the bedstead in a trance, and the bed clothes over him. In a few minutes he was restored to consciousness, when the alphabet was again called for, and we were informed that the performances of the evening were over, and we would be permitted to sleep. It was now our turn to say "Thank you," which we did with a good will, I assure you. Wishing us "Good morning," for it was near four o'clock, the invisibles withdrew, and we were allowed to rest unmolested.

Heavy indentations were made upon the head-board, and a lump on my forehead bore testimony to the fact, that I was not psychologized, while the confusion in the morning gave evidence that some very *odd force* was at work.

WM. M. LANNING.

My rooms, while in Baltimore, being in a boarding house, where there was a number of students residing, my first evening with Mr. Lanning could not pass without the nature of its proceedings being pretty generally known. During the night I had heard footsteps traversing the floor of the apartment over mine, and the next morning's repast had to be flavored by a spicy narration from me of my adventures during that season when "O'er the one-half world, nature seems dead, and wicked dreams abuse the curtained sleeper." I laid the affairs before my listeners in as mild a manner as I could—tempering the relation as much as a strict conformity with truth would admit, so as not to lay too heavy a tax upon their credulity. Considerable merriment was elicited by my strange story, and a challenge was tendered me by one chivalrous gent to pass that night in the room with him. Said he, "I'll put charges in my revolver, and I'll bet any amount we'll lie as quietly as kittens; for if any one attempt to play pranks on me, I'll blow his d——d brains out." I laughed at the idea of the ineffectiveness of his so boasted weapons on that which is "as the air, invulnerable," and on which his "vain blows" would be "malicious mockery." However, to cool his heated blood, I took up the gauntlet so valorously thrown down by the youthful knight, and bade him make any arrangements he deemed necessary, while *I* would request the presence of spirits, who would garrote him in double quick time.

Evening came, and with it a general anxiety throughout the household for the results of the night. Almost all the family retired before we did, as I had a private party in my room, and was not at liberty before half past ten o'clock. As my visitors left, I met my young chevalier on the stairs, and invited him into my apartment. He entered with an undaunted air, took from his coat pocket a small sized Colt's revolver, and laid it on the table. After some conversation, in which I explained to him the events of the preceding night, and showed him a shattered venetian blind, I inquired as to the location of the other lodgers in the house, least the pistol bullets might enter any of their chambers. I prepared to unrobe myself for retiring, bidding him follow my example. Taking his pistol from the table, he laid it on the mantle-piece, saying, "There you'll be ready in case of need." "Yes," said I; "and when you look where it is (like the paddie's ninepence) it won't be there." He took off his outer garment, and I being quite prepared to retire, merely waited (as the host of the room) his mandate to extinguish the light. I observed, while thus attending on his pleasure, that he was immoderately slow in divesting himself of his clothing, and seemed deeply ruminating. Being fatigued, and becoming impatient with his dilatoriness, I asked if I should extinguish the light. He stood a moment as if "waxing desperate with imagination,"—all was silent as the tomb—he looked toward the bed, then at the blind, next at the revolver. Seizing his coat in one hand, his weapon in the other, he exclaimed, while his whole frame shook with nervous excitement, "No, by G—, I don't know how the d——d things may be armed, and I consider the safety of the house." The soliloquy ended, he opened the door, adding as he made his exit, "I'll see you in the morning." I could not comprehend what he meant by "seeing me in the morning;" but not thinking it deserved much reflection, I got into bed, concluding that *time* would solve the riddle.

Morning, "in russet mantle clad," came walking "o'er the dewy east," and ere I had donned my day's attire, a rap at my door, elicited "Come in." Behold now before me stood our chevalier "*sans peur et sans reproche*," who then and there urgently importuned me to give no explanation to the family, of the valorous scene of the preceding night, but to leave all to him. To this I consented, provided he neither compromised the spirits nor myself, which being promised, I left the matter in his hands. The solution, however, at the breakfast table was any thing but satisfactory; the version of the affair being, "that his weapon was out of order and could not be used." I was silent; but the thought would present itself,

> "How now, Horatio? you tremble and look pale,
> Is not this something more than *fantasy*?"

This young man afterwards became much interested in our cause, and I hope, ere now, is an enlightened and sincere believer.

My southern tour was attended with felicitous circumstances. While in Washington, Miss E. F. Jay lectured, and the holy philosophy explained through her, rendered more comprehensible the tests and demonstrations given through my humble self. In Baltimore, Miss Jay and Miss Charlotte Beebe were alternately opening the avenues of inquiry to large and densely crowded assemblies. It was emphatically a *spiritual revival* in this great American seat of Romanism, and I think, even at this time, a repetition of such utterances as were then poured forth through the organisms of these two gifted media, would be highly acceptable to those thirsting after the real waters of life. But both these ladies have relinquished the evanescence of public sympathy and adulation, for the silken cords of hymeneal happiness, carrying with them into the domestic circle that amiability of character, for which they were so remarkably distinguished in single life, and proving, where there is mutual sympathy between the contracting parties, "each being to each a *dearer* self," that mediatorial powers are not incompatible with conjugal felicity.

CHAPTER VIII.

Return Homeward. Philadelphia. Circles. Professor Hare. Dial. Manifestations in the Laboratory. Death of Professor Hare. The Cup withheld. My stormy day visitor. Communication. Arrival in Boston. Continuation of home influences. Franky. Financial matters. Truth, not to be sold or bought. Father's message. Mr. J. V. Mansfield's letter.

"Who shall dare the gate of life to close,
Or say, thus far the stream of mercy flows."

My contemplated return homeward being known, I was solicited by the Spiritualists of the Quaker City to stop on my northern route, and sojourn a few days with them ; to this I willingly consented, and a notice of my intended visit was accordingly inserted in the Spiritual newspapers ; I likewise availed myself of Brother Foster's proffered politeness to make his home mine while in Philadelphia.

Soon after my arrival, arrangements were made for public circles, to be held at the Lecture Hall of the Spiritualists' Association, Chesnut street. My first séance was numerously attended, and, if I could judge from appearances, was enjoyed by all present : the tests were correctly given, and without hesitation.

These circles were repeated nightly, till I found accommodation for the reception of visitors, which was kindly tendered me by an opponent to our faith, but who afterwards became (as a matter of course, where investigation and reason move conjointly) a confirmed believer.

'Twas while in Philadelphia, at this time, that I formed the acquaintance of the venerable Dr. Hare, whose profound learning placed no barrier (as I am sorry to say it does in many cases) to his enjoyment of spiritual unfolding. The Doctor seemed much enamored with his dials, of which he repeatedly brought a supply, but, for myself, I could see no particular use or beauty in them, except for those who were but partially developed ; however, as they served the Professor's convenience, I have no comments to make. As a means of preventing the action of the dial by pressure, a plate of metal was placed upon two small globes, and the whole on the table of the dial, so that by the least motion, the plate would move upon the globular bodies, and thus prevent any interference on the part of the medium, when a communication was given. By an invitation from Professor Hare I called on him at his laboratory, where he instituted various experiments, with all of which he seemed gratified ; the physical manifestations were exceedingly well marked ; whether the apparatus suffered from the severe handling it received I am unable to say, but we would both start, from time to time, when some ponderable body, in the shape of a jar or battery, would come toward us.

The ingenuity, which the professor displayed in forming conveniences for a more independent mode of communication, was quite interesting; though many of his contrivances have never come before the public, as was designed by him. One of these, on which he laid particular stress, was a moving platform upon rollers, a bench, upon which the medium or mediums were to sit, crossed the platform, and it was supposed by Professor Hare, that the spirits might easily roll the contrivance from right to left, and thus cause a large wheel to revolve, in the groove of which was a strap, that communicated with a dial raised upon an upright staff; the desk was so placed, that an audience might easily recognize the letters to which the index pointed, and thus be able to receive communications. This enterprise never realized the Doctor's expectations; for, although he could have it moved in his own study, it would exhibit little intelligence. The mediums, with whom he was most successful in his experiments with this apparatus, were Mr. Ruggles and myself; while seated together on the platform the stage would be propelled with great velocity backward and forward, without tarrying at any particular letter. On one occasion the manifestation was in some degree successful, the index pointed to M; now, said the Doctor, "the next letter," the pointer slowly indicated A, "very good!" now again slowly, and the index indicated R; the good old man was in ecstacies, and, no doubt, pictured to himself the complete success that was about to follow. "Once again," said he,—the machine moved, but, alas! there was too much power, and the pointer whirled like a top, and stopped at X; the gentleman was confounded, but tried again,—this time, as before, the thing on wheels tipped, turned, rolled back and forth, till we were forced to abandon it.

While standing still in the room, two large brass balls fell with great force at our side, giving rise to a remark from Dr. H. that, "if the spirits were strong enough to do that, why could they not operate with his dial?" A wheel in one corner of the room started, and with busy buzz, revolved with great velocity. This forced a smile from the Professor. Then various small articles fell in different parts of the room; sometimes, also, a large weight would come in close proximity with our heads; at last, the Doctor thought it advisable for the party to leave the room. Repeated trials with the mammoth dial were attended with no more fortunate results; so we had to come down to the more convenient, though, perhaps, less physical mode of writing.

This life is full of change; the tree that bears fruit to-day, may be prostrated in the dust to-morrow; the fragrance of the rarest and sweetest flower is evanescent; change has wrought its work upon this patriarch of our cause, and he has passed through that valley, that must be traversed by all mortality; his, however, was no doubting, faithless passage; he had informed himself of that, to many, so much dreaded hereafter, and explored its intricacies; the veil of mystery had been raised for him, and when the summons came, he was ready, and went unflinchingly to meet those who had so long hovered around his earthly pathway, giving him hope and consolation. None that knew the earnest, sincere belief of Professor Hare in our faith, but will grieve, when they reflect how his last moments were embittered, at having that cup of life, from which he had imbibed such soul comforting draughts during the hours of health, withheld from his parched lips, when mortality's closing scene drew nigh. Charity compels us to attribute such heartlessness to mistaken zeal, blind fanaticism; and leads to the hope that the loved sister, who had guarded and watched him so long, with seraphic eyes, stood at that trying hour between him and the erring ones, and taught his spirit "what to brave and what to brook."

One stormy day, during which I had been almost entirely alone, I was called upon by a gentleman, who stated that he was about leaving the city, and had no other opportunity for a séance. His manners were the reverse of prepossessing; he seemed determined to sit in one corner of the room, and let me make the trial for manifestations. I assured him it was quite impossible for him to obtain any satisfaction, unless he calmly and sincerely desired to know the truth, and would seat himself at the table, so that he might hear and see whatever transpired. After some solicitation, he acquiesced, and we took our places. Twenty minutes passed without any response ; finally, the table rose, and tipped towards the stranger three times. I cannot say I ever felt, prior to that day, or since, the peculiar sensations which pervaded my system at that time. It seemed as though a solid substance were passing through my body, antero-posteriorly, and with that feeling came a sharp, stinging pain.

I explained the nature of the manifestation to the investigator, and, for the first time, he appeared interested: he asked, "How it felt, and whether I could tell what the substance was." I told him, it seemed like solid bodies of metal passing through me, and tearing the flesh as they went, at the same time, leaving a very disagreeable itching sensation where they entered. He asked the spirit to explain the phenomenon, when my hand slowly but intelligibly wrote the communication annexed.

My Dear Brother George—

I have been with you from day to day for a long time, and as you will see, it was with some difficulty that I prevailed upon you to come here this morning. Twice did you make up your mind to come, and twice did you break it; I have, therefore, to congratulate myself on the success attending my perseverance. I am a spirit, as you are well aware; and, I hope you may believe that it is I alone who write these lines: for after long days, weeks, and months in preparing your mind for this interview, to have you *then* doubt me, would surely be discouraging; and, I well know, I can give you some evidence that I am living, and not, as you suppose, dead, and not even immortal. 'Tis a hard thing, George, to believe we are but as blocks of wood, to rot out, and leave nothing but our ashes to tell we ever existed.

When I left the good old home at Columbus, little did I think that I should not survive to meet you again; but you know the only thing that prompted me to the step, was the cold-heartedness of Kate. I went to her but a few weeks before I enlisted, and she was not as one should be. I told her then, partly in joke, that I should go to Mexico. Her reply was, "If you go, you show more courage than I think you possess; if you do not go, you only strengthen the idea I already have of your boasting qualities." The result you well know, but never till now, did I open to you the cause. Before I left, I went to Eliza, and told her, I should *never* get shot. I knew it, I felt it, and my prophecy was true. I was in two engagements, the last at Monterey; and though companions dear to me were unmercifully deprived of their lives, still I was left to be killed, not by powder, but by that scourge of the South, yellow fever. I lay on my back eight days, and when my senses were my own, how I prayed for one smile from home; one word of love from those I had so cruelly left. As you may suppose, my nurses were not of the most effeminate nature: and under such conditions I left earth. I cannot say I had any distinct idea of the other existence; but, never mind, however much I could tell you of my feelings, you would say, others could write the same.

I wish you to see Kate; tell her, I loved her not wisely but too well, and that I was undoubtedly one of those few fools, who care more for others than for themselves. But I forgive all, and now wish to satisfy all, that I am truly living, and I hope more wise.

May I meet you again, and when ?

Thy spirit brother, HARRY COLEMAN.

The communication was written from right to left, as they usually are ; and I was called upon to read it for the gentleman. From the change in his manner and expression of countenance as I read, it could easily be perceived that his spirit brother had struck a vein in his heart, which previously had lain still and motionless. As I concluded, he took the papers, rolled them carefully together, and placed them in his wallet ; then, grasping the pencil, he asked various questions, which were readily answered. Although this visitor came in haste, and had affirmed on entering, that he could only remain half an hour, two full hours elapsed ere his departure.—As he finished, he simply asked, "What's the damage ?" and repairing it, bid me good day, and left.

The result of this interview was quite as conclusive to me as if the gentleman had admitted its truth, for I have not been constantly before the public for years without having acquired some knowledge of human nature ; and I would unhesitatingly predict, that the recipient of that spirit brother's message will ultimately become convinced of the reality of what he had probably before believed to be jugglery.

I remained but a week in Philadelphia, my engagements in Boston calling me thence, but I had a greater concourse of visitors while there than had been mine in any of the other cities in which I had held circles during my tour.

I arrived in Boston in the early part of May, and immediately resumed my seat in that temple dedicated to spirits, 45 Carver street. Much gratification did the old friends, who had received so many glad tidings through me, express at my return: prominent among these were Messrs. Bruce, Farquhar, Dow, Curtis, &c., &c., all of whom had been accustomed to hold regular meetings, and whose chain of evidence having been broken by my absence, they were much pleased to have the opportunity to repair it.

A few days after my return I was called upon by Elisha Hanson, Esq., of Salem, whose little Franky, a darling spirit, gave his father's heart much joy: he would invariably pat his father on the knee as a signal of his presence.

Franky was very active, and while my hand lay flat on the table he would take the ring off my little finger as deliberately as though he were a privileged character, and this, too, in broad daylight. I presume he supposed his right was prior to mine, as it had been his own ring, and had his name on the inside. I have sometimes had it on my finger at the table, and on rising would miss it, and it would be gone for weeks; then, at some interview with Mr.

H., the mysterious little present would slowly work its way on my finger, and remain undisturbed for days, then again take French leave; this same ring has been spoken of in a previous article.

At this stage of my development I met with a rather interesting, and to me, at the time, highly amusing coincidence—other mediums may have passed through similar ones, but I have heard none related.

I was sitting alone in my room, one Sunday afternoon, copying a communication that had been given a lady the previous day, and which she had left to have transcribed, when the bell called the servant to the door, and a gentleman was ushered into my apartment; he was a fine looking person, with dark complexion, and of remarkably urbane and commanding address. Judging externally, he was in every respect what the world would term a perfect gentleman.

I ceased my writing on his entrance, and looked up, when he introduced himself with the remark:

"Mr. Redman, I have heard friends speak of you very often, and have also read much about you in the papers. I suppose you are probably the best medium in the country, excepting Mr. Hume, are you not?"

"Well, sir," said I, "different persons entertain different opinions on that point. I am satisfied with my own developments, and when I find those who are as well pleased as myself, of course I am gratified."

"Well, I did not call for the purpose of having a sitting with you, but as it was Sunday, and I supposed you would be at leisure, I desired to have a little conversation."

"Very well, sir," I said; "sit down."

He took a chair at the table, and after remarking on the state of the weather, the progress of spiritualism, &c., he began.

"What are your manifestations, Mr. Redman?"

"Rapping, tipping, writing, are most prominent; but at times, even more extraordinary than these happen; it depends upon the character of the persons with whom I come in contact." I then referred him to Mr. Lanning's second letter.

"I have read that," he replied, "and have come for an especial purpose; one which is truly honest, dignified, and I hope will not prove unsuccessful."

"Well, sir, I will hear anything you have to suggest; but I cannot give you much time, as I have a number of communications to copy before evening, when I attend a party in the city."

"Then," he said, "we will come to the point immediately. You and I know well the source whence arise all manifestations, called spiritual, and that their explanation is but the work of a few moments."

"Well," thought I, "he must be a wiseacre assuredly; he makes pretension to wisdom, then flatters me with the same rare endowment." While these ideas were flitting through my mind, he continued: "I have come to-day for the purpose of making a proposition to you, which, I presume, you will not refuse; at all events, when you consider that the compliance will be locked in my own soul, entirely disconnected from the public, and I swear, known only to myself."

When he had arrived thus far in his prefatory remarks, I imagined, instead of the fine accomplished gentleman, I had unfortunately come in contact with a lunatic—or, more appropriately speaking, the lunatic had come in contact with me.

"I cannot conceive, my friend, what can be your meaning," I replied; "had I any suggestion of yours to comply with, I would as soon the whole world should be informed of it, as that it should be imprisoned in your soul; at all events, whatever I do I am perfectly willing to have subjected to the ordeal of public trial; I desire no secrecy. But if I can benefit you in any feasible way, be that by making a proposition (provided you enlighten me on the especial kind to be made), or by complying with any reasonable one, I am at your service."

At this moment, the visitor drew a paper from his pocket, and looking at me wistfully, resumed his colloquy thus:—

"Young man, here is my check for five hundred dollars. I desire that you tell me, frankly and fully, without concealment, the manner in which you make those raps, tip the table, &c.; the instant you do this, you shall have this check, and with it another for a similar amount. I came prepared for your refusal; but I wish you to understand, I am already aware that there have been mediums, who have freely made concessions in this way, and concluding you were equally as accessible, I have approached you with this inducement. Now give me the correct solution of the matter, for I feel if it come from you it will be reliable; I beg you will not refuse me, for, as I stated before, I seek the information for my own individual pleasure, and not with any purpose of making it public."

"You misapprehend me, sir," I answered, "I will tell you, frankly and freely, how I make the manifestations; therefore, your preparation for refusal is wholly unnecessary."

"Then here is the first check," said he, putting the note for five hundred dollars in my hand. I took it, and holding it between my fingers, addressed him.

"I do not know what mediums have made concessions, nor do I care; but if there be any assuming to be mediums who have professed to make concessions, and have explained how the raps are made, or the tipping of the table effected, I have little doubt but that you will find my mode differing entirely from theirs."

I looked at the note as it lay doubled up in my hand; the thought entered my mind, truly he has paid pretty dearly for information, which I deal out to hundreds for a very trifling remuneration; but, while cogitating over my good fortune, he recalled my wandering mind by notifying me to proceed, as he was anxious to finish the business.

"You shall have all the requisitions in as explicit a manner as I can give them," I responded. "The first essential is to place your mind in as passive a state as possible, then, either sitting at a table like this or at a small stand, to lay your hands upon it, and silently pray for some manifestation which may indicate that those who loved you in days gone bye are still near, to give assurance of the continuance of that affection. A number of sittings may be required, sir, but, by perseverance, I am quite positive you will obtain some manifestations; it was six weeks in my own case, from the time I first commenced investigating the subject, ere I obtained the sounds; how long it will be with you I cannot pretend to say, but if you go to work in this way, no doubt success will ultimately crown your efforts."

On casting my eyes towards the visitor, after closing my explanation, I perceived that his countenance had undergone a material change, the expression of self-gratulation which had pervaded it as he had listened to my promised exposition, had now given place to that of passionate disappointment;

he was nervously twitching his chair from right to left, and as I ceased speaking he remarked, "That's the way, hey? Well, I knew all that before—but —but—but—my money was given in good faith, supposing you would tell me the *physical* means you employ, and not imagining you would humbug me in this manner."

"Sir, I have told you all I know, you are welcome to the knowledge, for I repeat it ten times per day; but if you think the manifestations produced through me are made by me, you are most egregiously deceived. I return the amount you so munificently proffered, as undoubtedly you think the bargain an unfair one; but, let it be a lesson, how, like Simon of old, you offer to purchase gifts which are purely spiritual, as you may not be always fortunate enough to have your money refunded:" I then handed him the check, which he, without hesitation, took, and tore into diminutive pieces, and then exclaimed:

"You're a shrewd one, I have no doubt, Mr. Redman, and know your own trade better than those that have worked at it less time; but, I am sorry to say 'tis only knowledge deferred, for I am determined eventually to obtain it—I wish you good day."

"Good day, sir. I have a circle for the poor on Saturday evenings, and if any of your friends desire to investigate and are unable to meet the expense, you can mention the fact to them." To this last remark, my inquisitive friend gave no response, his form gradually diminished in the distance, and I resumed my copying, which had been interrupted by this little "affair of business."

Having finished my allotted task, I sat at the table, hoping to receive the views of some spirit on the event of the afternoon; I was silent but a few moments, when father's well-known signal gave evidence of his presence, and he wrote the following, not deigning, however, to make any comment on the occurrence.

My Beloved Child,

Has not my prophecy been fulfilled? Have I not watched thee in the seed, and in the bud, and behold now in the flower of thy success, as a divine teacher: yet even now thy path is but just entered upon, and thy duties but commenced: thine is a flower, that fades not by autumnal winds, nor is it weakened by the heat of the noonday sun. Thou shalt bloom even when others, that now flourish by thy side, shall have passed away, and the spirits made joyous through these realities shall, in the mighty future gather, to make thy reception into the second life grand and imposing. Mary, thy dear mother, is here, but I am better able to write than she, and her wish is that my words may be considered as hers also, and the love and care I bear you shall be from her the same. I frequently visit the old vault, that holds the mortal remains of Lizzie and myself; but 'tis not instructive, the only pleasure exists in gazing upon that structure, which was a tabernacle for the same individuality that now addresses you. How often have I wished that I could have known that what was by us called warnings, was the same priceless reality of the intercourse of those existing before us. I have often told you, my son, of the legacy left me by thy grandfather, which consisted of his old leather apron ; I see him often. and he says to me, "tell George you have left him a richer prize than that ;" and, well he may so say, for this development, is to open a path, which will need little modeling in after life, and thy entrance into the future state will be far easier and more comprehensible to thyself than mine was.

Although I am not happy, still I find great pleasure, and I may say comparative happiness, in knowing that through thy hand I can at least advise those who are our kin on earth. I shall respond to a call from you to advise and counsel on any of thy actions or thoughts. With the love of thy dear mother and sister I close. Thy Spirit Father and Guardian,

ALEXANDER.

The communications received from my guardian parent are very frequent, but I give only a few. In all my acts, spiritual or material, his counsel is ever ready, and thus whatever is undertaken, there is a preceding knowledge of its success and benefits. In the discharge of any duty, or the indulgence of any thought, his admonition is at all times ready and acceptable. It may be imagined that this in a degree might impair self identity, but to *me* it does not in the least, for his caution to use my own judgment first, always is the precursor of whatever response he gives to my interrogatories. Such a guide is invaluable, and truly makes me, even when most melancholy, feel there is

"A true, a kind, a faithful friend,
That's always near his aid to lend;
That such a friend I have above,
To cheer me with his guardian love !"

Below is given a letter from Mr. J. V. Mansfield, which I have selected from my bureau of correspondence, as possessing claims to the interest of the reader.

Mr. Mansfield was at the time of this séance totally uninitiated in the sublimity of spiritual realities, and this his first circle was probably the means of moving the vast river of susceptibility within himself, for, as is well known, he occupies an eminent position among the mediums of the present day; Mr. Callagan and his enemies to the contrary notwithstanding.

Boston, Nov. 17th, 1856.

To George A. Redman:—

Dear Sir:—Will you please pardon the intrusion upon your valuable and much occupied time, while I relate the experiences of a sitting with you some weeks since. I was then and still remain a stranger to you. I did not register my name, neither did I tell it during the hour of my visit. Now, after sitting at the table for perhaps two minutes, raps were distinctly heard, or might have been, in any part of the room. You then remarked, if I would call on my spirit friends, no doubt, something would be received, by which I could identify them. I accordingly wrote names on pieces of paper entirely concealed from your sight, rolled them up into small balls about the size of a large pea. This I did to the number of three, and placed them before you, saying, "As I had called on several friends, perhaps some of them would respond, if not, I could call on some others." Now these pellets did not leave my sight, neither did you touch them with your hand; but, with your pencil you separated them perhaps three inches distant from each other, then you wrote out the name of my father, giving it in full, while I had only written his first name.

You next gave the name (which I had not written) of a very dear friend of mine, whom I supposed then to be living. I was so certain this was the case, I would have risked all I possessed, (though that was not much) that the person who purported to be a spirit was as much alive as yourself. I could not refrain from laughter at the idea of communicating with the spirit of a living party; and if you recollect, I remarked, "I was willing to pay for that communication, for by it I had learnt I could communicate as well with spirit in the body, as one out of it." Now what little faith I had as to talking with my dear departed, before entering your rooms had vanished, and I left them in disgust with the whole thing. While retracing my steps homeward across the Common, well do I recollect how heartily I laughed at the communication I had received from my supposed living friend. Just as I was about leaving the Common, the thought struck me, that my friend had a nephew living in the city, and would it not be better to call and find out how the case stood. This I resolved to do. I made my way to his office, and after passing a few words, asked him how my friend was (from whom I had just received a communication.) Never, never, was I so completely taken aback as when I heard, for the first time, that the person had been buried more than three weeks; my laughter was turned into surprise. What could I think, but that I really had been talking with my dear friend; and on looking the communication over, I found some words communicated which were peculiar to that person and no one else; and here let me say, I do fully believe I had conversed with my once mortal, but now spirit, friend. I have many in spirit land, with whom I intend shortly to make an attempt to communicate; when I do so, I shall avail myself of the honor of calling on you. Again, let me say pardon this intrusion on your time. I dare say, the reiteration of my visit may not seem as interesting to you as to me. God bless you in this holy calling. Yours, respectfully,

153 Commercial Street. J. V. MANSFIELD.

CHAPTER IX.

The Mysterious Visitor. The Reality. Manifestations at Mr. Park's. Spirit Telegraphing. Mr. Bruce. The Carpet Stretcher. Progressive Spirits Strong and his Strength. Independent Spirit Communication.

"Cease not to explore
Th' unknown, th' unseen, the future,—though the heart,
As at unearthly sounds, before them start,
Though the frame shudder, and the spirit sigh,
They have their source in immortality."

WHILE running over the keys of my piano one morning, to pass away the tedium of an idle hour, I was aroused from my musical mood by the entrance of a gentleman: I had heard no bell ring, and he had come into my apartment without even the customary signal of a knock on the door. I was somewhat surprised, not only at the uncerimonousness of the visit, but at the unusually early hour of the call, it being before eight o'clock in the morning. My irascibility, which had been rather excited at this breach of etiquette, was however appeased when I recognized in the intruder my friend Mr. Palmer, of Portland. I immediately extended to him my hand, and was not a little astonished at his taking no notice of my proffered greeting. With much brusquerie he passed me, and took his seat in the place allotted to investigators, and without any delay or parley, I following his example, drew my chair to the table, and patiently waited to hear him, as was his wont, ask questions, or address himself in some way to the invisibles ; but, to my surprise, he did neither, but resting his folded arms upon the table, and fixing his unwinking eyes upon me, sat like a statue.

"Well, Mr. Palmer, suppose you begin the circle by putting questions to your friends ?" said I.

My answer was a continuation of the same immovable attitude.

"Are any of Mr. Palmer's spirit friends present ?" I asked, thinking to conceal my annoyance by drawing a response from the spirits ; but not a rap. Again and again, I repeated the query, but the invisibles were as taciturn and inflexible as the visitor. My organ of combativeness began to feel uneasy ; but I thought, "Well, I can sit here just as speechless as he, and, perhaps, shall enjoy it fully as much." So taking the pencil, I began sketching human faces, during which employment I could see his elbows on the table ; I looked up, and his keen eyes were fixed immovably upon me still. It now occurred to me that should he have suspected me of any wrong, and I evaded his searching glance, his impression would be strengthened. So, assuming a position similar to his own, I "fell to such perusal of his face," as though I would draw it, being very determined that nought should divert my fixed, untiring gaze, till he was perfectly convinced I feared to look no man in the face. We sat thus, as far as I could judge, five or ten minutes—my eyes absolutely ached with over exertion. Finally, he either seemed to recede from my view, or I was becoming mesmerized, I could not tell which, but he gradually faded, till he was gone. I rose, and approached the chair he had occupied. It was empty. I went into the hall; no one was there. I inquired of the persons in the house, but all positively affirmed that no one had entered by the front door. I therefore concluded that Mr. Palmer had suddenly passed from earth, and had returned in that manner to identify himself to me, and give me evidence of his spiritual nature. I noted the occurrence in my journal, expecting to have the fact corroborated by time. The same day, after dinner (which was about two o'clock), I again took a seat at the piano, and was playing a lively air, when the hall door bell rang, and a rap soon followed at my door. I opened it, and to my unutterable astonishment, there stood the *identical Palmer*. "How do you do, Mr. Redman," said he, at the same time extending his hand.

"Well, sir," said I, "I do well enough, but you don't catch me napping again, as you did this morning."

"What," he said, "I do not understand you."

"Now, sir, first tell me, are you a spirit, or are you a mortal?"

"Take hold of my hand and see," was his response. I did so, and found that this was indeed the veritable Mr. Palmer himself. I then explained to him the visit he had paid me in the morning, and that that was the cause of my hesitancy in recognizing him. He could not account for it in any way, except, that about that time he was thinking of paying me a visit, and that his spirit must have, in that instance, preceded him. Again,

I attended a circle in company with Mrs. Helen Leeds, at the residence of Mr. Park. We had been sitting but a short time, before a communication was spelled by the alphabet, thus,

"JENNIE IS HERE."

"Jennie who?" we asked.

"Jennie Keyes," was the response.

Now we were not aware of the departure of Miss Keyes, who is the niece of Judge Edmonds, and we felt, moreover, assured that she had *not* passed into spirit life, because Mrs. Leeds would have been notified of the fact. We continued to question the spirit, and received answers, the purport of which was:

That the body of Miss Keyes was lying at her home, in New York, asleep, and that her sympathy with Mrs. Leeds had attracted her spirit there, to announce itself. A loud call was made for the alphabet again, and—"I must return to the form, for Laura has just entered my room, and is to arouse me." The spirit then left us.

Here, indeed, was a most remarkable instance of the independent action of the spirit during sleep, though we are unconscious of it at the time, and remain so afterwards. Mrs. Leeds informed Miss Edmonds of the fact, and it was ascertained that Miss Keyes was *actually sleeping* when her spirit declared this to be the case.

Mrs. Leeds has often told me (and even when I have been in company with her, it has happened) that she has seen Miss Edmonds come into her apartment, and give a message, that had been agreed upon by parties in New York, which was thus transmitted to us in Boston, without any other intervention than a spiritual one.

A regular circle was formed for the special purpose of establishing the fact of the possibility of spiritual communication between the two parties. They met on appointed days, and particular hours, and the trial was attended with considerable success; quite sufficient to demonstrate, beyond a doubt, that it can be done.

With the foregoing data before us, can we doubt, that though absent in form and divided by space, we may still linger around those to whom our affections cling! Certainly these instances, to which I have casually alluded, are but a grain in the scale of evidence, which is continually being presented of the existence, not only of communication between man and the spirit, that has left this place of existence; but, that while that essence of divinity still dwells in its earthly tabernacle, it can hold communion with the in-dwelling intelligence of another, likewise surrounded with its clay incumbrances.

Mr. Charles Bruce, a number of whose manifestations have been already given, resumed his weekly séances. The usual time taken by him was from 7 till 8 o'clock on Thursday evening. We verily feared, that the manifestations would become so strong, as to compel us to petition for mercy; although each tangible demonstration only tended to fix, more firmly, the knowledge, that when we go hence we do not become children, but absolutely possess physical force in even a greater degree, when conditions are suitable, than when here on earth.

The hands of our spirit friends were displayed with perfect indifference, and Mr. B. asserted, that on a number of occasions, he felt the wedding ring on the spirit's finger. They would take us by the arms, and with an unceremonious rubbing over our heads, would cause our hair to stand on end, not from fear, but from disorder; our boots and stockings were almost invariably taken off, and sometimes, the latter articles would be closely knotted, and pushed into the toe of the boot, so tightly as to occasion some trouble before they could be drawn out.

In short, nothing was left for them to accomplish except showing themselves in as tangible a manner as they exhibited their hands, which (although our friend expected it) was never realized.

I leave the reader to philosophize upon some, if not all of the above, as undoubtedly it needs much philosophy (that perhaps we have not) to explain them. We already agree that the ring was not the same Julia wore in life ; but if it felt the same, and it sometimes seemed similar, what was it ? Time will answer these more intricate queries, as it will others of the same, or of similar character, that will be given as we proceed.

A carpet was being laid in one of my rooms, and at each stroke of the workman's hammer, a similar sound would respond, as if in echo, on the opposite side of the room. I saw that this confused the carpet stretcher, for at each sound, he would turn partly round, as if to ascertain from whence the noise proceeded. But presently the reverberations came faster and at shorter intervals, till the man imagining that I was taking the job out of his hands exclaimed, " Doctor, you must not aid me, as I can do it better alone, it needs stretching." " I am doing nothing," I replied. " But you were tacking down your end of the carpet, were you not ?" said he. " Certainly not," was the response. He said no more, but (I dare say questioning my veracity) proceeded with his work : the same knocking being kept up, I finally left the room, no doubt to his great relief.

About this time I commenced a series of circles, alternately, at the residences of Messrs. Wm. Story, Eldridge and Appleton—these gentlemen, and at times Mr. Henry W. Longfellow, constituting the investigating party.

Our first séance was held at the house of Mr. Story, and although the manifestations were not as strong physically as what took place subsequently, still there were certain evidences of an unseen intelligence being present, that all admitted.

We were repeatedly touched, and sometimes so powerfully as to cause those who were thus complimented to cry aloud. A large bell, that had been placed beneath the table gave evidence of life, and was passed into the hands and upon the laps of some of the party; the bell also rose through the divided leaves of the table, and its form could be seen distinctly, the cover being on the table at the time, various communications were received, but as the meetings convened especially for physical demonstrations, they were not of sufficient character to note.

To obtain powerful physical manifestations, it is essential to form a select circle, that will meet regularly at a specified time. The members of it thus become more or less *en rapport* with one and another, and this harmony creates confidence, which should be one of the governing principles of every meeting of a spiritual nature. The necessity of frequent meetings, where manifestations of an extraordinary kind were desired, this circle of gentlemen fully understood, hence their arrangement.

One trait I observed in my interview with these gentlemen, which was, that however skeptical or incredulous they were, there was a manifest effort to keep it to themselves to enable me to enter into as passive a condition as possible, and at every meeting the same spirit of consideration was beautifully manifest.

How much wiser was such a course, than *à la Agassiz*, to make a pretence of expressing sincere desires to witness these truths, and when introduced to those, who, at some personal inconvenience to themselves, had assembled for their accommodation, to offer insult on the first introduction, before even an attempt had been made for demonstration of any kind.

Our third séance was at Mr. Eldridge's house, located on Summer Street. Here we were treated to a variety of manifestations, which were certainly not on an anticipated programme.

We gathered round a common three foot and a half table, and after some interchange of sociality, we were welcomed by raps of a most ponderous kind, and our table began exhibiting various gymnastic feats. We asked for the name of our demonstrating friend, when S. T. R. O. N. G. was spelled by the alphabet.

"Happy to see you, Strong," said Mr. A.

"You don't see me," replied Strong.

"To hear you then, or see your power. I hope you are going to give us something nice to-night."

This was answered by a most prodigious thump of the table, which certainly gave indication of the power of our visitor. Various small articles were now moved from point to point, without human intervention, and as the evening drew near its close, after having been amused, and I hope enlightened, by many pleasant occurrences, Mr. Eldridge proposed, "If Strong were going he should bid us good-night."

To this our invisible guest readily assented, and a slight tremor was perceptible in the table; finally it rose with a resolute effort to a considerable height, and descending with immense force, broke into pieces—the bed piece lying flat on the floor, and the legs strewed in various directions. We collected the fragments with a cry of Bravo! Mr. E. deposited them behind a door for the purpose of exhibition.

Our acquaintance, Strong, was always a welcome guest, and was never tardy in showing his force—in fact we were compelled occasionally to request him to desist, for his power could be felt by those on the floor beneath.

On one occasion, a very large bedstead, standing in an adjoining room to that where we were sitting, took upon itself the responsibility of motion: it came with great velocity towards the entrance to the room where we were, and wedging a corner between the sides of the door, seemed determined to force through; different other articles joined in this spontaneous locomotion, so that we were compelled to return the bedstead to its original position and shut the door. If we partook of refreshments when the evening closed, Strong manifested great desire to be considered as one of the party, and we always had the politeness to gratify him.

How many circles, like those described, were held I do not remember; but there were sufficient to clearly demonstrate that the repeated meetings of the same persons would have strengthened the results to almost any degree.

Though, from time to time, parties are found imbued with this harmonic principle, who are wise enough to see what is to be seen, and sufficiently shrewd to *know* what they see; we find persons who require long and repeated séances to accomplish the results that would accrue from the meeting of the former class. Many, also, more imbued with ideas of spiritual trickery than of charity, refuse to sit at the table; for the reason, that in such a position deception cannot be detected: to such, I would repeat what I have often told my visitors—take nothing for genuine except what you know to be beyond the power or knowledge of human. If the table tip, consider it the act of some one present, if this accord with your preconceived ideas ; but if it rise in mid air, and you can see above, below, and around it, then give the truth its due ; or, if from those who have passed on you receive what is known only to yourself and the communicating intelligence, then judge accordingly. If persons desire truth, they will put themselves in a receptive condition ; if they wish to overthrow truth, or have no desire to ascertain wherein they err, they will erect every possible barrier against it, and this has been the case in numberless instances within my own knowledge and experience.

The communication given below is a somewhat remarkable production, as it was written without hands, while the paper lay on the floor ; it was received by Mr. Edward Bill, of New York City, at a circle composed of six persons.

Productions of similar character are generally noted for their brevity ; but this deserves particular attention for its length, the consideration of its having been produced in a lighted room, and in the presence of so many witnesses.

Copy of a communication received at Doctor Redman's, being written by spirit hands upon the floor.

Indeed it may seem strange to you and miraculous, that unseen fingers can trace a word of love, or a line of consolation —but witness its truth in these lines ; and, also, know that every mark my spirit makes hereon is in itself an emblem of my long love, my devoted affection, my unchanging desire to make thee better prepared to enter a life which is at present dark—lighted only by the dim flickering glare of faith—still, herein is an avenue of knowledge, an amount of fact, that leads where faith alone fails to approach, and where creeds of the day are forgotten, or never known. Let not a moment pass without improving thy stock of this life-principle, and be assured my spirit perception is, as the air you breathe, ever present to give life.

Thy own guide upward,

LIZZIE.

CHAPTER X.

Abbott Lawrence as a Spirit. Mr. Potter and his unseen Antagonist's. His Sanguinary Encounter and Defeat. Communication from the Ayrshire Poet.

Thy spirit like the rivulet goes coursing on its way,
A stone, a snag; perhaps a tree, may its pure progress stay:
But still toward the ocean, its source of life doth run,
And finds its dearest resting place, though it had just begun.

SOPHIA.

FIRST experiences of Abbott Lawrence, upon entering the Spirit Life.

Given at the residence of Mr. Alvin Adams, of Boston: a weekly meeting having been held for that purpose. The communications will be numbered as they were received, though owing to want of space some of them have been omitted.

No. 1. While I lay upon my couch of death, or rather life, I tried to imagine the future state, and I can now see where I received impressions from those in the spirit spheres, who had passed before me. I was unconscious of my position about two days before I departed for spirit life; though my friends supposed I was rational, still I dwelt in a kind of misty atmosphere, my spirit all the while bringing up some scenes of bygone days. While thus I lay, Adams, scenes of my boyhood passed before me as vividly as though they were but transactions of yesterday; and I sifted the various incidents of life, to see where my talents have been misapplied.

All my hours, for two or three days before my last of earth's life, were spent in perusing the volumes of the past, and being impressed by unseen influences around, with reminiscenses of what *had* been. I heeded not the many mortal eyes, that were dampened with tears, neither did I sob in spirit to hear or see the falling drops of affection, that fast trickled down the face of my earthly companion.

Oh! could I point thee to those hours of solemn, silent thought, while my mortal frame was unconscious of the actions of the spirit! Believe me, Adams, I did not even know the moment, when the body struggled last with its Parent, nature, for my spirit was employed in reviewing the hours fled no more to return, and in looking toward the future. I had heard of persons drowning being favored with the panorama of their lives, but I was not aware of the same advantage being enjoyed by others. I attribute my apparent favor in that respect to my comparative knowledge, or silent belief of the actuality of spirit intercourse, for since I have become enlightened on my developments, I find there are few who were even as conscious in their last moments as I was: whether the velocity with which I was carried through space had any connection with my sight, or consciousness, I know not; but true it is, that I felt a soothing susceptibility as I was thus propelled by a force, which you will probably better comprehend, when you are favored with its locomotive character.

I was taken, by the loved ones, into a strange atmosphere, that seemed exhilarating; its very presence, as my spirit breathed, seemed to quicken a circulation within me that bade my internal senses open and view the objects around.

Presented to my gaze were myriads of beings of various

forms, sizes, and color. I afterwards learned, that these varieties were only the objects of optical delusion, and had I been clearly initiated into the sphere, where the good ones conducted me, all would have been as open and comprehensive as the elements of my own family home. Be this as it may, the exquisite pleasure of my bed of down, as I call it, was far from producing any desire to be moved.

The mental impressions of the high walled-neaven, and the fiery-gated hell, came like a vision before me. I congratulated myself on escape from the latter, and hoped that my present condition was but preparatory to my entering the former; still, as I before said, I had little faith in such contrasts to nature's teachings, although the atmosphere of the old stone church, surrounded by its cold graves, instilled into me somewhat of that feeling.

Time-pieces were objectionable, or not necessary, I hardly know which—therefore, the length of time I reclined on my downy bed, I know not, but I was visited by Amos, who desired me to accompany him. As if only by desire, I felt an action in my frame, and a dizzy motion was given me; I could not clearly perceive Amos, nor others that accompanied me; but, as we advanced, I understood we were to revisit earth, from which I had been removed; and, also, that the cause of my being taken back was to give me a consciousness of objects around, that I might have the pleasure of witnessing the last and most solemn rites of earth's vanity—my own funeral services. What an idea! thought I, here to hurry me from such repose to the scene of grief, where, unless I am materially changed, I shall surely join with my friends and shed silent tears, not for myself, but for those who cannot see me, and are not aware of my better condition: but we sped on, and finally came within the atmosphere of earth, when the previous giddy sensation was increased, owing to the greater density of the elements surrounding it. As we drew nearer to our point of destination, my dizziness gradually abated, and I could discern the different objects as we approached; but never had the thickness and unrefined condition of the atmosphere been so perceptible to me as it was now; the striking contrast between it and the refined elements from which I had been taken, made my spirit probably more *alive* to the change. I could see a self-congratulation in the feelings of my accompanying guides, that they had been enabled to render my spirit so susceptible in such a comparatively short time; they seemed especially happy, and their thoughts were mysteriously known to me without utterance. I was in constant wonder and study how to account for my sudden and painless transition from earth's sphere, and also for the ease with which I comprehended the wishes of those around me: but my philosophizing was interrupted by our arrival at the house from which, but a short time before, I had been taken. Brother told me I had been absent from the form about nine hours—it seemed to me so many days or weeks.

On entering my former abode I saw eight persons in the room—they appeared to be females—but I could not discern the countenances, as they seemed enveloped in a misty vapor peculiar to all mortality. Brother remarked, "It is nature throwing off the influences of the flesh." These eight persons were standing around the bedside, apparently grieving at my having left that form or mortal house, where I had been an inmate for sixty years. I saw no reason why they should not grieve, for if they could see me no plainer than I could perceive them, I, too, would have grieved, and, indeed, should have done so now, but for the assurance of Amos, that "as my spirit grew finer I should be enabled to comprehend the nature of all earthly things;" I understood him to mean that I should be more and more refined in spirit. My interest was intense: I watched every motion of those who stood around my body; Amos said "he had watched me with as much interest from the moment the conflict between nature and disease commenced."

I saw tnose in attendance when they left the room; witnessed the arraying of my mortal limbs in uniform; which ceremony struck me as quite unnecessary, for why should mortal garb be put upon an inanimate form? I almost expected to see the body rise up and walk. You may imagine the gratification I experienced in beholding the attention bestowed upon the worn-out frame: the thought arose,—how they love my body! could they but be aware that the life exhibited once in that dust was near them, standing by their side, how that would likewise be loved and cherished! Amos said, "I understood not the laws which separated mortal from immortal, but would as soon as the various duties and restrictions of spirit life should be pointed out to me." For many hours I watched the movements of those dear friends, whose eyes were filled with symbols of grief: it was about eve, all had left the room save Amos and myself: there lay the dust confined in mortality's last abiding place, and the spirit standing by it a silent observer of its passive obedience to the commands of the Angel—Death.

No. 2. I paced the room arm in arm with my guardian; we spoke of the days of earth life and the coming moment, when those who were weeping for my apparent loss should be laid low themselves, and be brought to witness the same scenes that were passing before me at that moment. We had remained in the room for some time discussing the separation of electric fluids from the body, when the door, that then stood ajar, opened, and two ladies, with a gentleman, (whom I learned was Mr. L., my pastor,) entered, and with a slow tread approached the coffin that held my remains. A tear trembled in the good man's eye, as he gazed on the features that had been a surface, whereon time had ploughed its broken furrows. I was conscious of a low sound from the lips of the party, but my sense of hearing being deficient, I could not comprehend what was uttered. Presently our number was considerably augmented by the entrance of several persons, who, from friendly sympathy, had come to console and comfort our family. While they were dilating more or less on my earthly pilgrimage, Amos and myself found abundance of food for thought by contrasting their belief with the true condition of things, as I had found it since the opening of my morning existence.

Amos and myself left the room when the visitors retired, with the determination to return on the following day and accompany the body to its quiet house—the tomb. We had ascended only a short distance when we were met by a vast concourse of spirits, who seemed much gratified at finding me with so attentive and competent a teacher, thus complimenting Amos, who acknowledged the politeness and we proceeded onward, mentally rehearsing the hymn,

> Mortal life, like fleeting day,
> Cannot with the spirit stay.

We were now joined by an aged ancestor, named Jacob Lawrence, who seemed to have progressed much towards the higher spheres, and as we passed swiftly from earth, he gave me a short sketch of his visit to the planet Saturn, (whence he had just returned) and assured me he would be my escort thither at some future time, and unfold the realities of other spheres. I thanked him kindly, thinking how much interest *you* would take in my relation of the life and habits of the Saturnians.

Thus our travel was made pleasant and agreeable by the incidents of Jacob's spirit life; and ever and anon a momentary conversation with any spirit who passed us while wending its way toward some mortal habitation to give light to others, as I labor to enlighten you. Journeying onward, I observed in the distance an immense number of starlike objects, which Amos told me was the Zophanium, or delegation to initiate me more fully into a realization of my own character. Drawing nearer I could distinctly see their forms, which were of the most angelic perfection; approaching, they divided and formed to represent a hollow cone, through which we slowly passed.

10

During our passage not a motion was perceptible on the features of those surrounding us, although the placidity of their smile indicated an interior happiness. As we emerged from their influence, I inquired of Jacob the meaning of this manœuvre, and received the following answer:

"My Child—

Mortals, on entering these regions, are surrounded by doubts of their real spirit existence. Mortal education and influences having nurtured them in fairy dreams of heaven, their conception is difficult to overcome. This demonstration, my child, is to eradicate these influences, and more perfectly open thy interior, that with a sense of philosophy, thou mayst realize the progressive beauties of surrounding objects, and thy soul flow onward, toward the great expansive ocean of joy, where floats the bark of Divinity."

"Do you feel a change?" he asked.

"Certainly!" I replied. "I can now see more distinctly the elements around me. I can discover why I have been through this change, and likewise that some good has resulted from my doubting the correctness of my senses when I first entered spirit life." Gratefully I thanked my good progenitor, and as I pressed his spirit hands, the emotions of my soul were plainly seen in the pulsation of thought, that forms the principal sense in the spirit organization.

What a harmony pervaded the region around; all seemed passive as an inland lake; no angry element disturbing the sweet calmness of the scenes before us. Did I ever pass a happy moment in the mundane sphere? thought I. My friends would ask if I were happy. I would refer them to the perfect lily, where nature shows externally its condition; therefore, where externally I was joyous, then my answer would be affirmative; but now, how could I be otherwise than progressively happy, though unseen to many. A life of experience had been concentrated into a few short hours, and I a recipient of all this! indeed it was gratefully acceptable.

Amos reminded me, that to witness the services of earth, it was requisite to return. So absorbed had I been in the wonders of sphere life, that an attendance to the disposal of the mortal part had not entered my thoughts, but I expressed a desire to witness the attention bestowed on the body, so we once more descended to earth and approached the scenes of my rudimental life. A line of vehicles marked my former home; the countenances of all around were indicative of that gloomy sadness, which ere many years must be converted into joy—when mortality assumes its higher, purer garb. We entered the room as the remains were being removed to the edifice where once I sat beneath the voice of him you call "servant of God," or "a chosen messenger sent to teach poor erring mortals the way of life." With what deep interest I followed the procession you may easily imagine. While the mourners formed on each side of the entrance, my small tenement was carried into the church. We listened a short time to the words of the devout man, who was extolling my career and representing my spirit as an angel of the highest development, though no doubt to him an angel, was such, be its development what it may. I wished to walk by his side and move his organs of speech to give forth facts that would, perhaps, astound, and truly convince; but no! I was to farther progress before that power could be mine. We remained not long in the sanctuary—we left and walked together the paths where my mortal formerly trod, to enjoy the attentions shown by my friends at my life, not death; at my resurrection, not decease.

We passed toward the Common, and viewed the display of mourning at sundry points; a sense of pleasure came over me, on witnessing these tokens of esteem, though they did not accord with my ideas of *propriety*.

The time now arrived for the conveyance of my form to the garden of the dead: the cortége slowly wended its way to the spot; Amos and myself joining in the procession; the tomb was reached, the parting tear dropped on its cold stone floor; —how my spirit yearned to tell them I still lived, and to enjoy that life with me, but I could not, and as they derived consolation from their tokens of grief, I was content.

Jacob, Amos and myself, were all that took a parting glance at the corpse, then resigning it to the mould of time, we departed, leaving our dear earth ones to retrace their steps homeward, whilst we sought a higher, purer, and more joyous atmosphere.

EXPERIENCES OF MR. E. B. POTTER.

Mr. Potter, who had almost daily correspondence with the spirits through my mediumship, became, as a matter of course, quite harmonious with the influences that naturally surround every medium; and although his manifestations are upon the same plane as those of Mr. Bruce and others, still, in many respects, they differ; and in order to present the various shades of the same original color, I give them.

Coming into my room, it was not an uncommon thing for this gentleman to suddenly miss his hat, coat, or gloves; and a patient search of some minutes would elapse without their being produced; relinquishing the idea of finding them, and flattering himself they would be brought back before actually needed, Mr. P. would resume his sitting, and as the time drew nigh for the articles to be required, they would return, and resume the place in which they had been left. So frequently would this be the case, that he had quite ceased to notice it, and then it also ceased to be an uncommon occurrence.

On one occasion, I had to remain a night in the hotel with Mr. Potter; we retired about ten o'clock, and the nasal vibrations of my friend soon gave evidence of lassitude and unconsciousness. Suddenly, the clothes were all pulled from the bed—being drawn down from the foot. Mr. P., with slow wakefulness, exclaimed, "Come, Redman, give me some ot the blankets." I remained quiet, till he had become fully conscious, when he discovered that we were both minus those warm commodities. We labored to replace them, when a large pitcher of water was emptied over us, much to our annoyance, as we had no relish for a cold bath on a winter's night. Hardly had we changed our clothing and settled down comfortably in bed, when the movement of the furniture warned us to cover up or be injured. The bedstead became so unruly we were forced to leave the room minus some of our garments, which had been scattered over the floor; 'twas after midnight that we were forced out, and knowing not where to go, stood shivering in the hall, ringing the bell, in the hope of bringing up a servant. The proprietor ultimately appearing, the tale was soon told. "Why do you not go in and get your clothes?" said he. "As we put our heads inside of the door, some article meets us half way," said Potter. We were ultimately forced to accept the landlord's offer, and take separate apartments, thus eluding the powers *regnant* that night.

At another time, after retiring, a large rubber cane, the property of Mr. Potter, was vigorously applied over our bodies; the room was quite light from a jet of gas on the opposite side of the street, and Mr. P. seeing the cane in mid air, reached to grasp it; in doing so, he was struck upon the hand, which somewhat disabling him, caused it to be speedily withdrawn, and placed under the bed-clothes. Again the cane presented itself in battle array, and descending on the scapula of my bed-fellow, he quickly caught it, and after a few minutes exertion, during which much force was exhibited, he succeeded in wrenching it from his invisible but determined assailant.

The alphabet was called for, and "Put your heads under cover" was spelled. I quickly obeyed the warning, but Potter refused, saying, "I have the cane now, and we'll see who is the master." Quickly as thought, another cane, which proved to be my property, came through the door. As it approached, my valiant bed-fellow assumed an attitude of defence, and the rencontre began. I cried for him to desist, as, while striking in the air, and defending himself from his opponent's cane, he every now and then brought his blows down on my quiet, unoffending body.

"Get under the clothes, Potter," I cried.

"No! I'll not give in till I'm beaten," said he.

Simultaneously with the utterance of the resolution, the poor fellow dropped upon the bed; all noise ceased, and with a stifled utterance, Mr. P. exclaimed, "Redman, they have put my eye out; get up quickly and light the gas." I instantly answered his call, and he emerged from the bed, the blood dropping from his hands as he held them to his face, at the same time crying out—

"I'm blind, get me water! water!" I led him to the Cochituate, and assisted in dressing his wounds: it was some time ere the hemorrhage ceased, and then his eye presented a pitiful plight; after dressing it we again went to bed, but no sleep for Potter, his was a night of pain; I told him he deserved punishment, but not to the extent of having his eye put out. Morning came, and Mr. P. asked, in a subdued tone, what time it was, requesting me to put my hand under his pillow and look at his watch. I did as he directed, but no watch was there; I searched again and again, but alas! for the watch! we removed the pillow and coverings, but the timepiece was gone. Visions of thieves passed swiftly through our minds until we entered the front room, when lo! the long gold chain was seen dangling in front of the portrait of Washington, and over the picture hung the watch: the walls of the apartment were on a lofty scale, and the nail, from which the articles were suspended, was in so elevated a situation, that a chair had to be placed on the top of a piano ere we could reach the wandering bijou. Mr. P.'s feelings were now relieved, except as far as his eye was concerned, and that for some days bore marks of violence.

From this night, never did our chevalier of the cane attempt another combat with spirits; he usually declared "'twas all well enough, only you couldn't see where to strike, whereas the invisibles brought down in the right place every time."

In cases of this nature I think prudence the best part of valor, and follow the maxim—

> "He that fights and runs away,
> May live to fight another day."

COMMUNICATED BY THE AYRSHIRE POET.

A noble knight an' I one day
Wi' bonnie lassies gude did hey,
Frae broome clad brae, an' childre all,
Toward Roderic Harlow's Gothic hall.
St. Francis there wa' sayn to come
An' sing a merrie Te Deum;
Sae all the folk went flocking thither
Wode to convince their senses wither
St. Mark, or St. Francis they'd meit,
An' how they should conseil the spreit.
Thai enter'd the portal sa wide,
An' squeezed thei as Marjorie site;
Then ta'en a seat neighe th' aisle
They thought to rest silent awhile.

When lele and lassies gathered in,
Then did the merrie welkin ring;

For sang 'twa said, hae raised th' dead,
Hae made St's Mark and Francis tread
These halls sae many times before,
An' bro't wi' them, ye knights o' yore.
Wai scarce had sang twa stanzas o'er,
When straightway fram a magic door
Came angels full a score or more,
Wi' statlie step, they crossed the floor,
A few sma' sunbeams answer'd stools
To sit upon instead o' mools.

Sae sat thai down an' seemed enjoying
Silent thought, an' still decoying
Everich nerve, an' sense, an' feeling
Till I felt my hot brain reeling:

"Awa' wi' your witchcraft, I cried,
An' my Marjorie, come to my side;
My soul is by Devils opprest,
An' the hall is by imps possest.
I winna sta', till night sets in,
An' walk wi' ghaists across th' plain."
But as I spake, there came a light
As if from Heaven, sa' very bright,
It changed on every face expression,
An' of our fear made full cónfession.

Then as by magic, very full
O' bonnie Angels wa' the hall,
Auld men, merrie maids, an' lassies,
Childre, babies, an' all classes,
Filled the nooks an' corners tight
Wi' their bodies o' sweet sunlight;
When nooks wa' filled, an' all the cramming
Ceased, an' there wa' no more jamming,
Then the stillness wa' gently broke
Like pipe stems made o' Elder smoke,

An' the gude people from letharg woke,
To hear St. Francis: Thus he spoke:

" Ye mortal men an' cannie maids,
" Frae heav'n's bright portals, holy glades,
" We angels come, na' to destroy,
" Na' weak thy treasure wi' alloy;
" We come, wi' luve's light melodie,
" To chant o'er death our victorie:

" Although thy kind faith be but sma',
" All thy luv'd ones, that's lang been awa',
" Wi mingle again at thy door,
" An' repeat, wha' they've seen o'er an' o'er;
" Na' more shall auld grim death be seen
" Striding proudly o'er valley an' green,
" Fa' he' bones wi' his body is lain,
" Wha' thai never can rise up again.
" On Cassilis* Downans we'll come
" Or meet thee wherever thou'lt roam;
" We'll tak' thee to bonnie bright glens,
" When thy mortal in immortal ends;
" Sa' hie ta thy hames an' proclaim
" These truths to the blind an' th' lame;
" The hour glass of death hath been broken,
" An' man wi' the spreit ha' spoken."

The luve light now vanished the hall,
St. Francis, our dear ones, an' all,
Like vapor passed out thro' the wall,
An' left us to reason recall.

We truly were favor'd with a',
An' we turn'd from the hall awa'.

* Little romantic hills in the vicinity of the ancient seat of the Earls of Cassilis, where fairies were said to have enjoyed their midnight gambols.

But our spirits were joyous now,
Grim death had been slain by a blow,
Our joy like bright embers did burn
That those, who had died could return.
Sa now each short week as it comes
We at Roderick's sing Te Deums,
An' the spreit appears as before
Laying open the book of The Law.
He calls on all Scots to gi' ear
That luved ones an' all that are dear,
Shall na' in some deep hell complain
But wi' us, make happy our hame.

BURNS.

CHAPTER XI.

United States Ship "Ohio." Mr. Bigelow's Letter. Abbott Lawrence's Experience Continued.

> "Dieu ne veut point d'un cœur ou le monde domine.
> Qui regarde en arrière (douteux en son choix)
> Lorsque sa voix l'appelle écoute une autre voix."

EVERY location has its peculiar influences; and none are more susceptible of those influences than media. The surroundings of one city differ materially from those of another; and the demonstrations that can be received in one locality, will be of a decidedly different nature from those of another. My manifestations while South, varied essentially from what I had in the Northern cities; so did those West from what were given in Boston.

One of my most interesting séances while in Boston, was held on the deck of the United States receiving ship "Ohio." The commodore and officers made all arrangements; and one beautiful evening, when Cynthia, floating in the blue ethereal, cast a silvery hue on all things earthly, I ascended that spot dedicated to importance and etiquette—the quarter-deck of a man-of-war.

My presence was the signal for piping all hands on deck that were to compose the circle. This consisted of ten persons, four of whom were ladies. Boldly did our good spirit friends proclaim their presence, and loudly did they make the deck of the good old ship resound with their powerful vibrations. Communications were few and short, the invisibles evincing more inclination to exhibit their physical power, by handling the table, and compelling the party to follow it round the deck.

From the influences of that evening, I formed the conclusion that, with a harmonious circle and favorable atmospheric surroundings, manifestations could be produced more easily, and of a more powerful character, upon the water than on the land.

When any unusual exertion is taking place on the part of spirits, I can always, more or less, feel their efforts ; but in this instance, there was no more impression made on my sensibilities, than if I had been quietly sleeping. The circumstances that led to the above sitting, being rather peculiar, may not be uninteresting.

At noon on the day previous to it, I was taking my accustomed walk, and was passing through Washington street when I felt a strange but powerful influence gradually taking possession of my locomotive powers ; suddenly I was wheeled round and made to take the hand of a gentleman behind me ; his dress declared him a naval officer. I apologized for the strange movement, assuring him it was perfectly involuntary, and then introduced myself; he seemed fully aware of the cause of the salutation so unceremoniously given, and told me he had for some time been interested in the subject of Spiritualism, and was then returning from a circle. This gentleman proved to be an officer of the Ohio; our singular introduction led to numerous interviews, and resulted in a general interest in the subject of Spiritualism among all the officers of the ship, and some of the attachés of the navy-yard.

Whether an interest in spiritual things will tend to develop the Christ precept, "If thy neighbor smite thee on one cheek turn to him the other also," in the war department, or the opposite teachings of Moses will still predominate, remains to be seen; one thing is certain, however,—seed has been planted in one of our national vessels, that probably will never be uprooted.

Below is a letter from an investigator, who has been long a confirmed infidel; having had the waters of truth presented to his parched lips at his sittings, it is to be hoped he has been enabled to take long draughts from the refreshing springs, whence he sought his first drink, and has by this time had his sensuous theory smothered and destroyed by life-giving streams from immortality's fountain.

I saw Mr. Redman for the first at 45 Carver street, Boston; we were entire strangers to each other. A test of his power at this sitting, (no other person but ourselves in the room) was this. Mr. Redman was sitting at a table in the middle of the apartment; leaving him there, I took my seat on one side of the room at a table about twelve feet from him, his back towards me, and my face towards the wall, leaning over the table to conceal the motion of my hand. I wrote with a pencil ten names of deceased friends upon as many separate slips of paper, equal in size and appearance, carefully rolling up each slip (as written upon) into a hard compressed ball, like a large pea; in this way losing all power of identification on my part: holding the ten balls in my hand I seated myself at the table with Redman—without hesitation he took up one of the balls from my open hand, and placing it upon the table, wrote the name of my deceased wife, Elizabeth, before opening the paper ball; correct answers were given in reply to my questions, which answers were only known to *me*, *not* to Redman. The paper ball was opened, and the same name found thereon. Redman's hand was then moved to take another paper ball from the nine still in my hand; not giving the name at once as he did before, he drew with his pencil the figure of a bottle; this not being at the time intelligible to me, or indicating the possible name upon the paper ball, I took it and moved back to my seat near the wall, fully ignorant of the name, but requesting him to write the place of decease of the person whose name was on the paper I then held in my hand—in a minute I went back to the table, and there found written "Keene," and drawn with a pencil, a square figure, with "Medicine Chest" written upon it. No more had yet been given, nor the paper ball opened. Redman then began to write in his peculiar way from right to left, and upside down. While he was writing I expected to have a communication from an intelligence purporting to be my wife, but in a moment, the finished sheet was handed to me, and I read the following:

"I am here too, and labor to make you know that we are not *mesmeric* spirits, but real friends of thine. Now, perhaps, you are thinking that I am Elizabeth, but I am not; she is standing on your right, and I am by your left. I love to come to you, for you are true. Thy guardian,

AMOS".

I opened the paper ball, and the name "Amos" was there, the same, or that of Dr. Twitchel, who died at Keene, N. H., in May, 1850; a relative and early friend of my youth, also an intimate friend of my wife, and her father's family physician. No two names could have been selected from the ten on the paper balls who, when living, stood towards each other, and to myself, in so friendly and intimate a relation. I am skeptical of conscious individual life after the death of the body, but I know that in this case, as well as in many others in my own experience as an investigator of the phenomena of Spiritualism for the last six years, there is often found in some way connected with mediums, an intelligence, not only able to gather up facts in my own experience, not at the time present to my consciousness, and put them together for an intelligent use; but to see or sense the name on a hard, compactly rolled paper ball, in a way completely independent of any conscious action of my own mind.

The ballot test (as it is called) I have tried repeatedly with Redman, and am convinced that there is in some way connected with him the power to see or sense material objects without the use of the external senses.

L. G. BIGELOW.

Burlington, Vermont.

CONTINUATION OF MR. ABBOTT LAWRENCE'S EXPERIENCE IN THE SPIRIT WORLD.

No. 3. My spirit guides now left me, and I was alone. As I saw their forms gradually fading in the distance, there arose a realizing sense of my position. Objects around me, though differing from those on earth, seemed wisely adapted to my better development. My first surprise was, that I suffered no weariness from the activity to which I had been subjected since my change. I had no desire for sleep, rest, nor food, except, that I experienced (but in a much greater degree) the same wish I had had while a youth, to acquaint myself with the objects growing around me. I really felt that I was a child, and that my years of observation on earth were but as an alphabetical cradle, in which I had not been rocked half enough.

My love for flowers was satisfied, for all around me was a perfect growth of the rarer beauties of nature; and a genial warmth, that was accompanied with no glaring sun, pervaded the atmosphere. Light seemed to give to each bud a smiling language, that invited me to inhale its fragrance and count its virtues. All was busy life, and though young in such realities, I could but take the hint given by surroundings: the outspreading carpet of emerald life, the busy humming bird darting from flower to flower, the waving lily-heads, all seemed to utter one universal cry, "Work! work! for by thy industry shalt thou pass upward."

I now began the first study of the spirit, which is, a comparison between the animal and vegetable. My pristine instruction had given me little idea of vegetation in the spheres, and I had supposed outward things would be swallowed up in inward psalm singing, praise making, and God worshiping, but I saw that the true way to worship the Divine Being was not to bow and do him homage, nor to kiss some golden sceptre outheld by his majesty, nor twang the strings of an instrument of harmony; but the true devotion to his holiness was to study, appreciate, and understand his works, and thus inwardly unfold that parchment of divine principle, that he hath transplanted from his own divine interior, to ours: to comprehend this was, indeed, a change, and where it was well digested, I could contrast the ever unfolding knowledge with the monotonous glorifying, that is so highly eulogized by mortal prayer-makers.

I compared the vegetable kingdom with the human, and in the shrub as in the oak and willow, I could perceive a perfect bodily development; in the one was a heart, veins, skin, blood, &c., so also in the other; if you bruise the one, it bleeds; so also does the other. A glowing life is manifested in both, and if the human has an immortal principle, has not the vegetable likewise a never dying germ? In the fragrance of the garden shrub, we behold its *spirit;* in the exhalations of the oak also, we microscopically perceive a never dying principle, that though unseen by mortals, is both felt and appreciated by spirits. As I realized these things my appetite, I perceived, underwent a change, and where the crude substance only was digestible, now the dynamized material was preferred.

Instead of using the powers of mastication for the conveyance of food, as in material life, I found the spirit form was nourished and developed by endosmose, and was sustained almost imperceptibly to the mind; the waste particles passing off by exosmose; thus the whole surface of the refined body acted as one combined organ of receptivity, while the same surface, under other circumstances, rejected the material as it assumed the non life-giving character. The pleasure of taste was transferred to the spirit, thereby rendering that principle more acute, while at the same time, a pleasurable sensation is derived from the inhalations of that God fluid, that sustains and keeps in action the spirit centre.

If I possess a desire to pass from one location to another, the will-power alone is of itself locomotion. How strange! you think; however incomprehensible to you, to us it is hourly demonstrated. If one wish to pass from point to point, the spirit instantly reaches that position; and it is as real to the spirit sense, as the surroundings of the body are to its organ of vision and the disconnection of the soul from the body is the only barrier that destroys its identity, I mean the identity of the location on which thy thought is centred. Does not thy spirit feast, gambol in fields, and visit the scenes of actual life, while thy body lies quiet among feathers? Is not that enjoyment as sensible and as much a reality as though the earth-form were there? Certainly; yet you call them delusive dreams, because the body is not fed also.

One of my first thoughts, after being left in my garden of reflection, was, Where is God, Jesus Christ, and the multitude of saints, that are to greet the pure in heart?

The answer came thus:—"The mighty ladder of principles must be surmounted, before that haven is reached. The first round is, to understand thyself; the second, to comprehend the relation of vegetable life to thyself; the third, to consider thy *neighbor* as thyself; and so on." Well, I cannot say that I have reached even the second, for I find I know as little of myself as others do of me; but the few first principles toward that end, I have labored to give thee.

I cannot describe the spirit to thee, Adams; suffice it to say there is a form which envelopes the intelligence, and it grows, not in size outwardly, but in *refinement*, inwardly, by the process above given.

There is no dividing line between thought, mind, and spirit; they are but one, as wind, atmosphere, and air; *wind* is the *activity* of the *atmosphere*, *thought* is the spirit in motion.

As we loosen the bonds of mortality, I find we repair immediately to a sphere or condition best suited to our developments while on earth. Thus, I say, that my thirst for flowers was gratified; also the desire to improve upon all objects surrounding me. As I before said, the mysterious faculty of understanding the thoughts of those around us without outward speech, renders deception and hypocrisy strangers to these abodes, and a knowledge and clear sight of the happiness of those more highly purified than ourselves, awakens in the anxious soul an intense desire to expand its chambers of receptivity, and inhale the unfolding god-like principles. All is outward here, Adams; and *family secrets* have to become questions of nationality. Thus, plainly is seen the evil man's hell, and the pilgrim's heaven--the hypocrite's damnation, and the Christian's bliss.

No. 4. The popular theology that taught me to view the lightning stroke as providential, that to kneel three times a day in secret, gave more chances in the great lottery of eternal happiness, and daguerreotyped the various scenes of the spirit world, as 'tis pictured to millions—all these, my friend, I have found to be mere empty vagaries, necessary, perhaps, to withhold the ignorant from evil-doing, but of no possible benefit to the more intelligent and self-possessed. While undergoing the change from such educational prejudices, to more truthful and philosophical realities, I could but pray that the day might soon dawn, when

> "The nation will rise regenerate,
> Strong in her second youth and beautiful;
> And like a spirit, that hath shaken off
> The clog of dull mortality,
> Arise in glory."

My reverie was broken by the appearance of Amos, who desired to instruct me farther in the beauties of my life; we were joined by good old Jacob—I say old, applying the term to residence in the spheres; for age here has no tottering steps, neither are the windows closed, nor the wheel at the well impaired. I followed my guides. They led me far beyond the multifarious stars I had seen, while enjoying my more tranquil thoughts. As we sped on, I could perceive, though very indistinctly, what appeared to me like a gilded city; as we approached it, a strange fascinating melody broke on my ear, unlike earth music; it seemed to kindle every spark of the divine within me, and, verily, I was astonished, when that spark was irradiated, to find how great a share of the devotional was mine. I felt inclined to pause, that I might enjoy the sweet strains more quietly, but Amos objected; and as on the wings of the wind we nearer drew, the harmony became more entrancing and more enjoyed. I could now see the inmates of the gilded city flitting to and fro, like dazzling gems floating in an atmosphere of light.

We reached the entrance to the city (for such I call it, knowing no better term), and were greeted by a number of its residents. Jacob said they had been notified of our visit, and had come to welcome me as a pilgrim from earth. I received the most attention. I was quite bewildered with this novel but pleasing feature in my present existence; and the willingness with which every thing around me was made comprehensible by the kindness of my new associates, rendered every moment a living life, a pleasing recollection. I was now surrounded on all sides by those dear ones, whom I had either known on earth or read of, and considerable time elapsed in merry greeting and congratulation. Some of my spirit friends seemed cognizant of earth scenes, and freely alluded to events connected with myself during my last few years of mortal experience; others desired information about the same, and it was only surprising to me, that with all this activity of mind I experienced no weariness, but seemed to have more elasticity of spirit as I continued. Having gratified all inquiries, as far as in me lay, I turned to seek Amos and Jacob; but they had gone. I was left with my new friends, perhaps to undergo farther initiations, for which I was ever ready.

I inquired of a sage looking immortal near me, the locality of this heavenly city when compared with earth; his answer was as follows:

"Thou art now in the third sphere; it is situated far above the rudimental life, where oxygen is not so abundant nor as necessary for animal life, for its presence obstructs, to a greater or less degree, the vision of the spirit. This is thy home; but thou art yet to be initiated. Amos and thy ancestor Jacob abide in the sphere above thee, called the "Sphere of Comparison." All higher beings, discerning the conflict between the elements of spirituality and mortality in those they love, are at liberty to descend to earth; and, by their influences, aid the germ of divinity to free itself from its prison house of clay, give it electric power, assist its formation for the higher life, and conduct it to its appropriate condition in the spheres. The various changes thou hast undergone, have been but preparatory to this step: now thou art free to expand thy intellect and progress upward with the myriads of intelligences before thee.

Spheres or conditions are not to be measured by distances, they are as unbounded as every eternal element; they are known only as conditions, limited by the scope of the soul alone. Thou art but a child,—go bathe thy intellect in the stream of wisdom, and form thereby a tie of affinity with the companions of this life-condition; be assured every thing thou meetest is but existing for thy improvement; all shall tend to make thee most happy. Throw away thy mundane nature, for now thou canst not even see the star called Earth; its existence is swallowed up in space. When thou hast become as yonder shining light, giving brilliancy to all around, then wilt thou be permitted to visit thy friends, and polish that immortal gem within their souls, now left to tarnish. We'll call thee brother, and on thy brow place the vizor of truth: the orbs that twinkle shall be as nails, whereon to hang thy purest thoughts, the elements around shall lull a dulcet harmony into thy spirit: join in this strain of angel melody, let thy tones praise the all-controlling power, that gave life to thyself and all, that makes thee what thou art. Look forward, onward, upward, every thought of progress shall yield more clearly to thy interior, visions of the fourth heaven."

How fairy-like are all these things, thought I. I was directed by my host of friends to seek a certain stream of water, whose murmurings alone would give my spirit wisdom: I obeyed, and as I sat by what appeared a rivulet of flowing silver, I received this message:

> "Doubt not thy life, and progress mar;
> Think what thou canst be—what you are."

As hours passed, my fairy-like dreams vanished, and I accepted everything as an actuality. I found that the extreme contrast of the two lives, mortal and spiritual, rather increased my imaginative powers; but still the change was great, and I accepted it with awe.

CHAPTER XII.

Visit to New York. Committee. Rooms in Canal Street. Diabolism exemplified. The loaded table. Father's guardianship and garroters frustrated. Engagement at Buffalo. A fireman's influence. Affecting seance with Mr. Farwell. Skepticism unmanned. Mr. Sprague's test. Visit to the Immaculate Church and forced departure. Felicia Hemans.

> "A treasure, but removed,
> A bright bird parted for a clearer day,
> Thine still in Heaven!"

Mr. John W. Norton, as agent for a committee of gentlemen in New York, engaged my services for a series of circles. Accordingly I made arrangements to visit that city. The séances were to occupy two hours per day for one week. On reaching New York I took rooms at the Bancroft House, and on the evening of my arrival commenced my interviews with the gentlemen. I had understood that a report of the results was to be published, but it never, to my knowledge, reached the press. The decision of the committee was unanimously favorable as to the spiritual origin of the manifestations. One of the party, Captain Steward, was especially enthusiastic, in consequence of tests received by him relating to matters at a distance of which he was totally ignorant and which proved to be facts. The precise nature of the test I am unable to give, as they were kept from me, a usual occurrence in assemblies of the kind. I, however, had the pleasure subsequently of meeting some of the members of that circle, and the satisfaction of hearing them avow their entire belief in the reality of Spiritualism. Concluding my engagement with the mentioned circle, by advice from father, I located myself at 391 Canal Street.

I had thought my rooms filled to overflowing in Boston, but here it was a perfect inundation, composed of investigators from all grades of society.

Among the most prominent of the visitors, soon after my being settled in these quarters, was a party of men, who, from accident or design, called during my absence. On presenting their inquiries at the office for me, and being informed that I had gone to my tea, they thereupon commenced having various demonstrations on their own responsibility: one among them, diabolically influenced, broke the leaf of the table with his fist; another, probably an amateur fresco painter, threw the ink bottle violently against the wall, thus breaking the vial and leaving a full length caricature, or possibly, sketch of some incident in his own erratic life, indelibly delineated on the paper; a third held a glass lamp filled with burning fluid, to assist the optic nerves of his comrades, while this illuminated statue shed its rays around. Medium, No. 4, with an uplifted chair broke the lamp into fragments, driving the glass into the lampholder's hand, thereby causing the blood corpuscles to ooze pretty freely from the wounded member, and to aid this ensanguined investigation, the inflammable material with which the lamp had been filled, as if desirous of enlightening them to the utmost of its power, ignited and wrapped my new carpet in flames. All hands now set to work, and by the aid of the ever ready Croton the fire was extinguished. The party now, I suppose, thinking it advisable to withdraw, left one after the other, but in doing so, they put their tarsal extremities into a large glass globe belonging to a solar lamp, and in passing down stairs each, in turn, gave the hall lamp a parting salute, which much diminished the symmetry of its fair proportions.

I returned to the scene of destruction too late to encounter these *bellicose mediums*; but in the centre of the room, enveloped in darkness, stood poor David (the young man who had charge of the apartment in my absence) pale, and almost speechless. To my inquiries into the lugubrious appearance of the room, I was told "there was no lamp," and the ignition of a match exhibited the lamentable plight of the apartment; and David, in wo-begone tones, related what I have given above; the question "Why did you not seek the police?" elicited the admission, that he was so perfectly bewildered by terror, he knew not what to do. From the belligerents I heard not again; so considering this a *striking* initiation into New York experience, I quietly settled down, hoping that my manifestations might be fully as convincing of the presence of spirits, but less destructive,—have in them more of a *spiritual*, less of a *spirituous* nature, for to the latter influence I charitably attributed the unjustifiable conduct of these brutish bipeds.

A fair test of spiritual strength was exhibited, shortly after this affair, at a circle held at Mr. Spaulding's, 476 Broadway, at which I was the medium.

A pleasant little circle had convened for spiritual instruction: on my arriving and being ushered up stairs, I found some six or eight persons gathered round a table: I seated myself, and we were not long in ascertaining the presence of the desired friends, whose favors we had assembled to solicit. Communications were written to each of the party; they, in turn, severally asking tests, to identify the communicating spirits. After exchanging loving sentiments, we turned our attention toward the more tangible or physical indications of power beyond ourselves: we remained in perfect passivity, having obtained a promise from the invisibles that, if we would be tranquil, they would gratify us. Our patience was not long taxed, for a side tip of the inanimate body before us, notified the readiness of friends to respond to our wishes. The table rose and came down on the floor with a tremendous thump; it danced to and fro without human contact, at each of its movements making the very house shake. I did not understand why so small a table should make such ado; every motion would cause the chandeliers, in the parlor below, to jar, so that they could be distinctly heard by us. I found it quite as much as I could do, to keep my toes from under the legs of the table; finally, Mr. S. exclaimed, "That will do;" and instantly the inanimate object ceased its saltatory movements. Our circle now broke up, but ere separating, it was Mr. Spaulding's wish, that each should raise the table: all complied, alternately, and much to our surprise found, that although to sight it seemed anything but heavy, the united strength of the party was required to lift it. We asked the cause of its weight, when our host exhibited to us, on the under side of the table, a quantity of pig iron placed on cross bars, that were nailed to the side pieces, the exact number of pounds I do not remember.

Although Mr. Spaulding was an earnest and sincere Spiritualist, still, actuated partly by curiosity, and partly by a desire to satisfy friends, he resorted to this mode of convincing the doubtful, that there was, in reality, a power outside of mere electricity or muscular force, to accomplish the movement of a material body. The spirits probably were aware of the presence of the iron before our circle assembled, but we were kept sublimely ignorant of the fact, till afterwards, and then the cause of so much commotion below, (at each movement of the table,) was apparent.

Previous to locating myself in Canal Street, I had made arrangements to visit Buffalo, and the West; and though my time was much occupied, and my services in the cause of truth required in New York, still I felt it a duty to fulfill engagements with our Western friends.

A few days before the contemplated journey, I was impressed, or rather propelled to walk down Broadway toward the Battery; it was a rainy afternoon, and why this unusual influence on the part of my guardian (for I recognized the influence of father,) I could not tell; and as I was involuntarily moved along, wondered what it meant. On reaching the vicinity of Cortlandt Street, I was suddenly turned into a store, made to lay hold of a box lying on the counter, take a twenty dollar bill from my pocket, and hand it to the attendant. He gave me two dollars in change, wrapped the article in paper, and presented it to me. Like an automaton, I placed it under my arm, and my (to me uncontrollable) nether extremities propelled the body they upheld, back to the office: taking a seat at the table, my hand was influenced and wrote;

MY DEAR MORTAL SON:—

By my influence you have been controlled to act as you have. Unwrap the parcel, load the weapon, you may have use for it. 'Tis not our policy to kill; but to frighten others may often save thy own life; and also the lucre in thy pocket, that is so necessary for the conveniences of life on earth, especially to thyself as a journey is anticipated. Thy Spirit Father,

ALEXANDER.

I opened the package and was not a little surprised to find it contained one of Colt's revolvers, with all the requisites for its use. Never having been placed in a situation to require such destructive implements, and withal being somewhat of a non-resistant, I was at a loss how to place the weapon in a condition for use, or in other words how to load it. This difficulty was soon obviated, for father took possession of my arms, went systematically to work and soon arranged matters. He first took the caps from the box, placed them upon the tubes of the pistol, filled each barrel with its due allowance of powder, placed the bullets one by one, then drove them by the iron lever into the barrels, which done he quietly put the revolver into my breast pocket and retired.

Here, thought I, is a pretty specimen of a *spiritual* teacher; on one side of my breast am I carrying sentiments of peace, progress, happiness, and good will; on the other a loaded revolver. Who knows whether I shall not shoot the first man

I meet? for I must say, I felt as though I had the power to do some harm, and began to imagine how such and such a one would look, were I only to pull that trigger upon him; again, suppose the pesky thing should explode in my pocket. What then? why, there would be one less Spiritualist in the world, and the Kingsborough priests would rejoice at my providential removal from society; but where father had placed the weapon there it must remain till he gave further instructions.

At night I attended a place of amusement, and my pocket companion was not over and above agreeable, especially as it was not remarkably light. The performances over, I walked towards my boarding house, which was in the vicinity of St. John's Park. I passed down Canal Street, across to Varick, and as I was leisurely pursuing my route homeward, listlessly swinging a small cane in my hand, a stalwart Irishman sprang suddenly to my side, and seizing the stick said, "What are you doing with that cane?" "Does it concern you particularly?" I replied. At this moment another person appeared, whence he came, I knew not, but addressing his associate, inquired what I had said. "None of my business," responded the first assailant. At this moment I felt a stunning sensation as if struck by some heavy instrument, and fell staggering against a door near by. I now perceived my hand jerk suddenly, and though partially stupified, I had sufficient perception to see the ruffians backing from me with their hands before their faces; then dodging into a by-way, they disappeared. By this time I knew all; my arm was still raised, and in my hand the revolver. Almost involuntarily I pulled the trigger as though other desperadoes were near, but no report followed. On examining the weapon, I found it had not been cocked; the purpose nevertheless had been answered, and as I directed my steps homeward, inwardly did I thank that parent, who, seeing danger before me, had thus not only saved me many injuries, but likewise considerable inconvenience which, had I been overcome, would have followed from the loss of money on my person. Entering my bedroom, I immediately thanked father for his parental kindness, and he responded thus:

MY CHILD:—

Thou hast no more use for the weapon. 'Twas better that you should pay eighteen dollars for the prevention, than to have been robbed of a hundred. Had the pistol been minus even a lock, it would have answered all purposes, as such assailants are generally cowards. Fear not in any moment of life, for I will always protect thy body to give thee strength to protect the souls of others. Good night. Thy Father,

ALEXANDER.

On retiring to bed that night, I felt I should rest ever after secure from harm, and truly appreciated the guardianship of him, who was happy to call me child. Without the means used the evil could not have been prevented, and although I thought the whole proceeding singular in the commencement, I was perfectly satisfied, ultimately, of his far-seeing care, and willing afterwards to be contented with whatever my guardian parent might suggest.

According to arrangement, I proceeded to Buffalo, stopping on my route at Kingsborough, the place of my early developments ; as may be supposed, the Brown family were not unmindful of Auld Lang Syne ; we had a renewal of spiritual scenes ; and a few days of field sport (during which we were gratified by the attendance of our former good old spirit Swanee) recuperated the system for fresh labors in the west. Having tarried a week at Kingsborough, I resumed my journey, and soon after arriving at Buffalo, secured reception rooms directly over the publication office of the "Age of Progress," where every rap could be heard by the venerable editor of that small but truth-embodying sheet.

While at the hotel, I formed the acquaintance of Mr. S. J. Finney, and part of the time had the pleasure of rooming with him. One Sunday evening while sitting together in our private apartment, discussing theological questions, on which Mr. F. is quite *au fait*, the bells commenced tolling for the evening service ; a spirit instantly took possession of my locomotive powers and vocal organs, and throwing off my coat, and rushing down stairs, cried, "Fire, fire!" How far I went, I know not, but was aware of being propelled at no ordinary rate through different streets, and when consciousness of my surroundings returned, I found myself leaning against a pillar that formed part of an engine house entrance, saturated in perspiration ; my hat was no where visible, so after peering around to ascertain if I were noticed, I retraced my steps somewhat humiliated at having thus rendered myself the "observed of all observers." On re-entering my room, I found Mr. F. where I last remembered seeing him, and on asking the length of time I had been absent, he remarked, that "he could not tell, as he had suffered little anxiety on my account, for he had felt satisfied if those who influenced me desired I should run with a machine, they knew enough to bring me back."

As may be supposed, my engagement book was well filled, and prominent among the number of my visitors was Mr. R. Farwell. His first sitting was quite characteristic of a skeptic : he asked permission to examine the table, to which I of course acceded. So, carefully removing the paper and pencils, he inverted it, and began with his penknife minutely inspecting the holes in its legs made by the turning lathe ; at the same time apologizing for the little faith he evinced in his fellow man ; but assuring me he had heard there was a person in New York, that "manufactured tables for this kind of business." I requested he would satisfy himself on all points, and if he were successful in finding wires, or any other adjustments, he would be so kind as to inform me.

A careful inspection satisfied him, that the table was as harmless, and inefficient to produce raps or float in the air, as tables in general are wont to be; so placing it in statu quo, he took his seat opposite to me. Hardly had he become silent, when I observed a spirit enter the door, leaning upon two other spirits, its arms on their shoulders. It appeared to be a young man, his features thin, pale, and emaciated; his dress seemed carelessly thrown on, and consisted of a dressing gown, pair of linen pants, and on his neck a large black silk handkerchief; as he approached nearer, I distinctly saw even the color of his eyes. The two spirits with him I was unable to discern plainly enough to describe. He had lost the use of his legs apparently, his movements being made by the assistants raising him from the floor. As he stood by the side of the table, his head would turn first to me, then to the gentleman present, and as I was about describing the sight to the visitor, the spirit nodded, as if pleased. I gave the above description to Mr. F., and as I finished, my hand wrote:

DEARLY BELOVED FATHER—

Have I not redeemed my promise? Is there not another life? Am I not still living? Do I love thee? Art thou happy? What shall I do, that you may know me? I am not disabled now. I appear so, that you may know me. Is mother well? I have not seen her—tell her of this. My last words were of her.

I did not like the doctor's pinching me, I felt it. I could not move. I knew all you said. Why did they pinch me so? Tell mother, John, and Harriet, to come. I'm strong; I live to do you all good. Tell them all, I bless them for their love.

Thy son, free from pain. THEODORE.

The old man's emotions could not be concealed as I read the above to him, and presently ejaculating, "How true! How true!" his head sank upon the table, and he remained for some moments convulsed with grief. I folded the communication and sat passively, until the father rose from his recumbent position: shaking me by the hand, he left the room, saying, he would see me in the evening.

Surely such a scene of anguish would have touched any heart not made of adamant, and as I watched the recipient of that son's affection descend the stairs, drying those tear-bedewed cheeks down which, no doubt, many bitter drops had flowed since the beloved one's departure from earth, I inwardly exclaimed: "Blessed be this truth of heaven; for he that was lost is found."

The ensuing evening Mr. Farwell, true to his word, returned. He attended the public circle, and after they were dismissed, remained. He then gave me an account of the loss of his only son, which was substantially as follows:

His child, Theodore, was employed on one of the

vessels that navigated Lake Erie. He accidentally fell through the hold of the vessel, and his spine was so injured that his lower limbs were completely paralyzed ; not only his limbs, but his abdominal organs were likewise in a state of utter uselessness, and the poor boy was helplessly prostrated for ten days, when dissolution put an end to his misery. During his suffering, and from time to time, as he lay immovable, the attending physicians would frequently pinch him to see how far up the paralysis extended ; and also to ascertain if there were any increased sensibility in the benumbed parts. "'Twas painful," said the old man, "to witness them taking up his flesh and he looking silently on. We did not think he felt it, but he did, and we thus unconsciously added to his pain. Every word is true, my dear sir, and I shall bring his mother and sister to see you to-morrow—they know it all."

As the morrow came, it brought Mr. F's. family, and of all the spiritual meetings that I have held, that one will never be obliterated from memory's page. A free, open, and satisfactory interview of two hours, was spent between the spiritual members of that home circle and those still in mortal garb, and though tears fell thick and fast, they then and there learnt that on the starry shores, where move the footsteps of the dead,

> "Love, o'ersweeping change, and blight and blast,
> Finds there, the music of his home, at last."

Of the many singular tests received by parties during my stay in Buffalo, one of a very peculiar nature may find a kind reception here.

A private party engaged the evening for a circle, and met accordingly. Among the number was Mr. Sprague, the engagee of the time. About an hour and a half was spent in the receipt of pleasing physical demonstrations, such as rapping upon a card held under the table, moving the table, tipping chairs, &c.; also, in messages being given to most of the circle. Mr. Sprague, however, was singularly deserted, having received no intimation of his guardian friend's presence. The séance was nearly closed when, as Mr. Sprague termed it, a spirit hand gently patted him on the knee and ascended to his waist. Asking the name of the spirit, H. I. R. A. M. was given, and a question as to its relationship elicited "Father."

"How did you die, father—will you describe the manner through the medium's hand?"

Immediately he wrote:

I deid fo detalugnarts laniugni ainreh ym nos, ti saw ton deviecrep yllanretxe dna suht saw dewolla ot yortsed ym htrae efil.

It was some time before this singular production could be deciphered, and not then till the spirit spelt by the alphabet, "Reverse the letters." This rendered it comprehensible.

"I died of strangulated inguinal hernia, my son; it was not perceived externally, and thus was allowed to destroy my earth life."

Mr. Sprague opined to the truth of the statement, and expressed himself satisfied with the identity of the communicating party. A long message was then given, and Mr. S. was requested not to read it till he got home.

Evidence of this nature should be as satisfactory to a *party* as to an *individual;* although I find it quite general, and natural enough, that we are never content—as a class; without our own door of belief is knocked at, each individually wishes to be assured that

"Full and high"
Is his "communion with eternity."

I was induced, one Sabbath morning, to attend the Catholic church, with Mr. Henry Bellows; the object for this movement was to hear the singing, which, as is usual in the worshipping places of this denomination, was said to be uncommonly fine. The sexton showed us to seats in the centre of the building, and we were certainly highly delighted with the performance of the choir; but it was paying almost too dearly for such gratification, to be forced to listen to the

"Spavin'd dactyls," as they were "spurr'd into recitativo,"

by the monotonous chant of the officiating priest. Anon, however, came the sermon, and now we were amused at the responses of our *spirit* friends ; by an emphatic "No," they would signify their dissent to any clause in the speaker's harangue, and with yet greater emphasis would they respond "Yes," when they coincided in his forensic efforts : as he proceeded in his discourse, the spirits, more and more, evinced their disposition to notice the remarks I mentally requested they would desist, as it was becoming a source of annoyance to those in our immediate neighborhood ; but my silent petition was utterly disregarded, and, as if enjoying the discomfiture of the devout within the pale of this Holy Catholic Church, our communing saints rapped louder and louder. Mr. Bellows, turning to me, asked if I could not stop the spirits from making so much noise, as we should be turned out. I told him not to notice them, but to keep still, and the attention of the audience would not be attracted to us, Louder and louder, however, came the raps, until they seemed almost like reports from a pistol. The sexton pacing the aisle, paused opposite our pew, and with distended orbs scanned our immovable persons, for we were just at that moment, apparently, striving earnestly to digest the spiritual manna that was being showered down by this direct descendant of the apostles.

Rap, rap, rap, came an affimative to some remark,

then a succession of sounds, and the boards beneath us seemed to vibrate with the concussion. Perceiving no disposition on our part to interrupt the services, the sexton moved on, keeping a strict espionage on our actions ; still louder came the demonstrations, till friend B's. nervous excitability, becoming uncontrollable, he grasped his hat, saying, "I'm going out for 'tis as easy to go one's self as to be unceremoniously put out." This movement of my friend drew more attention towards us, and the demonstrations were most decidedly those of displeasure at our presence. Considering discretion the better part of valor, I took my hat, and assenting to the proposition of Mr. Bellows to leave this spot of righteousness, rose to depart ; the moment we did so the spirits, as if sounding an *au revoir*, produced the most vehement raps I ever heard in my life.

With some difficulty my friend and self made our way down the aisle (it was densely crowded with human beings) and on emerging from beneath the holy portals, we discovered one of the attachés of the church behind us. We walked on, but found where'er our wandering footsteps veered, they were tracked by the same tangible disciple of Catholicism. Reaching the hotel, he entered with us, but remained below. I learnt from the proprietor of the house afterwards, that he was very particular in his inquiries relative to our names, occupation and place of abode. Our address was readily obtained, but none the wiser was he of our profession, and thus terminated this adventure. We concluded no more to visit such consecrated spots least we should become involved in difficulties, which might end in raps more impressive and ineffaceable than pleasant.

In the chambers of the soul,
  Of the ignorant and sluggish ;
Lying quiet, is a roll
  Of white parchment, 'neath the rubbish.

Covered o'er with heaps of sin,
  Lies this multitude of pages ;
Looking tho', when viewed within,
  As if dormant there for ages.

Did they know the jewels bound,
  'Tween those leaves, they'd quick uncover;
And their darken'd souls resound,
  Thanks, these treasures to discover.

But a Priest, anointed stands,
  Lengthened visage, attention bent;
With the soul's key in his hand,
  Pond'ring o'er a book, content.

Millions listen at his word,
  And this key is grasp'd with power—
"I am authorized by God"
  Says he, "He's giver of the law.

Shouldst thou widely ope that door,
  And from rest the parchment sever;
Turn it's pages o'er and o'er,
  Hell would be thy lot for ever.

Reason is its title page,
  Its contents, Infidelity;
To read *destroys* the parsonage,
  And stamps God's word, *uncertainty*."

While he speaks, the angels come,
  And widely ope those leaves within;
The glittering pages call us home,
  To where Progression's seraphs sing.

In the chambers of the soul,
  Of the ignorant and sluggish;
Lying open is a roll
  Of pure parchment, *cleared* of rubbish.

And the vision lingers there,
  Tracing Angel truths, beseeching
With a solemn, silent prayer,
  That the world may know its teaching.—HEMANS.

CHAPTER XIII.

Extract from A. Simmons' Letter. Mr. Albro's Reply.

"Nearer than we think,
Are those, whom death has parted from our lot!
Fearfully, wondrously, our souls are made—
Let us walk *humbly* on, but undismayed!"

Extract of a letter from A. Simmons, of the city of New York, to Mr. Stephen Albro, of Buffalo, New York, late editor of the "Age of Progress."

"Other matters disposed of, allow me to enquire what effect has been produced upon your mind by all the exposed, fraudulent, spiritual manifestations, the confessions, the vacillations, etc., etc., which have so much occupied the columns of public journals, both religious and secular, and so stunned the public ear within a few months.

Is it true that a large majority of those who pretend to be mediums for spiritual communications and manifestations are impostors and cheats? And is it really doubtful that there are any such things as genuine spiritual phenomena in mundane society? As you are aware my faith is comparatively young, and of but slender growth; you will, therefore, not wonder, but have charity for me, when I candidly acknowledge to you that so many charges of fraud, and so many confessions and concessions as have been recently made by professing Spiritualists, have somewhat unsettled my convictions.

Hoping to derive sustaining strength from your reasoning on the subject, as I frequently have done in times past, I am anxious to hear from you, and to learn the present state of your mind."

MR. ALBRO'S REPLY.

ESTEEMED FRIEND AND BROTHER:—

I am both pained and gratified by the portion of your last letter, which relates to an unfortunate class of professing Spiritualists. It pains me to learn that the eternal truths of the Spiritual gospel, which the angels have brought us, are not sufficiently established in your mind to prevent it being swayed to and fro by the fitful puffs of inharmony which issue from the lungs of unsuccessful traffickers in the spiritual philosophy. And I am gratified—perhaps flattered—by your appeal to me, and the confidence which you manifest in my ability to aid you. Nor shall I, in the fashionable phrase of mock modesty, question the soundness of your judgment, in the selection of a friendly adviser on this subject; for, although I am as far as the humblest individual from making any pretensions to superior wisdom, or to any advanced position of philosophical attainment, my conscience tells me, that so far as ingenuousness and an ardent desire to benefit you are concerned, your confidence is not misplaced.

Before proceeding any farther, I will give you a direct answer as to the effect which has been produced on my mind, by the causes to which you allude. They have admonished me that Spiritualism and true Spiritualists have much more to fear from unsound advocates, than from the most boisterous and rabid opponents. And even from these there is nothing to apprehend as regards the final success of the spiritual philosophy throughout the world; but they are stumbling blocks in the way of honest, but cautious and timid investigators, and tend somewhat to retard the spread of celestial truth in the domain of terrestrial intelligence. And even this seeming evil may will be an essential good in disguise; for it is as bad philosophy to make proselytes faster than they can be spiritualized, as it would be to feed a gristmill faster than the stones can grind the grain, or to feed the human stomach faster than the digestive organs can properly dispose of the food. Faith in my mind as to the reliability of spiritual intercourse with mortals has given place to positive knowledge; and all the sophistry of pseudo philosophers, and all the cavilings, bickerings, counter-reasoning, and confusion of the light material, which agitation brings to the surface of the spiritual philosophy, cannot possibly cast upon my mind even the faintest shadow of a doubt.

Your mind has been thrown into doubt by the croaking voices of dissenters, who attribute the loss of their faith to frauds committed by pretending pedlars of Spiritual manifestations. You have heard and read exposures, coming from the mouths and pens of recanters, who publish their own shame by showing how they themselves practised the frauds which they are exposing; and you are at a loss to decide for yourself, whether they were greater rogues and liars when they committed the frauds, or when they confessed and exposed them.

The safe position, in such cases, is to give them credit for being really and continually what they report themselves to have been, on the occasions alluded to in their confessions. I shall not pretend to deny—nay, I *know* there are many itinerating mountebanks, who perambulate the country under pretence of being Spiritual Media, for the purpose of defrauding unwary wonder-mongers of their dimes. And what does this fact amount to? Nothing but another evidence that every genuine and valuable product, and development of nature, science and art, which is capable of being imitated by fraudulent genius, is counterfeited with base resemblances, wherewith to gratify the conscienceless spirit of avarice.

Those physical manifestations which the departed spirits of

earth have found it necessary to practise, for the purpose of convincing their incarnate friends that they still live, and are present with them, have been so startling and attractive, that they have drawn together crowds of men and women of all classes, wherever they have been allowed access to them. This general and natural desire to witness the manifestations, suggested to dishonest avarice the practicability of making money out of them or their counterfeit. Hence the many performers of mock-manifestations, by which the country is infested; and hence the evidences adduced by recanters, to prove that there are no genuine Spiritual manifestations.

There is one phase of these manifestations which is peculiarly favorable to the success of mountebank imitations; this is in those physical operations, by spirits, which cannot be performed in lighted rooms; because the light, whether natural or artificial, is a ready absorbent of the electrical and magnetic forces which the manifesting spirit must use in all heavy operations. By the use of these forces, spirits are enabled to raise heavy articles of furniture, such as bureaus, side boards, and pianos, and hold them suspended high above the floor; but whilst they are thus suspended, if a light be suddenly produced, or brought into the room, they will fall to the floor in a second. This is because the forces by which they are suspended are instantly dissipated by the light. And the circumstance, as above hinted, has afforded a wide field for fraudulent operations, by those prowling swindlers who feed upon the credulity of innocent and ignorant minds, who are too ingenuous in their own natures to suspect and detect villany in others. And, in many instances, adventurers in this ignoble field of enterprise, have associated with them genuine mediums of a low order, who, being destitute of the moral element in their natures, and free from the controlling influence of conscientious scruples, are ready, for hire, to enter into partnership with hardened villany, and to prostitute the gift of God, to the unhallowed purpose of making plausible the pretensions o. knavish counterfeiters.

Besides these, there are not a few itinerating practitioners in the profession of spiritual science, who are genuine mediums, and who are capacitated to do great service in the cause of truth, by aiding ministering spirits in their work of human redemption from the thraldom of religious tyranny; but who, when conditions will not allow spirits to manifest through their mediumship, as must often be the case, do not hesitate to carry out the advertised programme by fraudulent devices of their own, held in reserve by them for such occasions. For want of innate honesty, and true wisdom, this disgraceful shift is resorted to, rather than to adopt the honorable alternative of candidly declaring the philosophical truth, and returning to the assembled audience the money they have paid for admittance. And the most despicable of all the little-souled apologies by which such guilty ones attempt to shield themselves from the indignant scorn of those upon whom they practise these petty larceny tricks, when they are detected in them, is the disavowal of any fraudulent intention on their part, and the criminating of the manifesting spirits, stoutly and persistently averring that the fraud was perpetrated under their positive control.

It is right and highly necessary that all fraudulent practices by pretended or real mediums, for Spiritual manifestations, should be promptly and publicly exposed and condemned, by all true Spiritualists to whose knowledge they come: nor should any censure, either expressed or implied, fall upon those who honestly make the exposures. But who, let me ask you, are these several gentlemen who have figured so largely, within a few months, in both spiritual and secular journals, as exposers of fraudulent practices by Spiritual Media, and as dissenters from, and repudiators of the spiritual faith, on account of these frauds; pretending to have been convinced that all manifestations, purporting to be spiritual, are false and fraudulent? Who are they, and what have been their antecedents? You understand that I put these interrogatories to you, for the purpose of answering them myself. But I shall not answer the question, *who?* for this would lead to personal allusions, which it is always best to avoid, if consistent with the requirements of truth and justice; I shall, therefore, confine myself to *what* they are, and what have been their antecedents.

Every one of these exposers, of whom I have had personal knowledge—and I think that knowledge embraces every name that I have seen conspicuously figuring, as above named—has been, for years past, a professed propagator of the spiritual philosophy, and a practical speculator in the spiritual phenomena. They went from city to city, from town to town, from state to state, and from section to section of the country, loudly proclaiming the glad tidings of great joy to all people, that open intercourse had been established between Earth and Heaven, and earnestly inviting every man and woman, boy and girl, who had dimes to spare, to come and see, and hear if not see, the indubitable evidences which they were prepared to adduce, to substantiate the truth of their loud sounding annunciations. Then, as now, they were among the most honest of Adam's progeny; but they warned their customers against being duped by the tricks of those who might not be quite as honest as they were. And they kept on exchanging the communications and manifestations of their coadjutors in spirit life, for the dimes, quarters, half-dollars, and dollars of the people among whom they traveled and sojourned, as long as the material receipts were sufficiently ample to meet all expenses, and afford a handsome income for all concerned in the divine speculation.

Why did they discontinue their labors of love? I think the true cause may be found in the now nearly established fact, that ministering spirits have unanimously determined, that none of their legitimately adopted mundane helpers, nor any of those who volunteer their services for pelf, shall ever be bloated to *super-crinoline* rotundity, by streams of material wealth, flowing from their patronage. Think you, these recanting exposers would have been such, at this day, if their labors in the service of ministering angels had met the pecuniary reward, which their thirsting spirits longed for? I tell you nay; for the whole genus, speculator, by common instinct, will think well of, speak well of, and endeavor to protect, if need be, by legislative enshrinement, the traffic by which the greater amount of gain can be made.

Some of the present exposers of spiritual humbug, who failed to make its advocacy a paying vocation, have been, for many months past, and probably are still, endeavoring to mend their fortunes by exhibiting to audiences of scoffers at Spiritualism, the manner in which they practised bogus manifestations, when they were traveling advocates of the spiritual philosophy; charging a dime a head for admittance to the show. Maryatt tells of a gin-drinking mother, who took fire, and was reduced to a heap of cinders, by inhaling the flame of a candle. And he tells of a son of that mother, who gathered her charred remains into a bag, and exhibited them in public places, at a penny a sight; recounting at each exhibition, the cause and manner of his mother's death. Which of these two charlatans should you consider the most loathsome, in the estimation of honorable minds? If you find it difficult to decide, I will not press the question.

From what I have written, you will learn, I think, pretty clearly what effect has been produced on my mind by the recantations, confessions and exposures to which you have called my attention. But you seem to be almost ready to yield the point, that there is no reality in the proposition that enfranchised spirits *can* and *do* revisit their friends in the flesh, and make their presence known to them by physical effects, produced through mortal media. In this state of mind, you cannot, of course, feel assured that there are any true mediums;

but you merely cling to the hope that they are not all impostors and cheats. On all these points you invoke an expression of my sentiments in the present state of my mind; and you intimate that you have great faith in the correctness of my reasoning, and the truthfulness of my representations.

For your good opinion of me, and for your unchanging confidence in the correctness of my conclusions, I am truly grateful to you; but I intend to be the last person to advise you, or any one else, to abandon your own individuality, or to adopt the opinions of another person instead of your own, without first bringing the whole force of your own reasoning powers to bear upon the facts and circumstances of the case in controversy, whatever it may be, although that other person should be myself. Thus premising, I feel free to give you the result of my investigations and experience in my researches after spiritual truth, and I find it necessary to narrate a few facts which have come under my personal observation. I hope you will not feel that I am over-taxing your patience; and I promise to be as brief as practicable.

My course of investigations has resulted in the following conclusions:

Spiritual intercourse with mortals, or the visitations of spirits to their mortal relatives and friends, and their efforts to influence and enlighten their minds, commenced with the first development of the human spirit to immortality. Many of the reputed sooth-sayers, seers, and prophets of ancient history, were mediums for spiritual intercourse; and many others were mere pretenders, for, as before remarked, every good thing, in all ages of the world, has had its counterfeit. Jesus of Nazareth was a medium for spiritual manifestations, both inspirational and physical, and probably the greatest, in some respects, of all that have yet been brought into the service of ministering angels. Both the inspirational and physical phases of His mediumship, were manifested in that single scene with the adulteress and her accusers. When the Jews, who brought her before Jesus, asked him if she should be stoned to death, according to the law instituted by Moses, he stooped down and wrote with his finger on the ground. This writing in the sand was physical. The answer which was written by his finger, and which he gave to the accusing Jews when he arose from his stooping posture—"Let him that is without sin cast the first stone,"—was purely inspirational. When he had given the answer he again stooped down and wrote on the ground. Again he arose, and gave utterance to what he had written—"Woman, where are those thine accusers, hath no man condemned thee?" She replied: "No man, Lord." And he said, "Neither do I condemn thee; go and sin no more." The wisdom of the answer to the woman's accusers surpassed anything that has been reported as having come originally from the lips of Jesus; and the forgiving sympathy manifested in the words addressed to the woman, were sweetly angelic, and evidently fresh from Heaven. It is true that, as the case is reported, Jesus is represented to have stooped down and *pretended* to write, merely to make the accusing Jews believe he heard them not. This explanation of the act, however, is unsustained by any of the attending circumstances, and at war with common sense. To practise a deception of this kind, especially in the absence of any circumstance which could be supposed to make it necessary, was inconsistent with the purity of his character; and no other rational conclusion can be arrived at, than that he wrote, as a medium, the sentiments of a controlling and inspiring angel, and delivered them in that capacity.

Constantly in all ages, since man became immortal, have the inhabitants of our spirit-world, or Earth's Heaven, been endeavoring to open a free and general intercourse with their kindred spirits of earth: but they have never before been as successful as they have in this general effort of the nineteenth century. Here the religious fanatic elongates his countenance and asks: If God desire the accomplishment of that object, what is to hinder it from being accomplished at once? and if it be not in accordance with his will, why do spirits, as you pretend to say, continue their efforts? Are they in a state of rebellion against God? and are they so stupid, as to believe they can effect their purpose, in opposition to his will? A sufficient answer to this kind of argument would be to say, that neither the inhabitants of earth's spirit land, the angelic hosts of all the higher spheres, nor even the Infinite God himself, can accomplish anything outside of, or in opposition to, the laws of nature, in which laws may be said to exist the *vis vitæ* of all living entities in all worlds. That Infinite One in whose being is aggregated the totality of life, spirit, power, wisdom, goodness, truth, and love, that pervade the entire universcœlum, hath decreed, and doth eternally will and decree, that nothing shall ever come into organic being in full ripeness and perfection; but that all things shall come into existence in a state of crudity; and progress continually from degree to degree of ripeness and perfection; and that those beings which are not endowed with the principle of immortality, shall so progress till they reach their climax of perceptibility, when they shall pass through the destined change of organic existence. This being the pleasure of the Infinite One, expressed in the great book of nature, spirits from earth may continue to labor in the glorious cause of human redemption, and still pursue their noble project of opening that free and general intercourse between the inhabitants of the two kindred countries, in which so many millions of them are engaged, without fear of being arrested for high treason, or of running counter to the will of that all-loving, all-directing, and all-comprising One, of whose being they are constituents. Nor need any mortal doubt that an enterprise which so many millions of God's constituent spirits have been engaged in, perhaps for many millenniums, will ultimately be accomplished. Indeed the fact that they are engaged in it, should be proof positive to every thinking mind, that there is no possibility of failure.

When they meet with reverses and are foiled in their endeavors, as it happened with them after the crucifixion of Jesus, when deteriorated Christianity amalgamated with Judaism and Paganism, and when they were encountered by that tripartite amalgam whose power ecclesiastical, was concentrated in the established churches of that age; and as it happened with them when they made the extra effort at Salem, in the seventeenth century, where they found superstition and religious fanaticism not dead, as they had hoped, but warily watching for prey, they profit by their experiences, fortify the weak points which are thus discovered to them, and renew their labors with ever increasing energy. And the lesson which these failures of our brethren and sisters of the spirit realm should teach to us mortals is, that although they are a step in advance of us, they are neither omnipotent, omniscient, nor infinite, but finite man and woman, dependent upon instruction, experience and observation, for what they know more than mortals. These convictions are the effects produced upon my mind by my investigations of the spiritual philosophy; and how much should you think those convictions could be changed by the puerile bickerings and fooleries of pretending dissenters and real exposers of their own shame?

As respects mediums of spiritual manifestations and communications, there is much to complain of and to be ashamed of, and much to rejoice over and to be gratified for. It is a fact to be regretted that there are so many of the class before alluded to, who either have a mere germ of mediumship, or unite themselves with media of small development and flexible morals, and go prowling through the country, seeking whom they may devour, regardless of everything but pelf and sensual gratification. And it may well seem strange to superficial thinkers, why disembodied spirits should aid them, as they frequently do, in their dishonest operations. But those who look more deeply into the philosophy, are not at all surprised at such collusions. They see, at once, that the mundane, and super-mundane spirits are congenial in their natures, and equals in development. The vicious and undeveloped mortal attracts to him associates from the spirit world like himself, who are as capable of mastering the science of manifestation and communication as those of superior qualities and developments; and they can readily supply their want of philosophical knowledge by random or evasive answers, or by false assertions, any of which will pass as currently with ignorant minds as the choicest philosophical truth. But there is always some good resulting from even the most gross and stupid falsehood communicated by spirits, for when they are known to be thus communicated, as in most cases they may be, they prove some important truths. No rational man will deny that a man is a man because he tells a falsehood; neither can he deny that a spirit is a spirit, because it either wilfully or ignorantly makes a false representation. The lie of the communicating spirit proves the great truth that it does exist, and the farther important truth that spirits do manifest their presence and hold intercourse with mortals. So you see the dark side of this part of the subject presents a streak of light. Now for the bright side.

That there are many mediums whose integrity of character cannot be justly questioned, and whom no consideration could induce to act the part of knaves, I do positively know—both male and female mediums do I know, in whom there is no propensity to deception. Communications through these may be always relied on as being genuine. Whether communications are always true or not is another question. Well developed spirits will frequently contradict each other in their philosophical communications; so do the most truthful spirits incarnate. The philosophical opinions entertained by disembodied spirits are frequently speculative; and they may as rationally be allowed to disagree honestly, as may spirits occupying physical forms. Among the many mediums of this character, with whom I have had the pleasure to become acquainted, I know of but two, who are probably known to you; and it would be scarcely worth while for me to go into detail of facts witnessed by me in connection with media, of whom you know nothing.

The two, whose names I was about to mention, are residents of your city, and are generally known to all Spiritualists there; they are Dr. G. A. Redman, and J. B. Conklin. They are both test mediums of a superior order; and, as I confidently believe, perfectly reliable, as far as their own moral integrity is concerned. I have witnessed many beautiful, and thoroughly convincing tests of spirit presence, intelligence, and power, at séances held by Mr. Conklin, in this city; but for want of any record of the particular facts, I dare not venture to detail any of them.

With respect to tests given through the mediumship of Doctor Redman, I am more fortunate. He was, at each time when he was here, located in an adjoining room to my editorial sanctum; and it was convenient for me, at all times when he had no other company, to occupy a chair at his table; and I rarely failed of embracing such opportunities, when my own duties did not peremptorily require my attention. A few of the facts thus witnessed, and recorded by me, will, if you believe me, convince you that there *are* such things as genuine spiritual manifestations, and reliable mediums.

The first of the facts, to which I will call your attention, I find recorded in the "Age of Progress," of September 6th, 1856. Thus reads the record:

AN EXTRAORDINARY SPIRITUAL TEST.

A gentleman who resides in this city, but who has not authorized us to give his name, called at Mr. Redman's room, on Sunday last, for the purpose of introducing a friend who was visiting him. Besides this friend, a brother of the gentleman first named, was also present. This brother was an inveterate skeptic, without the least fellowship with Spiritualism. He called for curiosity, but refused to sit at the table for investigation. The spirits, however, requested all present to be seated at the table. He complied; and, in a few minutes, the spirit of a deceased brother, who departed this life in England, at the age of 17 years, addressed him, through the hand of the medium, writing backwards, from right to left, and signing his name. The skeptical brother asked the spirit if he could tell the manner of his death. This was answered in the affirmative, by the raps; and the hand of the medium was immediately used to make numerical characters as follows:

9 23 1 19 19 13 15 20 8 5 18 5 4 9 14
20 8 5 5 1 18 20 8 4 5 1 18 2 18 15 20
8 5 18.

What the meaning of these figures could be, no one present could divine, till direction was given by the spirit, through the hand of the medium, to place the numericals over the letters of the alphabet, in their respective order, thus:

1	2	3	4	5	6	7	8	9	10	11	12	13	14	15	16
A	B	C	D	E	F	G	H	I	J	K	L	M	N	O	P

17	18	19	20	21	22	23	24	25	26.
Q	R	S	T	U	V	W	X	Y	Z.

By this key the reader will discover that the combination of characters given, spells—"I was smothered in the earth, dear brother."

The fact thus ingeniously and uniquely represented, was, as stated by the two brothers, "that he and another lad were at play in a sand hole, the projecting bank of which caved in, and suffocated him before he could be extricated." This test proved too potent for the skeptical brother's stoicism; and his tears confessed his conviction.

These brothers being Englishmen; the scene of the fatal accident to their younger brother having been England; and the medium having no knowledge of anything relating to them, or their connections; it strikes me that this single test of spirit identity, was sufficient to convince even Pope Pius himself of the fact, that the spirits of the departed have power to revisit their incarnate friends, and make their presence known to them, and that they do so continually, when conditions are favorable.

At another time, I went into the medium's room in the evening, when all visitors had retired. We sat by the table, and he took a small piece of paste-board in one hand, put a pencil on it, and held it by one end under the table; at the same time keeping his other hand on the table. On this paste-board, while he thus held it, a loving message, of some four or five lines was written, by the spirit of my mother.

One morning, about 8 o'clock, he and I went into his room, locked the door, took a piece of board some three feet long, put it under the table, with paper and pencil on it, and let one end of the board rest on his knees, and the other on mine. In less than a minute, our four hands being on the table, we heard the pencil writing. In a few minutes more the board, paper and pencil were thrown upon the floor. I took up the paper and found a message directed to myself, with the signature of my old friend, Stephen R. Smith, appended to it. The message was about the same length as this narrative of the fact.

I went into the medium's room, one afternoon when he was absent, and saw, on the table, some dozen of paper pellets or balls, which had been made by investigators, by rolling up inch-square bits of paper, with the names, ages and occupations of deceased friends written on them. They were in their tightly compressed, globular form, about the size of a pea. I took four of the square pieces of paper which I found there, prepared for the purpose, and wrote four names of deceased persons on them. One of the names was that of Thomas

Jefferson. I put the four, when I had rolled them up tightly, as the others were, among the mass, and stirred them up; as I was hustling them around, the medium entered and asked, "What are you doing there?" I replied, that I had made some pellets, like those I found on the table, and mixed them up with the others; that on them I had written names; and I wanted to ascertain whether either of the spirits, whose names I had written, in his (the medium's) absence, could choose out the one that had his own name on it. He sat down, and his hand involuntarily seized the pencil, and wrote: "I will choose out my name, Thomas Jefferson." As soon as the name was written, the hand of the medium was brought to the heap of pellets, and one of them was picked up and handed to me. I opened it, and found it to be the one on which I had written the name of Thomas Jefferson, when no mortal eye but my own could, by any possibility, have seen me.

Here evaporates the theory of certain philosophers, that the medium sees the upper end of the pencil writing names in the atmosphere, takes note of the shape of the pellets, and remembers the names and shapes of the whole batch! Is it not strange that persons who have credit for possessing sound intellects, and a fair share of common sense, will advance theories, in a hopeless controversy, which are so ludicrously absurd that they would, themselves, laugh them to scorn, if they came from any other mind than their own? It must be that such believe all persons, except themselves, are native simpletons.

In the forenoon of the day, when he was to leave for the West, Mr. R. was in my office, sitting within about two feet of my desk, which was a very heavy one, with a full book-case on it. I had laid by my pen, and drawn back from the desk, and was conversing with him about his journey West. Among other things, I reminded him that he had promised to sit for the spirit of my father to communicate to me, through him, before he took his departure from the city. He acknowledged the promise, but said, "It is too late now—I will sit for him at the first opportunity, on my way West." I agreed to the proposition, and remarked that I had no doubt my father would attend and improve the opportunity. No sooner had I done speaking than the end of the desk, nearest the medium, rose and made three concussions on the floor, which jarred the whole building. Neither of us was then near enough to the desk to touch it with our hands, without leaning forward. This proves the power of spirits to move ponderous bodies, without mortal contact, which, you know, is stoutly denied by some of our would-be sages, who would fain make you believe they had delved to the nadir, and soared to the zenith of the spiritual philosophy.

These, my dear friend, are all the facts I shall give you at present; and as I have spun out my letter to an unaccountable length, I doubt not you are ready to cry enough!

Truly and fraternally yours,

S. ALBRO.

CHAPTER XIV.

Spirit Interposition. Rooms in Cincinnati. Mrs. Young and her Sonny. The Sealed Letter. Electric Lights. Does mind control the communications? Letter from Mr. Williams. Spiritual power of healing.

"What lack you? and where lies your grief?
What good love may I perform for you?"

I HAD determined to leave Buffalo, and continue my journey West, and accordingly on the night of the 1st Sept., 1856, took the express train for Cincinnati.

Taking advantage of my conveniences, I was soon between a sleeping and waking state, though sufficiently the former to feel careless of outward objects. How long I remained in this position I could not tell, but I was suddenly awakened by my arm being jerked from under my head, bringing my face in contact with the arm of the seat—enough so to cause some little sensation. I looked for the cause, but could perceive none, till my arm began to twitch, as it is wont to do. The unceremonious manner of disturbing one in a pleasant dream did not render my mind any too passive, and after a little resentment, I resumed my position, at the same time making all allowances for another such manifestation. I tried to pass off again, but no ; impressions began to flow into my mind of a very decided character, and my arms also felt quite at liberty, for they began to make manipulations as if to pull the bell-rope of the car. With all my resistance I could not fail to observe that something was required of me. So placing myself in as passive a position as possible, both of body and mind, I awaited the wish of my friends. It came quickly and strongly. The impression was this : "Arise, go into the forward car. Danger ! danger ! danger !"

I obeyed the warning and arose, went to the door, but perceiving that the car in advance of us was a baggage car, I immediately closed the door again, and was about to resume my former seat, when by force I was turned round, made to open the door, and step across the platform, and take my position in the baggage car. I found two young men seated upon something, I could not tell what, for I was confounded at the singularity of the manifestation through which I had passed.

Again an impression came, " Stay where you are." I was content. Seating myself upon a bag of some kind, I awaited a further direction, but I received no other. All seemed passive, and my friends satisfied. I remained in these comfortable quarters, as far as I can judge, about half an hour, when we were suddenly startled by an extraordinary twitching, and then a great increase of speed, a sharp whistle, and after a short distance we stopped; my company rushed to the door, and upon opening it we were amazed to find that we had been disconnected from the passenger train, and by straining our vision, saw that the car directly in our rear had broken down, and had forced itself into a wood pile by the road side, one end of the car being partially demolished! I immediately realized the object of my former impressions, and hastily getting out of the car we proceeded to the scene of disaster, where we learned that a wheel had been broken, as we were going at the usual speed, and in an instant the car had been disconnected, and, with all the force occasioned by such power, came in contact with the wood. Efforts were immediately made to ascertain the extent of the damage. But three were materially injured, one an Indian, whose shoulder was dislocated, with some internal injuries; one whose ankle was sprained, occasioned by a stick of wood being thrust through the bottom of the car; the other was similarly injured in the knee. Upon inquiry, I found that the Indian had taken my seat upon its being vacated, directly over the broken wheel, and had it not been intercepted by a pile of wood, the car would have been precipitated down an embankment of some thirty feet or more.

Surely here is some practicality. My spirit-friends seeing the weakness of the wheel, labored to remove me from danger. They could not tell when or at what point it would occur, undoubtedly; but they knew the danger, and hence removed me from my critical position. Had the car detached itself five minutes later, it would have been thrown from a high bridge, at a risk of the lives of all the passengers. I felt thankful for my deliverance, and by my own feelings could discern the satisfaction of my friends. The pile of wood was removed, the injured car tipped down the embankment, and after leaving a second partially disabled, we proceeded on our way; but sleep was far from the lids of the passengers, for the remainder of the night was passed congratulating themselves upon their narrow escape from death, and wishing for the immediate coming of the morning.

Such is one instance of deliverance from danger, which is often termed providential, but if fairly understood may be traced to the direct interference of those guardian friends, who so kindly labor with and teach us.

As usual on reaching a city, where we intend remaining awhile, our first object is to seek appropriate accommodations; but on arriving in Cincinnati, I found these conveniences all comfortably arranged for me, by thoughtful and considerate friends—in the house of Mr. Waggoner, on Sixth Street, between Vine and Walnut. I, therefore, without any delay, prepared to give proper reception to investigators, and to deal out with an unselfish hand, portions of the life food which it was my province to scatter.

A small centre apartment, with a partition of green baize to separate it from the parlor, was my boudoir of mystic sweetness ; and, all in readiness, I there awaited "demurring wits, who dare dispute this revolution in the world inspired."

A lady dressed in deep mourning habiliments, and claiming the cognomen of *Inquirer*, by engagement seated herself at my table one morning, for the purpose of affording to her wounded spirit consolation for the loss (as the séance proved) of a dear and only child. "The ark fraught with her earth-ward clinging happiness," had been wrecked, and after long reflection, she had ultimately gained courage to test the truths of Spiritualism, and ascertain if the loved ones did come back from that bourne whence, many even now believe, that no traveler can return. I bade her write names on slips of paper, as it was my way of proceeding ; hesitatingly she drew some pieces of paper under her veil, and complied. She might as well have written them at home, as far as I was concerned, for so thickly shrouded was her face by the crape suspended over it, I could not discern a single feature, much less what she wrote on the paper. The writing finished, the ballots were placed on the table, and all remained quiet : shortly, raps were heard, and one of the pellets selected ; previous to its being opened, this message was spelled by the alphabet being recited:

"That is my name, dear mother.

SONNY YOUNG."

The lady took the pellet, opened it, and seemed much affected by the unlooked-for announcement. I requested she would write questions on the paper before her, and probably her child would answer them. She did so, and the replies were promptly and aptly given; while penning a question, she suddenly started from her chair, uttered a terrible scream, declared there was a cat in the room, and with a vivacious shake of crinoline, rushed towards the door. I assured her, that since my departure from Buffalo, none of the feline race had I seen, and that there certainly was not one in the room. Resuming her seat, she recommenced writing, but again came forth another shrill intonation, accompanied with the assertion, that she felt something touch her foot. I assured her it was my belief that the sensation she experienced was spiritual, and if she would sit quietly, very probably the spirits would manifest so tangibly, she might feel the impression of fingers. Incomprehensible as this was to the visitor, she expressed perfect willingness for the invisibles to exhibit their power by more palpable touches, if they pleased, adding "That Freddy would do nothing to harm her." As the remark was concluded, she told me her dress was being pulled "so strongly! so strongly!" Her spirit son seemed to enjoy the demonstration on his part, for he made repeated raps, as if laughing at her excitement. "Don't tear it, Freddy," the lady cried. Freddy, however, would not loosen his hold, but with a sudden jerk, he disconnected the skirt of the dress from the waist, for nearly half of its extent, then calling for the alphabet, he spelt:

"That will do, mamma. I only wished to leave my mark.
SONNY."

Bringing all the stray pins into use, the lady effected a junction between the component parts of the severed garment, and throwing back her heavy veil, desired me to listen, as she related the remarkable evidence of the presence of him, who but a few months before, had been taken from her.

"I wrote," said she, "on the paper the name of my son, Frederick Young, with others of deceased friends. I expected, if he could come to me, he would respond, as I had written; but no, he signed as you have seen. Although called Freddy, Sonny was an epithet of home endearment, and his giving that signature would of itself convince me, that his darling spirit still loves and hovers near his mother."

Her other questions related to the names of spirit brothers and sisters, all of which were answered correctly.

The following communication is full of interest, as tending to demonstrate the actuality of communication between this and the Spirit-world. Mrs. Clara Smith, daughter of Oliver Lovell, Esq., of Cincinnati, on the first of May, 1853, being in a condition physically, by which it became certain that she must soon enter the world of spirits, wrote a letter, sealed it and endorsed the following directions thereon.

Oliver Lovell, Esq., Cincinnati, Ohio.

Three weeks after my decease, and after communications approved of by my father, this is to be opened.

Let everything communicated be faithfully written down word for word before opening this, and then perhaps skeptics will be satisfied that there is something in spiritual manifestations.

Mrs. Smith continued to live in the form until about April, 1855. A short time previous to her decease, she put the letter sealed and directed as above into the hands of her daughter, to be delivered according to the endorsed direction.

Sometime in the month of September, 1856, Mr. Redman, a medium from Boston, was visiting Cincinnati, when Mr. Lovell called on him for the purpose of getting a communication from his daughter, Mrs. Smith, respecting the contents of the sealed letter. Mr. Redman immediately took his pencil, and the following was written by his hand:

Communications received through Mr. Redman in Explanation of Mrs. C. Smith's letter.

My Dear and Beloved Father:—Blessed are the pure in heart, for they shall see God. I shall go to that happy mansion, where angels shall love and help me.

Best and Dearest Mother:—I shall send messages to you from Lucy and grandmother.

My Dear and Bereaved Sister Sarah:—I shall be permitted by my Heavenly Father to come and be with you, and send you messages from beloved Reuben. I will aid thee to be pure and holy. Tell my darling children I shall be near them and often send messages unto them.

Their dear Mother, CLARA.

Dear Father:—These are what I can recollect of what I wrote. You know it is hard to remember every word; but my address to you is more vivid than all. O, I hope the skeptic will learn a lesson from this, and know that we truly come to teach them, and rejoice the hearts of loved ones at home.

Thy Spirit Daughter, CLARA. ALICE.

Dearly Beloved and Honored Father: May 1, 1853.

"Blessed are the pure in heart, for they shall see God. Blessed are the peacemakers, for they shall be called the children of God." Such words as the above, my blessed Father, in all sincerity, in every sense of the word, does your devoted daughter believe, belong to you; and if permitted, will develop the same words, when this earthly incumbrance hath left me, and I go to that happy mansion prepared for me in the spiritual world.

My Best and Dearest Mother:—I shall, if permitted, send messages to you from grandma, Aunt Lucy, and all others near and dear to you. Little Alice, I will ask many questions of her concerning our former communications.

Unto Dear and Bereaved Sister Sarah:—I will, if permitted by my Heavenly Father, try and assuage her grief by delightful and soothing communications from her beloved Reuben. I will also convey to him the love still borne unto him, as she wished me to do when I met him. I will ask him if he is not always near her; I will send her messages from her children—everything that I can to make her happy.

Dear Sister Eliza:—I will, if permitted to communicate with you, convince you, if possible, that it is myself and no false Spirit that has made its appearance. I will ask those good men, that is, if I am pure enough to approach them, such as Father Hurdus, Mr. Watson, and a great many others, if these loving communications unto father through yourself, were truly from themselves or false Spirits. I will try and send you a message from Mrs. Tuite, some questions I will ask her about Alice.

Tell my darling children I shall often send messages to them, if such things are, as have been developed unto me while residing among you all. I will tell them of their angel sister, and many other things that will convince them that it is their sincere and devoted mother that is watching over them; and her last prayer will be unto her Heavenly Father, to guard and shield them from temptation in their earthly pilgrimage. And O, may we all meet in Heaven, a joyful company!

Your fond and affectionate Mother, CLARA.

For the purpose of exhibiting the points of resemblance and difference at one view, we will place them side and side:

SEALED LETTER BY MRS. SMITH.	WRITTEN THROUGH MR. REDMAN.
Dearly Beloved and Honored Father: " Blessed are the pure in heart, for they shall see God. Blessed are the peace-makers, for they shall be called the children of God." Such words as the above, my blessed father, in all sincerity, in every sense, does your devoted daughter, believe belong to you; and if permitted will develop the same words, when this earthly incumbrance hath left me, and I go to that happy mansion prepared for me in the spiritual world.	" *My Dear and Beloved Father*-- 'Blessed are the pure in heart, for they shall see God. Blessed are the peace-makers, for they shall be called the children of God.' I shall go to that happy mansion where angels shall love and bless me."
My Best and Dearest Mother:-- I shall, if permitted, send messages to you from grandma, Aunt Lucy, and all others near and dear to you. Little Alice, I will ask many questions of her concerning our former communications.	" *Best and Dearest Mother*--I shall send messages to you from Lucy and grandmother."
Unto Dear and Bereaved Sister Sarah:--I will, if permitted by my Heavenly Father, try and assuage her grief by delightful and soothing communications from her beloved Reuben. I will also convey to him the love still borne unto him, as she wished me to do. When I meet, him, I will ask him if he is not always near her. I will send her messages from her children--everything that I can to make her happy.	" *My Dear and Bereaved Sister Sarah*--I shall be permitted by my Heavenly Father to come and be with you, and send you messages from beloved Reuben, and aid thee to be pure and holy."
Dear Sister Eliza:--I will, if permitted to communicate with you, convince you, if possible, that it is myself and no false Spirit that has	

SEALED LETTER BY MRS. SMITH.

made its appearance. I will ask those good men, that is, if I am pure enough to approach them, such as Father Hurdus, Mr. Watson, and a great many others, if their loving communications unto father through yourself, were truly from themselves or false Spirits. I will try and send you a message from Mrs. Tuite; some questions I will ask her about Alice. Tell my darling children I shall often send messages to them, if such things are as have been developed unto me while residing with you all. I will tell them of their angel sister, and many other things that will convince them that it is their sincere and devoted mother that is watching over them; and her last prayer will be unto her Heavenly Father, to guard and shield them from temptation in their earthly pilgrimage. And O, may we all meet in Heaven, a joyful company!

Your fond and affectionate Mother,
CLARA.

WRITTEN THROUGH MR. REDMAN

"Tell my darling children I shall be near them and often send messages unto them. Their dear mother,
CLARA."

"*Dear Father*--These are what I can recollect of what I wrote. You know it is hard to remember every word; but my address to you is more vivid than all. I hope skeptics will learn a lesson from this, and know that we truly come to teach them and rejoice the hearts of loved ones at home. Thy Spirit daughter,
CLARA. ALICE."*

There are several points in the foregoing to which attention is especially invited.

1st. It is most manifest, that by some means there was communication between the mind controlling the hand of Mr. Redman, and the letter written by Mrs. Smith more than two years previous to that time; and if that communication was not through the clairvoyance of some mind in the form, it must

* Alice is a little niece of Mrs. Smith, in the Spirit-world.

have been through the mind of some spiritual being; and that, probably through the one it purported to be, Mrs. Clara Smith.

It will be remembered that the letter was written by Mrs. Smith in May, 1853, and sealed up by her for the purpose of testing the faith of Spiritual communications; that the contents of the letter were known to no person living in the form, unless clairvoyantly read by them. A comparison of the letter with that written through Mr. Redman will show that it was not clairvoyantly read. The differences and omissions are such as to forbid that solution of the problem. Had Mr. Redman, or the mind dictating the communication, have read from the sealed letter, the many omissions would not have occurred. The mind that could have clairvoyantly read, "Blessed are the pure in heart," etc., could have read what followed. The mind that could clairvoyantly have noted from the letter the order of addressing father, mother, sister, and children, would not have omitted to notice the address to sister Eliza. These numerous and striking differences and omissions demonstrate that the communication was not obtained through clairvoyance. There remains then but one other hypothesis that seems rational, and that is, that the Spirit of the veritable Mrs. Clara Smith dictated that communication from memory; that she herself could not, at that time, read the contents of the letter written by her two years before.

These things being true, two other points are suggested by these phenomena: one, that the memory of the Spirit is liable to be defective, as in this life; and the other, that Spirits are not either universally or uniformly clairvoyant, respecting things pertaining to sense. That the disembodied as well as embodied Spirit, must depend upon certain conditions for its perceptions, and when those conditions are not present, it can not perceive, and when but imperfectly present, its perceptions must be imperfect. If skeptics and believers would remember this, it might do a good work for both, by modifying the skepticism of the one and the credulity of the other.—*Tiffany's Monthly*.

During my stay in Cincinnati, a fine specimen of spirit lights was presented to an investigator, Mr. E. Williams of St. Louis, and myself. It was the most pleasing of the kind I ever witnessed.

I had attended Mr. W. to his lodgings at the Walnut Street Hotel, and while we were sitting at a small table, the spirits intimated their sympathy with us: raps came on a wardrobe in the room, and the name of Mr. Williams's mother was spelt by the alphabet, and a request that he would write questions. The one relating to the age of his parent was answered 49, which was correct.

"Mother," said Mr. W., "how many children had you?"

"Five."

"This cannot be," was his rejoinder; "you had but four, and *I* the youngest."

"I had five, my child; you were not the youngest, for my last babe lived but a few days."

This response to Mr. W's. declaration caused him to ponder deeply; still he adhered to the assertion that he was the youngest of the family; but promised should he find the statement of the spirit correct, he would write and let me know.

Other questions were asked, and apparently answered more to his satisfaction, after which we proceeded to make the room as dark as possible, having received from the spirits the promise that they would exhibit electric lights.

We sat quietly with hands joined, and darkness so dense that no object could be seen. A perfect storm of raps resounded all over the room ; the key in the door was turned, and the lock snapped as though we were being locked in. Mr. W. declared the key was on the inside of the room, and if the door had been locked other hands than ours had accomplished it. We were discussing this point when a faint light, about the size of a silver half dollar, was observed in the farthest corner of the room ; it twinkled a few moments, gradually growing brighter and brighter, until it was painful to our eyes to gaze at it. The color was a most beautiful bright green ; soon a small ball of light, about the size of a common marble, issued from it, and shooting across the room struck another light of a similar character, but red in color, on the opposite side of the apartment. The concussion was about as loud as a gun cap. During this remarkable phenomenon, neither of us stirred from our places ; and it continued at intervals for some three-quarters of an hour. The balls would alternately assume different hues, and their velocity be lessened or increased at our request. Mr. W. suggested rising and intercepting them with his hand or some article, to see if there were actual resistance from their contact ; accordingly, folding some paper that lay on the table, he slowly moved toward the opposite side of the room, and as the light contracted to emit the electric ball, he held the paper in a range as near as possible ; the light passed directly throught it, but he averred there was not the least perceptible resistance from the object. Lighting the gas, a circular brown spot was visible in the sheet, but no perforation. Our eyes gave evidence of the strain they had undergone ; the sight was lovely in the extreme, and we availed ourselves of it as long as our spirit friends saw proper to gratify us. We examined the walls thoroughly, but nothing was visible to indicate the ingress or egress of electrc fluids of an unusual character. I have seen many similar phenomena, but none so tangible or developed as were these. Thanking our spirit friends for their kindness, we wished them and each other good night. About two months after the above occurred, I received the following letter from Mr. Williams :

St. Louis, Nov. 18.

Dr. Redman :—

You are, no doubt, in wonder why I have not written you before ; but I have been very busy, and not stationary a week at a time. You probably have still fresh in your mind the evening we spent with spirits previous to my leaving Cincinnati, and also, that I strenuously disputed the fact that my mother had five children. I have since learned she was correct and I in error. Her last child, a little girl, was born, when I was about six years old. It was a premature birth, and lived a few days only; this being the fact, it makes the number of her children five, as she stated, and also adds a link to the chain of my conviction, which can never be broken. Added to that, the fire balls gave both novelty and strength, and convinced me of the truths of spirit manifestations and communications. I visit New York the coming winter, and hope to meet you again.

Yours electrically,

E. WILLIAMS.

This is another of the many instances where our positive knowledge at the time of communicating sinks insignificantly before facts, that reveal our mistake on due investigation. Mr. W. was positively certain that the number of his mother's children was only four, and, therefore, gave the communicating spirit but little credit for its kindness, and the subject communicated was passed over as unimportant until such time as inquiry disclosed his want of knowledge and the spirit's reliability and truthfulness.

During our stay at Richmond, Indiana, one morning, I hastily entered the parlor, and found my wife reclining on the lounge; playfully throwing myself by her side, I felt a sharp pang at my elbow. Quickly rising and taking off my coat, I was surprised to find the blood flowing from my arm. Ellie had been paring an apple, and was holding the open knife in her hand, which being unperceived by me, had forcibly entered the elbow joint, and as I sprang up had been jerked out. The application of a little arnica checked the effusion of blood; but I remarked to my wife, that my right arm was useless both to the spirits and myself. A sensation of faintness came over me, when I was made to place my hand on the wound and make passes from my shoulder downward—my wife at the same time manipulating my head. The pain in the wound ceased almost instantly; and on inquiring of father if it would be serious, he replied: "No! have you not two arms? You will need no sling for the one injured; go to thy duty as usual." Severe as this wound was, by the healing influences of the spirit, it was quickly cured; whereas, without the mediation of my parent, my arm would have been useless for some time, for the knife, undoubtedly, entered the articulation, as I could readily perceive by moving my arm immediately after the occurrence.

CHAPTER XV.

Return to New York. Spiritual Vision Re-opened. Cousin William's Visit to my Chamber. How I Distinguish Them. New and Pleasing Phase of Development. Wm. E. Channing. Emily Drinkwater. Howard Peacock. Elizabeth Wade. Caroline. E. W. Walbridge. O. H. Blood. Jane English. Gall.

"Allons faire éclater la gloire de Dieu aux yeux de tous,
"Et répondre avec zèle à ce qu 'il veut de nous."

FROM Richmond, after answering a call at Dayton, Ohio, and stopping again at Cincinnati, I directed my journeyings eastward; and once more located myself in New York, at No. 784 Broadway, corner of Tenth Street. Here my Spiritual vision was again actively opened, and I was subjected to many annoyances more humiliating, if possible, than those experienced in Baltimore.

Hailing the stage one evening, I saw a lady cross the street, apparently for the same object as myself—a ride. As she approached, I held the door of the stage, and waited in readiness to act the part of gallant: she stepped on the lower step, and remained immovable: even to arrive thus far it took the spirit a minute or two. The driver called for me to "get in;" the passengers becoming restless ordered the driver to "go on," while I pointed with my hand indicative of my wish for the bashful dame to enter. She, however, continuing regardless of my intended politeness, I raised myself at one side, and jumped into the vehicle, not a little surprised to find no impediment in my way. Looking back, and seeing no lady near, it then first occurred to me that I had been extending all my politeness to some gentle daughter of Eve divested of mortal enfoldings. My traveling companions stared not a little, no doubt imagining me a crazy individual, nor could their impressions have been at all diminished, when reaching home, they saw me pause in the centre of the stage as I was about getting out. When I pulled the check rein to alight, a lady sitting opposite rose to precede me; being tardy in her movements, I delayed in order to give her an opportunity to make her exit, and, at last, discovered my second mistake; by this time the driver had started his horses, and indignant at my want of perception, I dashed through the stage door, tumbled over a boy, with a basket, sitting on the steps, and prostrated myself, with peculiar grace, in the centre of the street: arising from my recumbent posture, I found my clothes most delectably ornamented and besmeared with mud and water.

Another occasion, on waking in the morning, I was startled to perceive a young man apparently performing his matutinal ablutions in my room, and with the most perfect *insouciance* making free with all my toilet appurtenances ; the bathing part completed, he leisurely employed my comb and hair-brush, every now and then casting an inquisitive glance at me. Raising myself in the bed, and narrowly scanning my visitor, I was surprised to recognize in him a striking resemblance to my cousin William Pratt, of Charlestown, Mass., who had passed from earth some years before. Perceiving my recognition, and his other duties finished, he seated himself in a chair, and placing his elbows on his knees "fell to gazing" on me ; then with his finger traced in the atmosphere these words—"Can you tell the number I am thinking of ?" This test was the same as announcing his name, for when a child he had taught me the method of ascertaining, by a mathematical process, any number of which a person should think ; his interrogation, therefore, identified him to me unmistakably : pleased with my recognition, he left the apartment, bowing and smiling. On rising, I found the appendages of the toilet disarranged, apparently as he had left them—the brush and comb were on the bureau, the drawer of which was open, and clean water in the basin ; the bed-room door, however, was locked as I had left it on going to bed the night previous. His apparent departure, therefore, was simply withdrawing himself from human vision. No doubt our Spiritual developments will reach that point, ere long, in which disembodied friends will be able to show themselves at *will*—of course more plainly to some than others, according to the impressibility of the individual. Cases of this kind of sight have become very familiar to me, and I could greatly multiply the instances. Although at first it was exceedingly difficult to distinguish between spirit and mortal, I can now easily discern the difference, and hence their presence is not attended with frustration or inconvenience. The distinction consists in their appearing at such moments, and under such circumstances as may confuse me, and in the exceeding tardiness or velocity with which every movement is performed. If I meet spirits in the street, they either approach at a very rapid pace, or an exceedingly measured one, more frequently the former: there seems, also, a magnetic attraction to the spiritual object, requiring the utmost resistance from me to keep my eyes from it, and of whatever is transpiring in the vicinity at the moment of these visitations, I find myself entirely unconscious.

A new and pleasing phase of development it may be well to mention here, as it seems more or less connected with instances of spirit perception already alluded to. I mean the novel manner adopted by spirits to convey their names, and thereby identify themselves. At first, (as in most of the manifestations we receive that are new) the similes were not very clear to my mind, hence I failed to afford a lucid and intelligent interpretation; but time and experience have elucidated the subject, and when not very intricate, I can, with readiness, define the wish of the communicating intelligence; facts illustrative of this statement I will proceed to mention. Mr. Monroe, of Boston, with a friend, called one afternoon for the purpose of enlivening his own faith, and of affording some evidences to the inquirer accompanying him. The guardian spirit of Mr. M. purported to be Wm. E. Channing, and as the communications from this spirit are characteristic and attended with truthful results, nothing could dissuade him from the belief that it was the veritable doctor. After various questions were answered by the request of Mr. Morgan, the spirit wrote:

My Dear Friend and Seeker after Light:—

That I am pleased and happy to greet you, even though it were every hour in the day, you well know—I am aware of your sincerity in these things, and also your credulity. The latter trait of character I desire to improve and modify. Honesty begets credulity, but credulity does not beget honesty. Confidence in thy fellow man may at times prompt him to take advantage of you, and sell thee water for wine, or diluted fact for veritable reality. However, thou art nearer the friends, who have passed before when thy soul receives all, than when the sieve of thy nature is too firm, and confines actual life, that it cannot blossom in thy progressive spirit.

I have this day watched with intense interest the passage from mortal life of the spirit of a missionary at Agra; a devout thinker and an energetic disciple of what he believed to be just and true. This town or village, as you are aware, is on a branch of the Ganges. His change was made known to me by members of his family, who have been inhabitants of the spirit realms for years. As the old man entered his new existence, he anxiously gazed about for the expected glorification, and not unlike myself, he found, instead of a place of rest from labor, a field, where philosophical activity and observation are brought more forcibly into requisition. "I thought," said he, as he saw my spirit near, "that I was a child in soul, as far as goodness and purity of motive were concerned; but I find I am even now a babe in development, and I must, therefore, strive upward toward the manhood of a new life." He was unlike many, who entering, have inquired for the kingdom of heaven, the harp on which their fingers were promised many vibrations and invariably feel for the wings, which poets have so fancifully fastened to the shoulders of the pure in heart. I say he was unlike this class, (though similar to them in faith.) for as soon as his gaze met the true condition of things, he avowed his utter amazement and his regret, that years of such patient study and labored benevolence should have yielded him so little usury. I am gratified that I can assist him to a knowledge of the true condition of the spheres, as I have been enabled to aid you; but others are near and desire to speak to thy friend. With all good will I retire, that they may open new light to the mind of thy companion.

I remain your friend, WM. E. CHANNING.

Here a spirit presented itself to me in the act of pouring water from a small golden pitcher into a goblet, and standing by the side of Mr. M's. friend; the spirit seemed anxious to attract my attention, and I willingly yielded. Filling the goblet, she drank its contents, and continued alternately filling and drinking, pointing at the water then at her mouth, as if desirous of conveying to my mind some test of identification for her friends. It was long before I could understand the analogy, and not until she wrote through my hand, as follows:

I am thy spirit friend, EMILY DRINKWATER.

The vision was rendered perfectly clear by this announcement. The act of drinking water was to convey her name to me, but I not being sufficiently impressible, she was forced to write it. The gentleman accepted the test as proof of identity, which, indeed, he well might.

Another: the circle consisted of Messrs. Robert Bonner, Edward S. Ready, of Wetumpka, Alabama, and Elisha Wade, of Okapilco, Georgia.

The first indication of the presence of spiritual beings was made known by raps. Mr. Bonner then received a happy and pleasing message from a loved sister, who but a short time previously had entered the spirit world, and who, as earth's last convulsive sigh was drawn, closely grasped her brother's hand in token of the unfading love that would be his, long after the spirit's casket should have been deposited in the dark and silent tomb. This unexpected meeting seemed to be a source of ineffable delight to both Mr. Bonner and the spirit. After answering different questions, and writing a short communication, the spirit withdrew that others might be allowed an interview.

At this stage of the séance, my attention was attracted to one corner of the room, where a strange and singular sight was presented to me. I distinctly saw a male spirit, caressing and leading by a cord a beautiful *Peacock;* its plumage was exceedingly lovely, and I watched it strut back and forth. I could not conceive what imported. The spirit all the while pointed with its fore finger to the bird, evidently wishing me to understand the sign; but I was too dull of comprehension, and could not divine its meaning. I described the vision to the circle, but neither could they interpret it, and I plainly saw by the way they turned the subject, that it was thought a freak of imagination. My hand was now influenced to write a short communication to Mr. Wade, and affix the name of Howard Peacock.

Here was a direct and powerful test of the presence of that spirit; he had, by this simile, labored to make me understand his name, and failing to do so, wrote it. Mr. Wade entered into conversation with him, but of its purport I am ignorant.

My attention was next attracted to the opposite side of the room, when I saw a clear flowing stream coursing undisturbed from wall to wall. I looked again, and a lovely female form was slowly wading backward and forward; as she did so, she gently raised her white robe, that it might not be wet, looked at me, smiled, pointed at the bubbling rivulet beneath her, and stepped slowly as before. I knew from the preceding vision, that this was given for me to recognize her name. I thought of "waters," but was not impressed that that was correct; again "ripples" occurred to me, but neither did this meet a passive answer. I described this second vision to the circle, but they were as much in darkness as before: the spirit failing to impress her identity upon us, wrote:—

My Dearest Earth Companion,

I thought I would present myself to the medium in this way, to see if you would not recognize me by the emblem of my wading through water.

This is our first interview, and to me each moment is like gold. Oh! how I wish I had known this philosophy before I left you. But I am not separated from those I love on earth; but by a great Divine law, we are permitted to watch over, and smooth the path toward the future of those who think us dead, when true life exists only in a second existence. Yes, this is our first moment of sweet communion, since my form was placed beneath the earth; but it is only one in the long years that I shall now enjoy, talking almost daily with thee in this way.

Thy loving wife,

Elizabeth Wade.

It was perfectly apparent, that the spirit's *wading* the stream was to suggest her name, and the incident made a deep impression on the circle. With the exception of Mr. Bonner, the party had seen little before, and withheld their names, until the close of the séance, when they kindly gave the address affixed to the commencement of this article.

Mr. Sam'l. Morgan and wife, of Albany, in company with Ex-Governor Tallmadge, paid a visit to my room, and Mr. Morgan was the recipient of a favor of somewhat the same nature as the foregoing. A spirit addressed Mrs. Morgan thus :

DEAR, DEAR MOTHER:—

Did you know that while you sat at the table of the other medium (the company had just returned from a séance with Mrs. Hayden) I was standing by thy left, and I did want to unbosom my spirit as freely as though I was mortal, that you might know and feel these truths as I do? I cannot blame you for not receiving them with the same ease as ourselves, for I well know you are mortal, but still God hath decreed that all are immortal, and hence at some future time my spirit shall go with thee, and exhibit the beauties of these laws of divinity. I shall attend you at home, beloved mother, and even when thy needle mends some rent in mortal garments, I will labor to mend thy spirit with the needle of divine philosophy.

Thy Daughter, CAROLINE.

Father Russell sent his love to you, and bade me say, "his spirit would be with you often." He wishes you to keep choicely all communications you receive.

During this interview, I observed a spirit actively engaged, building a miniature bridge from the bureau to the mantle-piece, the distance between them being about ten feet. He carefully laid the planks across, then descended, took up huge stones, and began building a wall on each side of the bridge ; occasionally looking toward me and smiling, as if pleased with the attention I was showing him. As he progressed in these labors, I described them to the circle. I could distinctly see the water flowing beneath the bridge, and as his task was finished he pointed first at the wall then at the bridge, until seeing my inability to comprehend, he seized my hand and communicated,

"Why do you not understand? I want to make you know my name E. W. WALBRIDGE.

The incident it will be seen revealed his name, and general satisfaction was expressed by the circle at the result. The spirit was a brother-in-law of Mr. Morgan.

The communicating intelligence, in one instance, bade the circle keep quiet, and a vision would be given the medium. Immediately a spirit presented itself; standing by the side of one of the party he bared his arm, and drawing a lancet, opened the median cephalic vein, from which the blood oozed freely; the stream from his arm fell upon the table. Laying down the lancet, he pointed at the blood. This was, indeed, plain enough. I asked the gentleman who was sitting with me, if he had a friend by the name of Blood. His reply was in the affirmative, and the spirit quickly answered,

I am present. Thy Spirit Guide, O. H. BLOOD.

At one of my select public circles, a lady spirit

presented herself, whose entire dress was composed of English flags; she also waved a similar flag in her hand. This vision was described to the circle, when, with her finger, she wrote in the atmosphere the name of *Jane;* immediately one of the party recognized the spirit as a friend of his, calling her "Jane English." With this she seemed much gratified; and, as Dr. Orton remarks, in his letter to the *Banner of Light,* "the gentleman was so strongly taken hold of by some invisible power under the table, that he sprang from his seat, with evident marks of alarm."

At the same circle, an elderly male spirit, with a bald head, appeared rolling a ball across the floor, from which he took small round substances, and biting them, pronounced the word "Bitter!" A communication was immediately written to Mr. Barlow Smith, and signed *Gall,* in which he (the spirit) said, he had been endeavoring to symbolize his name to the medium, by representing a head, and tasting a gall nut. Mr. Smith was a phrenologist, and hence the affinity that existed between him and the immortal founder of that science.

Referring to the great truths of Spiritualism, a spirit, addressing an investigator, says:—

'Tis like the mirrored water
  Still wrapped in beauty pure,
Indulging angel laughter
  As it flows along the moor.

'Tis like the sweetest singing
  Of some warbler from the spheres—
A sweet love is that ringing,
  When it strikes on mortal ears.

Blest one, be faithful—onward wander
  Through the crosses you may bear;
Take the book of life and ponder,
  Fresher beauties still are there.

CHAPTER XVI.

Proceedings of the Boston Investigating Committee, Professor Horsford, Peirce, Agassiz, Dr. B. A. Gould, &c., held at the Albion Building, June 25th, 26th, 27th, 1857.

By request of Dr. H. F. Gardner, I became one of the mediums to meet the above named gentlemen for the purpose of affording them every facility in our power, for a scientific, rational, and honorable investigation of the phenomena of Spiritual Manifestations. Dr. Gardner was induced to give the above party all the opportunity in his power, from the appearance of an offer, through the columns of the Boston Courier, of five hundred dollars to the person or persons, who would give satisfactory and conclusive exhibitions of the supermundane character of the manifestations called Spiritual. Dr. G.'s acceptance of this offer was *not* for the money proffered, for this was withdrawn by his (Dr. G.'s) special request, but to satisfy the Courier that these developments actually originated outside of the influences of the media, through whom they were produced.

The mediums engaged for this purpose were, Miss

Katy Fox, Mrs. Brown, (of the Fox family,) Mr. J. V. Mansfield, Mrs. Kendrick, the Davenport boys, and myself. To obtain this combined mediumistic power, Dr. Gardner spared neither time nor expense; and the outlay was not inconsiderable, as most of the mediums resided at a distance from Boston. Undaunted by difficulties, the Doctor made all due preparation and the media assembled to meet the honorable savans.

The referees were the before mentioned gentlemen, viz: Professors Horsford, Peirce, Agassiz of Harvard College, Dr. A. B. Gould, and a Reporter of the Courier: the apartment selected (which was tendered for the occasion by the kindness of L. A. Huntington) was room No. 12, Albion Building, corner of Beacon and Tremont Streets. A raised platform was placed in the centre of the room, that the vibrations or raps might be more distinctly heard: all being arranged to the satisfaction of the committee, the first meeting was appointed for June 25th, at 11 o'clock, A. M. On the side of the Spiritualists were, Dr. Gardner, and Alvin Adams, Esq., of Boston; Mr. Allen Putnam, of Roxbury; Major Raines, of New York; Mr. Robert Carter, of Cambridge. Miss Katy Fox, and Mrs. Brown as mediums.

The circle formed consisted of Mr. Adams, Major Raines, Dr. Bell, and the mediums. Loud raps were soon heard on the platform, and the intelligence requested, that the room should be more thoroughly ventilated. Communications were short and few, the company being more desirous of ascertaining the *cause* of the raps, than the matter elicited from them. The ladies were requested to stand upon a stool; but the same demonstration by raps continued; then they were asked to step on a chair, which was attended with the like result. The spirits were asked to rap ten times, to which they responded by loud concussions, of the designated number.

Professor Peirce asked several questions, and received unsatisfactory replies. The pine table was changed for a long extension, and all requested to join the circle; to this some acceded—among the refusers was Mr. Agassiz. I would say here, that previous to the meeting, the committee (with the exception of Mr. Agassiz,) had made an agreement in writing to organize according to the received rules of circles, and conform, as far as in them lay, to make conditions harmonious; here was deviation No. 1. The very refusal of Agassiz to sit at the table and thereby form a complete circle, tended to produce disquietude and restlessness on the part of all. The issue was (as might have been expected) unsatisfactory, and nothing was obtained but a few indistinct responses to questions put by Doctor Gardner. It being asked, why the manifestations were suspended, and who (if any of the party) were the cause? The answers intimated Mr. Agassiz and the other members who, like him, refused to comply with the requisite conditions. The objectionable party left the room, but their absence created no change; they re-entered, and the mediums standing on a sofa, answers by raps were given to inquiries; the mediums touching the door, sounds were likewise readily produced, and after a few demonstrations of this kind, the party retired to meet again on Friday 26th, at the same hour.

Friday. Present, Messrs. Gardner, Gould, Bell, Peirce, Raines, Huntington (lessee of the Albion,) Putnam, Adams. Myself the medium.

One leaf was taken out of the table by Dr. G., and the formation of the circle was delayed till the arrival of Mr. Agassiz; he shortly came, and eyeing me with no benevolent expression of countenance, said to a by-stander, "That's Redman, is it?" He was told that it was. "Well!" said the *hero*, "I should know him to be an impostor at the first glance." This remark was related to me after the adjournment of the circle, by one who heard it; and I must say, such a comment argues little in favor of the claim to the title of *gentleman*, or to the character of Christian in any man, especially in one professing to examine a subject presented to his investigation with an impartial and unprejudiced mind. The circle was formed on the entrance of the Professor; Mr. Agassiz, however, and two others remaining out of the party, as on the previous day. Inquiry was made, if there were any spirits present, and an affirmative response given, upon which, Mr. Agassiz, to more closely inspect my acts, moved cautiously behind me. Some one in the circle suggested the propriety of writing names on ballots: the members commenced complying with the proposition, subject of course to the yea and nay of Mr. Agassiz, as to what names should be written, as he demanded of one of the party to throw away first one pellet and then another. He was importuned to join the circle; but, no, he averred that he had sworn never to sit in a circle, and he meant to adhere to his oath.

Query—For what was he present?

Receiving no manifestations of any consequence, Dr. Gardner and myself retired to an ante-room to inquire what next should be done, and the cause of the apparent failure. Scarcely were we seated at the table, when it moved violently, and a communication was written, from right to left, to the purport, that unless all present were willing to receive, and shaped their actions accordingly, nothing could be done. We announced the substance of the message to the party: Mr. Agassiz desired to see the manuscript; it was shown to him, when, without hesitation, he declared *I* had written it, and "that it was sheer humbug;" that "any one could have written the same." This harangue was entirely unnecessary on his part, as we were well aware that the thing could have been done by practice, and had it been done in the usual manner, we should have given it the same credence, so the denunciation of the Professor was wholly uncalled for.

I now politely invited Mr. Agassiz to join me in the ante-room, and we would try alone, that no doubt we would be more successful, and perhaps receive the same demonstration which had just been given to Dr. G. and myself. "Sit with you," said Mr. A. "No! I have resolved to sit with no one. I made up my mind before coming here, that nothing would come of it, and I am only the more convinced it is all deception." I could say no more. The opportunity was afforded him to enlighten himself, his refusing to do so manifested little inclination to test the subject, the object of his assumed examination seeming to be solely for the purpose of casting upon a sacred theme ungentlemanly ridicule and ignorant sarcasm, which might have weight with those, who being unenlightened themselves, and trusting to his supposed candid investigation of so all-important a subject, would probably be influenced by his representations. Dr. Gardner remonstrated against the refusal of the committee to investigate fairly, reminding them of their written agreement to abide by the ordinary rules of the spirit circle. Some discussion ensued, and we broke up in disorder to meet again at 4 P. M.

Dr. Gardner reduced the size of the table, and a circle formed around it, composed of Mrs. Kendrick, Mrs. Mansfield, Messrs. Bell, Mansfield, Peirce, Adams, Putnam, Gardner.

Mr. Mansfield, being known as a test medium for answering sealed letters, one had been prepared by Professor Horsford, and was submitted to the circle. Mr. Mansfield was influenced to take the letter, and his hand passed over it, as if the spirits were reading its contents, through the influence obtained from his finger ends, but no answer was given. The medium changed seats, and another sealed note was laid on the table ; but it shared the same fate as its predecessor ; no satisfaction could be obtained as to its contents. The circle remained in situ till near five o'clock, without any intelligent sequence. Mr. Mansfield and Dr. Gardner repaired to a small room alone, and the spirits through Mr. M. declared their inability to proceed for the same reason they had assigned before. Thus two days had passed without the committee attaining any nearer approach to the truth than when they first began. They again adjourned to renew efforts (rendered futile by their own acts) on the morrow.

Saturday, at half past ten o'clock, a circle was formed, consisting of Mr. Mansfield, Dr. Gardner, Capt'n. Ailing and myself, the rest of the company scattered over the room in no very orderly manner. Three-quarters of an hour passed, and not one trifling indication of spiritual presence was observed. Mr. Adams and myself went into the adjoining apartment, and manifestations were instantaneous; still in the large room with its unquiet surroundings nothing could be obtained. Another adjournment till four o'clock ensued.

At this hour the committee were present with the exception of two, who were elsewhere engaged.

The utter inutility of attempting to induce any demonstrations of merit from spirits or mortals in such a confused and confounded mass of opposing influences was so apparent, that we (mediums) unanimously declined subjecting ourselves longer to the sneering ridicule of certain members of the committee. The séance was, therefore, abandoned to be renewed at 8 o'clock.

8 o'clock, P. M.—Present: The Committee, Messrs. Adams, Bell, Huntington, Gardner, Carter, Putnam, Davenport and his two sons.

This meeting was arranged for the purpose of testing the Davenport Manifestations. A rough pine box had been constructed large enough to contain the two boys, and on its inner side were two benches or seats for the accommodation of the mediums. The box stood upon four upright posts; holes were bored through the sides for the passage of the ropes with which the boys were to be tied, a large door with a bolt inside completed the coop. The boys entering were securely fastened with stout cords, by three of the committee, Dr. Gould, Professors Horsford and Wyman. The cords were first passed tightly round the wrist, giving only room for due arterial circulation. The wrists were then brought close together behind them ; their ankles were similarly confined, and the rope carried through holes in the seats, brought up over their chests, put through holes in the box over their shoulders, then firmly knotted outside, and the ends carried back through other holes into the box. A rope was likewise passed on each side of their necks and also secured. Dr. Wyman and Dr. Bell tied the cords which fastened their wrists with threads ; passing the threads between each finger on each side. The young men were certainly as secure as prisoners need be ; but not yet contented, and fearing lest the boys should untie themselves, a semi-circle, composed of Professor Agassiz and others, faced the box, and Professor Pierce entered it, taking his seat in the rear between the boys, who were *vis-à-vis* to each other. He next gathered all the instruments, consisting of two tambourines, one violin, a tin horn, banjo, &c., between his legs. Truly ridiculous must he have appeared to those out of the form who were observing him, as much so I think, as if entering an operating telegraph office he should take the battery wires and all the other apparatus between his knees, bind the operator with two hundred feet of rope, and then command him to send or receive a message from New

York. If passivity be a requirement, by which the manifestations of our spirit friends are to be forwarded, the condition in which the Davenports were placed, would scarcely tend to develop that principle. I am inclined to think, also, if the learned gentlemen ever expect to obtain even a glimpse of spiritual demonstration under such a high pressure of determined resistance and bigoted prejudice, they will be most egregiously disappointed. Notwithstanding the galaxy of science, the array of caution, the Argus-eyed intelligence of old Harvard's learned Dominis, one of the mediums was freed, and the carefully knotted rope was found lying untied at his feet. Because the spirits did not untie the finely knotted thread, it was pronounced imposture. I would enquire of the august body, if they would stop to untie a needle full of cotton, when by a simple effort it could easily be broken? I do not believe the gentlemen would hesitate long were they in durance and had power to liberate themselves. The Davenports were not to be tied with threads, but ropes, long and strong, and it was reasonable to suppose that on untying the ropes the threads would be broken.

Thus terminated the so-called Boston Investigation! It was asserted by Mr. Agassiz, that he would produce a person who could make raps accompanied with intelligence, and perform other feats related by Dr. Gardner. This, however, has never been done. The report of the committee, long and anxiously looked for, has also failed to make its appearance before the public.

I have endeavored to give as nearly as possible, a correct statement of the proceedings as they occurred. The result ultimated precisely as foretold by me to Dr. Gardner, previous to my leaving New York for the purpose

> "And shall we own such judgment? No!—as soon
> Seek roses in December—ice in June;
> Hope constancy in wind!"

CHAPTER XVII.

Abbott Lawrence as a Spirit, Continued. Mr. A. C. Fletcher as an Investigator. H. B. Witty's Experience. Mr. P. R. Skinner's initiation.

"From the bright stars, or from the viewless air,
Or from some world unreached by human thought,
Spirit, sweet Spirit! if thy home be there,
And if thy visions with the past be fraught,
Answer me, answer me!"

Abbott Lawrence as a Spirit.

No. 5. Here I was joined by a circle of spirits, with whom, on earth, I had the utmost sympathy; and although they occupy different spheres, yet they were permitted to greet me in this stage of my interior development; this circle was composed of my guardian Jacob, Amos, Benjamin Franklin, Isaac Newton, Margaret Ossoli Fuller, Wm. Penn, Martin Luther, Philip Mowbray, Walter Scott, and Benjamin West. The presence of such a group, all happily welcoming me to the seraph land, was indeed a stimulant, and after exchanging a few words of friendship with each, I joyously agreed to accompany them to the Temple of Unity. With Franklin I was especially charmed; he seemed so anxious to open to my mind the modus operandi of communication with mortals, and invited me to go with him to a circle, of which he was a member, as soon as I had received the initiatory degree of the Temple. By Mrs. Fuller I was cordially greeted, and as her little angel boy stood by her side, she graphically portrayed to me, her first sensations on entering the second stage of exisence. Her husband was absent; she assured me, however, they were together, but duty to a lower sphere had called him from her at that time. A free and hearty shake of friendship was mine from Wm. Penn; delight pervaded his countenance, every lineament of which was expressive of wisdom and piety. Next came Martin Luther, with him I was not so familiar; but his noble qualities of simple purity, and his apparently deep interest in my progression, bade my soul blend with his, and in brotherly love we embraced. Walter Scott, with his friend Philip Mowbray, next approached, and I was the recipient of their kind offices to add harmony to my thirst for progression. Last came Benjamin West, and instinctively I clasped his hand with a warmth of fellowship which, (though we had never met in earth-life) seemed to have existed through all time. This meeting of congenial souls over, we turned our steps towards the Temple, and with little effort, an immeasurable distance was overcome.

I beheld, on drawing near, a second city as it were, lighted by illuminated globes, apparently suspended over its centre. "This," said Jacob, "is the City of Temples: here all newly initiated spirits receive the degree of progress; the talents thou hast employed on earth are to receive addition to the principal, and the usury delivered to the owner." We entered a mammoth edifice, where crystal walls seemed windows of light, and on each of the four domes, that surmounted it, stood a reporting angel. Our group did not enter alone, for in our rear were thousands with the same intent as ourselves: as we passed beneath the porch, our names were registered by the angelic scribes above us.

The interior of this lovely palace surpassed all description. On an elevated circular-platform, in the centre of the vast hall, stood a spirit clothed in flowing garments of lily white; his very presence diffused a holy light over the apartment: and near him, on platforms apparently of polished silver, sat six others less elevated than himself; there seemed to be a gradual diminution from the exalted seraph, to the lowest of the seven. My new nature could hardly comprehend the sight, and the vast multitude assembled, appeared as much paralyzed with the holy scene as myself. A heavenly melody pervaded the space, and the spirits swayed to and fro as if in tune with the harmony from unseen fingers. I turned toward Franklin, he understood my desire, and informed me that here my stage of development would be revealed; that in this sacred Temple, mothers, fathers, sisters, brothers, husbands, wives, and friends, received their respective degrees, and were from here transported or directed to their several circles by the attending guides of the Temple. As he spoke, there seemed to be involuntary divisions in the surrounding multitude, and when I looked again, we were divided into seven distinct triangular groups, each facing one of the seven Celestials. The group of which I was a member, represented the third, and from this division I was made aware of my spheric condition in the realms eternal. A complete separation being established, there arose a harmony more heavenly than before, and I was surprised to perceive the two lower triangles appeared to be stung to the soul by these notes of perfect bliss; each strain seemed to gore their very vitals, and the pitiful expression of despair there pictured, I pray never more to behold. The first evinced more distress than the second; while those in the triangle above my own, entered into the harmonic loveliness with more rapture than I did.

Franklin, again approaching me, said, "Those above thee have progressed from thy circle; those below thee, are fresh from the garden Earth, as are many in thy own condition. The happiness of those above, stings the polluted centre of the less elevated; and as thou dost rise in the scale of love, purity, good-will, and truth, as thou art here divided and promoted, so shall thy joy be measured."

At this moment a chant, as if from millions of voices, rent the holy air around, and the seven divisions separated, each to its given sphere. As I passed beneath the high arch of pearl, that gave me exit into the soft atmosphere without, I distinctly caught these words, chanted by angelic voices:

"Hasten, oh! ye hosts of heaven,
Prune the vine within thy bower;
Drop in famished souls, the leaven
Of God's goodness, love, and power."

Emerging fully into the sublime world without, I was joined by my friend Robert G. Shaw, who evinced great delight at seeing me; with him was Wm. E. Channing and Melancthon. Joining our already glorified band, they all conducted me to my study in the Third Heaven. Here I was left in the temporary charge of Franklin, to whom I am indebted for my present knowledge of spiritual communion. Without his kind and voluntary efforts, I might, perhaps, now have been a comparative stranger to its philosophy, although in time I should have become fully acquainted therewith.

I was first introduced by Franklin to a circle in Philadelphia, where I saw collected about twenty or more persons. As we approached the scene, we observed below us, and above each member of the circle, his or her guardian spirit. When within about twenty feet of the party, Franklin bade me approach no closer, as the method of communicating could not be as effectively perceived on a nearer proximity.

Conceive, if you can, the interest I experienced on distinctly seeing the table rise without mortal contact. There was more than one circle of mortals, one being formed within the other. As the table rose I saw a distinct electric light emanate from each of the guardian spirits present, and all converging to the centre; then by quickly withdrawing that influence, it acted as the power of loadstone upon steel, raising the table at each successive withdrawal. I also observed a peculiar floating fluid above the medium, and as these converging lights, or any one of them came in contact with this peculiar and (as I learned from Franklin) negative principle, concussions were produced loud enough to be heard at some distance. As the medium asked questions, the responses would be given by an attending spirit, by the contact of the active fluid with the inactive or passive. I observed two other immortals approaching, and learned they had been summoned by a desire of the circle. They saluted us as they came up, and passed to the opposite side of the room, keeping at the same distance from the gathering as ourselves. The guardian of the medium recognized them, and the three joining hands, I beheld two streams of the refined fluid passing from the brain of the spirit attendant on the medium to the *medium's* brain. I inquired of Franklin the cause or philosophy of the two threads of light. "They are called," said he, "the afferent and the efferent pole, and govern the corresponding nerves of the person through whom we desire to hold communion." As the hand of the medium moved, the effect was almost dazzling, and to my inexpressible delight, I found I could, in a trifling degree, influence the hand of a young lady, in the same manner, though with less result, by a concentration of the will.

This was to me a most instructive and gratifying period in my new existence, and the reflection of one day placing this experience on the memory of earth friends was intensely inspiring.

I returned to my studies in the spheres, and found Jacob and Amos ready for my reception ; and as I related the occurrence of my first communication with earth, they congratulated me on the prospects of my glistening future.

My principal study here was the relative density of the spiritual essence compared with the elements, that give it action ; also the comparative degree of refinement necessary for a spirit to attain a certain degree of locomotive velocity ; because, as you are not aware, the more sublimated the progressed individuality, the greater is its power over the atmosphere in which it moves. As you may imagine, this is no simple primary problem, and a certain portion of my time is daily spent in its solution. I have free communication with the higher conditions, though I cannot pass into them. My interviews with their inmates is by their visits to me, which are, indeed, advantageous and necessary for my desired development. I am visited by many whom you know not, and also by those whom history has crowned with earthly honor. Among them may be noticed many of our revolutionary celebrities, and indeed the very act of declaring their independence in that instance of our country's welfare, has linked them in brotherly bands, which though they are in different spheres still enables them to energetically labor for the grand union, which awaits us all in the seventh heaven.

I wish to give you, as near as possible, a description of what I designate as my studio; and when I declare to you the existence of things similar to those you have on earth, think it not strange, for the beauties of the mundane life are not destroyed on entering the immortal home, as many suppose, but are in fact continued on a scale of supreme grandeur as you progress. The All-Wise Creator did not place beauties before the material sympathies to have them blasted by opposite conditions in a future state. No! his wisdom decrees, that

"On one grand whole, the basis of our love shall stand,
And, as we rise, our wisdom view them grand."

An immense plain, dotted with miniature lakes, and studded with circular gardens that contain never withering flowers, whose fragrance renders the atmosphere one continual breath of sweetest fragrance, where no uninstructed gardener mutilates the beauties that present themselves constantly to the spirit vision, is the scene of my diurnal routine of study. An elevated point, which is reached by a winding staircase conducts to a small but busy mansion, whence with this vast field of perfection before me, I can expand my powers of comparison, the better to solve the problem given before, which is the base of the third principle presented to the mind of the freed mortal.

As we rise in spirit-life, we are located where surroundings may better conduce to the acquisition of the principles before us; hence my present locality affords me every opportunity to separate, one by one, the component parts of that question—"The velocity of spirit compared with the density of surrounding elements."

Combined with my daily study, I am required to lend developing influences to those in the second sphere; this duty consists in visiting the twelfth circle of that condition; in teaching, strengthening, and giving hope to those whose organized ambition bids them strive for our higher home.

The problem of the second sphere is, "The formation of the immortal germ, its requisite proportion, and the manner in which it enters the human organization."

My *third* duty is, to visit earth and assist in severing the imprisoned spirit, as the mortal form desires to part with its life principle. I am not confined to any particular class of persons to accomplish this end, as far as sex is concerned; but I can only attend those, whose developed intelligence and acuteness of perception qualify them for the same degree from the Temple as myself. It is indeed a holy, pleasing sight, to see the myriad angelic beings hastily overcoming space, for the purpose of extending a helping hand to those whose earth lamp is flickering in its socket, and waiting only for the guardian of its peace to give it a new flame, a brilliant resplendence.

These are our three most important duties, which, together with the time devoted to feeding the infant of "communion with earth," deprives us of the epithet of *Idlers*.

He, who imagines that Heaven presents simply flower-beds of rest, where he pillows his head in orange buds, and fills his mattress of indolence with flowers of the cape jessamine, is deeply at fault; for where we rest on earth, we toil in spirit life, and where we toil on earth, we doubly labor in our second home.

I was introduced to this medium by John Hancock, who was one of the first spirits that developed the *floating* susceptibility above him; and I can, through him, quite freely give expression to my thoughts, my ability to do so continually increasing. At first I experienced much difficulty in giving my ideas clearly, even through him, and frequently was forced to use a second medium: but now I come personally, and can, with comparative freedom, open to you the journal of my daily progress in spirit life, which, though at times, you may not comprehend, yet it may serve as a preparatory lesson, and possibly fit you for the same circle, in which I enjoy a knowledge of the Divine attributes.

MR. A. C. FLETCHER AS AN INVESTIGATOR.

In the month of August, 1856, began my acquaintance with Dr. G. A. Redman. Agreeably to appointment, in the afternoon of the day of his arrival in Cincinnati, I visited his room to obtain a séance. We took our seats at a table about four feet square, and at his request I wrote upon small bits of paper the names of several relations and friends. These bits of paper were afterwards rolled up and thrown together in the centre of the table. I took them up one at a time, asking aloud, whether the spirit answering to the name I held in my hand would communicate with me. After taking up several and receiving no response, for I had purposely written the names of those who were still living, I wrote a few more and added them to the others. From among these I then took one, and upon the instant heard a succession of loud raps, which were accompanied by a violent rocking of the table towards me. I asked if the spirit present would write the name inscribed upon the paper in my hand. The hand of the medium was seized, and the name, "Emma," written. I opened the bit of paper and it contained the name "Emma." Convinced then of the identity of the being I had met eight years before, with that of the intelligence, whose presence had been just manifested, I sought eagerly to enter more closely into rapport with her, and for that purpose the medium was entranced, and his body for a time became the receptacle of the purest and best spirit that ever dwelt among men. Then truly we conversed face to face, and the past returned like a forgotten dream. I recalled the brief hours we had enjoyed and my parting words, now after a lapse of nearly eight years realized, "We may never meet again on earth, but I'll meet you, Emma, in heaven." She recounted the circumstances of her departure from the body, and her experience in the inner life; with what labors and struggles she had guided and impressed me almost from the hour she became a spirit; our destiny on the earth and in spirit life, in language so exquisitely beautiful, that while she spoke, I seemed to be enjoying the perfume of a garden of roses.

For several days afterwards, each afternoon, I enjoyed these delightful re-unions, asking questions of earth and heaven; the past and the future, until the day of departure of our mutual friend and brother was announced. At the conclusion of one of these meetings, Emma presented to me the pencil (of gutta percha) with which she had written through the medium, which I still retain and value as a cherished memorial of the happiest hours of my life.

I went one Sunday morning, previous to the medium's departure from the city, to have (for a length of time) my final séance. Taking my seat at the table, Emma informed me that she intended to write me a communication with her own hand. For this purpose a piece of paper and the gutta percha pencil were placed upon the lid of a paper box reversed, that they might not roll off, and held under the table by the right hand of the medium with one end resting on my knees, while the left hand of the medium, and both of mine, were placed upon the table above. After a moment of quiet, the pencil was seized, and I heard a slight scratching upon the paper. Suddenly it fell, and the box was placed upon the table, when I beheld written in most delicate characters the following communication:

MY DEAR, DEAR, ONLY COMPANION—

Thy sweet presence fills my spirit with the deepest sense of joy. O! how can my spirit breathe the emotions that fill its interior. Great is thy duty, blessed one, and thy future shall be greeted by unseen millions. O, Addie, I love thee, and am ever present. Ever do I walk with thee, and when thy soul responds to mine, heaven shouts with joy.

Thy angel mate,

EMMA.

Of the hundreds of communications I have since received, not one remains. This brief and simple note embraces all, and this alone I have retained.

A few months after Dr. Redman left the city, I addressed a letter to him, (he at that time residing in Boston,) and accompanying his reply, received a note from Emma. This was the commencement of a correspondence that, ever since then, has been uninterrupted, and which has afforded to me a solace and comfort in the mental anxieties of life, so far transcending every earthly sympathy and affection, that disappointment and self-denial have been to me a blessing and a joy.

In the Spring of 1857, I visited the City of New York, and there received a hearty welcome from the spirit land, through my dear friend, who had removed thither. Our delightful meetings were again renewed, and during my stay of three weeks, I received a daily offering of truth and hope, from the beautiful spirit, whose presence, like the sun, was a radiance of unceasing light. The correspondence was continued until the ensuing August, when Dr. Redman visited Cincinnati a second time, accompanied by his wife. During this visit, two little incidents occurred.

One day, Dr. Redman and myself took dinner at a restaurant, and having occasion there to make use of the pencil Emma had given me, it was accidentally left behind upon the table. Leaving the saloon, I had proceeded more than a square before it was missed. I returned immediately, and after searching in vain, inquired if any waiter had taken it: they plead ignorance. As soon as we had returned to the Doctor's room, I related my misfortune to Emma: she quickly wrote upon the paper, "I know where it is. Shall I bring it to you?" "Yes, by all means, if you can," I answered. Hardly a minute had elapsed before the medium's hand was seized, and the words written, "The pencil is here; it was taken by one of the waiters, and was undergoing a minute examination, when I snatched it from his hand and brought it here." "But where is it?" I asked. "You must look for it," was the reply. I then searched the room carefully for some time, and was on the point of giving up, when 'twas found lodged in one of the openings of the cane bottomed chair, on which I had been sitting.

Shortly after this, one afternoon, just before the close of a séance, Emma said to me, (the medium being entranced) "I have brought you a little present." "What is it?" I asked. "A flower: I have been to the old home at Opelousas, and passing by the kitchen, I saw two growing on a bush near the door; I took one of them, and have brought it to you. After I leave the medium, look into your hat." I did so, and found a beautiful dome-shaped flower, of a species I had never before seen in this latitude, in field, garden, or hot-house. This flower I still possess, having carefully preserved it at the time.

On two subsequent occasions, I met Dr. Redman at Philadelphia, in the Fall of the same year; and at New York, in the Spring of 1858; and every time that I have been permitted to converse with my friends of the inner world, through him, the communications received, have been characterized by a spirit of reason, candor, and justice, that independently of their origin, would entitle them to that regard which all truth must receive, at the hands of every patient and investigating mind. A. C. FLETCHER.

I give below an unusually interesting letter from H. B. Witty, Esq., of Brooklyn, N. Y., a gentleman whose well-known veracity and shrewd perception, should entitle any statement of his to the entire confidence and belief of all honest and candid minds.

Being acquainted with Doctor Redman through his world-wide reputation as a Spiritual medium, and, also, from his being my family physician, I was induced to engage his services for an evening party at my home, No. 310 Navy Street. Punctual to the moment, the Doctor arrived, and found us all awaiting him—without other preliminaries than the usual introductions, we took our places round a common table, in order, if possible, to obtain some evidence of the communication of spirits with mortals. I cannot say I was skeptical of the fact myself, for I had had evidence of the presence of our spirit friends ere this; my chief object, therefore, in soliciting the presence of the Doctor, was for the benefit of friends, who were more or less doubtful and unconvinced.

We remained quietly seated, a stifled grin now and then the only disturber of the silence, till the table slowly tipped to one side. We moved back to give it room, and it continued to place itself at an acute angle; raising our hands, the table, thus disconnected, continued to rock slowly back and forth, we at the time, scrutinizing by the assistance of glaring gas light the whereabouts of the medium's feet. He moved away, and still to our astonishment the table continued its movements. We were at this time certainly from six to eight feet distant from it.

A large rocking chair that stood in one corner of the room started, and came very leisurely into the centre of our circle, taking the place of the table, which by its uneasy motions had changed its position. The chair was then elevated in mid air some two or three feet from the floor, no one being within yards of it, and all eyes fixed in wonder on its antics. Scarcely had our amazement commenced to wane, when the sofa, as if covetous of its neighbor's frolics, trotted out also, and we were preparing to witness a gay cotillion among the various articles of furniture, when the gas was slowly lowered by invisible power, and by the dim light, the dance began and continued unabated for some time, during which the gas was repeatedly turned on to its full strength, then slowly lowered to a dull, faint glimmer. This latter manifestation was to me as beautiful as any of the evening, for we could certainly feel we were on holy ground; no person was within possible reach of the fixtures, and we could plainly see each other. The large seven octave piano catching the contagion, performed its pas seul, so that the very walls shook—whether there were any invisible musicians I cannot say. We heard no music; but the instrument kept time as if cognizant of a spiritual orchestra. Three gentlemen thinking to put a stop to its fantasms, took their seats on its top; but lo! it tipped as before, and that too on the very side on which the party sat. Various questions were correctly answered by it, while in this condition, and after short communications were spelled out in the same manner, satisfied with the wonders of spiritual realities, the company adjourned.

At another time and with partly the same persons, we had the pleasure of an evening with the Doctor, after which I prevailed on him (as it was stormy) to spend the night with me. I had read his experience with Mr. Lanning, and I prepared myself with an armor of firmness and courage to encounter anything that might take place. Our sleeping apartment was the back parlor, shut off from the front by folding doors; our bed, a large French one, probably a counterpart of our friend Lanning's; the furniture of the room consisted of two large bureaus, some four or five chairs, mantle clock, and a settee. After my friend had tucked himself beneath the linen, I lowered the gas so as to afford us a dull light, yet sufficiently strong to enable me to dodge any pieces of the room's contents should they be thrown at me; then placing myself by the Doctor's side, I awaited the result of my recklessness. I began, silently, rehearsing the scenes of Redman's former visit, when a small chair came with great force, struck immediately above my head, and with a rebound fell upon the floor. The chair had been left in the front parlor, and been taken thence by this wonderful force. This startled me, and R. asked, "What was to pay?" His answer was given by loud raps, or rather thumps from all parts of the room and on the bed; and simultaneously with these he was lifted bodily in the air, carried over me, and thrown on the centre of the floor. "That's extremely cool," said Dr. R. I was about to respond, but I saw a daguerreotype start from the front room, and I dodged under the cover just in time to save myself, for it struck directly above me; the likeness proved to be one of my former wife. Redman scrambled back into bed; no sooner was he quietly covered up than the bedstead began to quiver and shake, as if with palsy, and raising like an air ship about three feet from the floor, sailed through the apartment, R. and myself clinging to each other in nervous fright; finally our aerial journey suddenly terminated by the bedstead bringing up against the wall on the opposite side of the room, where we landed. The bureaus now, each weighing, at least, one hundred pounds, shook themselves, and with a leap, bounded to our side and wedged our poor craft against the wall, so that we were indeed imprisoned. At this stage of the proceedings we were belabored most unmercifully with a pair of pants, which had been taken from a nail in the room, the while closely protecting our craniums with an extra amount of bed clothes, and holding each other's hands.

A pocket slate came rattling past our heads, and struck the wall. A second daguerreotype followed, that had also been taken from the adjoining room, and as it struck, opened, and I found it to be another miniature of my deceased companion. Sleep was impossible ; our eyes would hardly close before the bed would rise, or some inanimate object would assume the attributes of life, and start us from a labored doze.

I cannot say I objected to the dawn of that earnestly looked for morning, by which our night's experience was to be terminated ; and on turning the matter in my mind, at the present time, I do declare a few hundred dollars would not tempt me to a repetition of these tangible realities.

I would say to doubters, that in every instance related, I took all the precaution that my ingenuity could suggest, to detect deception ; but, in no case, was I the least able so to do, and I know—as I know I live—that the events of that night were super-mundane.

H. B. Witty,
316 Navy Street.

Mr. P. R. Skinner, of Anamosa, Iowa, and his first knowledge of Spiritual Communion.

Mr. Skinner, accompanied by two friends, per agreement, occupied my time, as a medium, for one hour, during which, Mr. S. was the grateful recipient of no ordinary tests of the fellowship of immortals.

We had been at the table but a short time, when a spirit announced himself as Gilbert Buckingham, and was readily recognized by Mr. Skinner ; a few written questions were responded to, and all influence in my arm ceased.

As I was writing of my own accord, on the paper

before me, a moving object in the distant part of the room, caused me to lift my eyes, and a lad presented himself to my vision. On his shoulder was a pole, and hung thereon were numerous skins of various animals; pacing the floor backward and forward a few times, he suddenly darted to one corner of the room, and seized what appeared to me to be a cat; then drawing a knife from a belt encircling his waist, he prepared to skin the animal, which he did with all the ease imaginable. Again catching another intruder, in a different part of the room, and stripping off its fur, he added it to his already accumulated burden. A lady in the circle immediately understood the significance of the vision. The spirit continued his operations of catching and unhiding these unfortunates, till I requested him to write; his compliance produced the following:

MY DEARLY LOVED FATHER—

I have come to meet you at this time. Oh! how my spirit loves to meet you here. I have furnished the vision to the medium, though it seems ridiculous, still I see you recognize it: it means *Skinner*, which you know is our name. I was happy in an instant, when I saw thee determined to come here, where I could make thy heart glad. Our dear friends are with me, and join in showing thee the laws of development. They all say they will work, that the river of thy impression may not be dammed by the impediments of earth, and especially those of church creeds. I know, you may think it strange, dear father, my thus speaking to you, but I have the help of those, who loved us both on earth. I shall never forget this meeting, it will be a gem of joy to be looked back upon. I shall remain and return with you, loved father, and when at home, I shall try to shed my genial influences over thy loving spirit. Thy son,

ALVIN R. SKINNER.

Mr. S. exhibited, by his countenance, the effect of his child's appeal, and though a few moments before he may have said

"We mourn thee! yes! thy place is void
Within our hearts—there veiled, thine image dwells."

He now could draw aside that veil, and bid the affections of a father meet in daily intercourse the object of his parental regard.

CHAPTER XVIII.

Leaves from the Experience of Mrs. M. R. Tucker.

He, that hath passed o'er life's heaving billows,
Still guides my canoe toward the opposite shore,
Where loved ones united on eternal pillows,
May rest thro' all time, to be parted no more.

The loss of a dearly cherished husband directed my attention to the excitement of the day with regard to the subject of Spirit Communion. Till this overwhelming affliction I had been a firm believer in the doctrines of the Roman Catholic Church, but when

"With him
Joy had gone forth, and left the green earth dim;
As from the sun shut out on every side,
By the close veil of misery,"

I found its teachings wholly, absolutely, totally inefficacious in affording any relief to my sorrow-stricken mind. My loved one, while on earth, had ever maintained that its inculcations were utterly at variance with reason and common sense. I was well aware what was the Catholic doctrine relative to those without its pale, and feeling that its local heaven would be no place of happiness for me, unshared by him (he was an Episcopalian) I revolted at its exclusiveness, and resolved to ascertain if there were one particle of truth, one shade of reality in the Spirit Manifestations, whether the sun of my existence were, indeed, entirely shut out by death's ruthless hand, or could still enlighten and cheer me with its beams through the remnant of life's lonely way.

In this frame of mind, I visited various mediums. You were not in New York in the dawning hours of my researches, but, having heard of your extraordinary mediatorial powers, the announcement in the Spiritual Telegraph of your arrival in the city, was the signal for my presenting myself at your abode, trusting that the hope, which had been enkindled in my crushed and sinking soul through others, would be confirmed by you. Truly, gratefully, thankfully do I acknowledge that it was, and repeatedly since have the sweet words of consolation, given through your hand, gladdened my desolate heart, and nerved my drooping spirit to the patient endurance of life's trials and toils, till my mundane mission accomplished and this earthly form laid in its lowly dwelling, I shall be reunited to him, my guardian angel, in that Morning Land, where sorrow, suffering, and above all, where separation can no more come.

You must pardon this dilation, for 'tis to me unavoidable, and now for some of my circles, which I cannot more fittingly introduce than by our first meeting.

Entering your room, and seating myself at a table, raps, loud, firm and clear, were immediately heard on the floor close by me; you, at the time, standing near the fire-place, which was at some little distance; you then taking your seat, and your hand being influenced, wrote:

"My Dear Wife.—'Tis I, your loving husband,

Robert."

Questions, unimportant to any save myself, next ensued, to which pertinent answers were returned, when I inquired,

"Do you know where I have been?"

"You've been to see me," and with the reply, you drew a coffin lid and on it a bunch of flowers. I had just returned from visiting his body's resting place, and on the coffin had left a bouquet.

After this I appointed an evening at my own residence, and the following is a succinct account of the physical manifestations of that to me never to be forgotten circle.

I first received a written communication, appertaining to private matters, when he added:

"We will make it a little darker, and then wait."

The gas being lowered, I placed my hand under the table, having previously, in compliance with your suggestion, enveloped it in a full-sized gentleman's pocket handkerchief; at the expiration of a few moments the handkerchief, after two or three powerful jerks, was pulled off my hand, and thrown on the floor, touching and resting close to my feet as it fell; the tips of my fingers were then several times distinctly touched, by other fingers which were warm and life-like. A pillow was taken from a bedstead, standing on the opposite side of the room from that on which we sat, dragged under the table towards me, (here let me remark, I distinctly heard the scraping of the pillow over the carpet, as it was drawn along,) and placed on my knees, where, after being left a few minutes, it was withdrawn, again dragged across the carpet, and replaced whence it had been brought. Next the handkerchief, which had been taken off my hand, was returned tied up in knots, and its dimensions reduced to a compact little package, of about three inches by two; this I prize most highly and have carefully preserved; therefore, if any one be desirous of viewing it, I shall always be happy to gratify their curiosity. Experiencing an intenseness of delight, which words can but feebly portray, and wishing to prolong moments so dear, I presented the loved promoter of this heaven-born bliss, with a case containing a daguerreotype of himself, that had been taken after he passed away; this was withdrawn from my hand, and in a little while, the likeness, without the case, returned; having been left in my hand some time, it was, at last, retaken by my dear one, replaced in the case, and handed back to me. When the case was closed, I distinctly heard the catch snap as it was fastened. I inquired of my husband, if the daguerreotype were one which had been given me by him;—rapping for the alphabet to be called over, he replied, "It was taken after I left."

At the close of the manifestations, he indicated the pleasure he had experienced, by loud raps, as if done by both hands, on the side of the bedstead, and so near to my feet, that the vibrations were plainly perceptible. The gas being relighted by his desire, he wrote through you:

"Don't you think, love, I've had a real jubilee? Indeed, I have enjoyed it more than I can express, and as I've been pretty active, I will not manifest more this evening, only remain with and bless you."

I asked if we should not thank the medium for the gratification he had been the means of affording us, and he answered:

"We are so gratified, that thanks are but poor words to express our obligations."

I will here observe, that it will be a work of supererogation for any one to attempt saying, what is here related was *not* spirit act, because I was sitting in such proximity to you, that it was in toto out of your power to have moved, without my being conscious of your doing so; that I was in full possession of my senses, and that no mortal being was in the room but you and myself.

I must not omit to add, it was at the termination of this, to me, most highly exciting but precious evening, that, as I was accompanying you down stairs, Cornelius Winne favored me by dropping one of his spinal bones in the passage-way, in a full blaze of gas light, and under circumstances that admitted of no collusion, for we were standing facing each other, you holding in one hand my spectacle case, and opening and shutting the top of it with your other, as we stood conversing at the bottom of the stairs. Concluding that this occurrence will be alluded to, in the account which I suppose you will give of Cornelius's wonderful performances, I merely refer to it here, for the purpose of saying, that having been deeply interested in the various reports which had been given, of the transportation of those bones from Hartford, I have ever thought that my husband induced Winne to drop the bone for my gratification; the *use* of it originating in his desire to do his utmost to strengthen my faith in spirit communion, knowing that by it alone would I be sustained and comforted, in the turmoil of life's heartless, weary way, which I was henceforth to tread, unblest by his visible presence.

This feast of delicious things only increasing my

desire for more ; on your return to New York, after your painful sojourn in Hartford, I appointed another evening for blessed commune. Dear and holy it was ; but for fear of intruding too much on your valuable time only one manifestation will I relate.

The gas was requested to be lowered, and with the request was subjoined the following :

> "'Tis not that our deeds are evil, nor that we wish to hide them under a bushel ; but it is, that we may silently approach each other, and feel as if naught else were near."

The gas was now put out, and by the alphabet was spelt to put my hand under the table. I was then touched by fingers, as distinctly as I ever felt fingers ; then there was something of a smooth glossy nature rubbed gently over the ends of mine, and ultimately to my extatic delight given to me. This little gift I put in my left hand, and replaced my right one under the table with the palm upwards ; it was taken and turned over, and on the back firmly clasped by a perfect hand, and not only clasped but held for a second or two. And where were the medium's hands? says the reader. Well, doubter, on the table under my left hand. A few other manifestations ensued, when we relighted, and this was written :

> "You see, loved one, my great joy is fulfilled. I have grasped thy hand again, and I pray, that as the compass guides the mariner on the sea of life, so shall I guide thee through these waves of mortality."

Alluding to this, my inestimable treasure, in a subsequent communication, he says :

"It was a great undertaking for me, love, but still I worked for weeks to bring about what I accomplished that night, and to see you prize it so much makes me enjoy it more. May it serve as a link to show us that the spirit world is but a hair's breadth from the material."

The following communication I send because I think it peculiarly characteristic of my husband. He was in his early days, what is technically called a "sea-captain."

"My own bark on a mortal ocean:—

While thy hull is floating on the sea of mortal trials, and the waves of perplexity run high; when the east or the south wester blows, and makes thee anxious; when thy masts of patience seem sprung, and thy cargo of hope and happiness seems dampened by the waters of earthly care; when the wheel seems broken by pain, or the bulwarks disturbed by any element, whatsoever, during this voyage of life; remember, there is a Captain at hand, whose love is like a doubled cable, and whose firmness equals and strengthens that love. He will brace up thy bowsprit, and cheer thy drooping sails of hope with gentle breezes of affection from the south. Who is that Captain? Dearie, it is old Captain

TUCKER,

Who ever knows, or tries to know where to drop his

ANCHOR."

At another session with you (and for the benefit of those, who love to cavil, I would state that it was in the early part of the afternoon, and as no measures were taken to darken heaven's light, your every act was clearly visible) my husband wrote for paper and a pencil to be placed on the back of a book, and for you to hold them under the table; this you did, your left hand at the same time resting on the table. While you were thus situated, I heard the pencil as it scratched over the paper, and when it was dropped, and the book withdrawn, I received this:

"Our little darlings have written, and Lovedrop is the correspondent. Ah! dearie! stranger things than these shalt thou see ere you come to your

ROBERT."

I must confess I did not exactly understand what was meant by this, at first; but concluded, as I had had a promise that my children would some day write to me, that he had made an error, and meant merely to renew the former assurance. He, perceiving my want of comprehension, wrote through you for me to leave the table and take a seat in a rocking chair on the opposite side of the room. I complied, and then first perceived a piece of paper pinned to my veil, which had been hanging on one side of my bonnet while I was at the table. Opening it, I found, in printed capitals, the ensuing little effusion. I am aware of all its defects; they are as obvious to me as they can be to others, but as a genuine spirit test its intrinsic worth is very great; and to me, the lonely mother and devotee to every thing truthful connected with spirit communion, the original is invaluable. Ere writing what was given, let me state that I was told after the circle, that one little darling wrote, and the other pinned the production to the veil:

"You think I'm not near you, dear Mother;
Thou hast two little guardian stars,—
I am one, dear sister's the other,
And we hear every moment thy prayers.

Our dear father, he learns us to spell,
That one word of delight we may give,
For we know thy dear nature so well,
We determined to tell thee, we live.

LOVEDROP."

Yet another communication, written without assistance from mortal hands, and I am done. The paper, on this occasion, was placed on the carpet, and I, the custodian of those hands of yours, through which flow such streams of soothing comfort to the joyless and disconsolate.

"MY DEAR WIFE—

How cold that seems beside the many epithets of endearment dealt out so freely by the world; but you alone know my soul, and know, also, that an eternity of dearer things than words dwells there; even a love surpassed only by God himself. I do not wait for thee to come, though thy body would fain place itself, this day, where decayed mortality finds a decomposing bed; but thy fruit hath not all dropped from the tree of usefulness; still many hang, as tempting morsels to the weary traveler, and though thy limbs will scarcely bear the tread to reach them, still they can be plucked by a voice and hand, that will but ask thee to shake thyself—I mean, shake those truths from thy soul. God bless you; and if there were a million gods, I'd beseech them *all* the same.

Thy faithful, loving husband,

ROBERT."

DOCTOR REDMAN,

DEAR SIR:—Having seen your notice in the Telegraph, I send you the foregoing. If among the multifarious experiences, which doubtless will be handed you, mine be deemed any way beneficial, I shall be pleased by your inserting them: but *you* alone can judge of this, and I, therefore, leave it entirely to your discretion to use them or not, as you may consider most advisable.

With much respect, I am,

M. R. TUCKER.

The Messenger Bird, as communicated to the "Banner of Light," by Dr. Orton, deserves insertion here; and I append it.

One of the most beautiful and extraordinary incidents in my spiritual experience, has occurred on this, as I write, Friday morning. At this very moment a beautiful white dove sits within a few feet of me, alternately gazing into my face, and adjusting its feathers, and stretching its wings, as though in anticipation of regaining that freedom from which I have temporarily restrained it, and soaring away in its native air. I am loath to part with it, for to me it was a messenger from the skies. It brought me a note, this morning, before I had risen, and delivered it at my bedside, from one who has many years been an inhabitant of the spirit-world. The note I have; and the bird I have; and the floss which bound the missive about the little postman's neck; and am able to give something of a satisfactory explanation of the way in which the messenger obtained an entrance to my chamber, while the door was shut and locked, and the blinds closed. The circumstances are as follows:

On Thursday, while sitting with Dr. Redman in his office, the spirit of a dear friend wrote through his hand the following sentence:

"Did you know, *******, I was preparing to make thee a present—a present in which I shall take another *form*, and be with you, so that you can *see* me?"

"Please explain," said I.

"No; time will explain," was written in reply. Keep this to thyself till that time comes."

Lost in wonder, I asked if this would soon occur. The answer was:

"*Yes!* within four days. Let this suffice, ****; do not wonder, but let thy mind *pass to something else.*"

Of the purport of this conversation, I am satisfied, Dr. Redman could known nothing. In giving the part of the spirit, he reached across a good breadth of the table—the full extent of his arm—and wrote on the paper lying before *me*, placing the letters in the natural position for me to read, but which made them to him inverted; and though I exhibited some surprise at the nature of the communication, I gave him no information on the subject.

The evening which succeeded, I passed wholly with Dr.

Redman. Between ten and eleven we retired to the same room and bed. I was a few minutes in advance of him, but he soon followed; we extinguished the light, and, after a little conversation, went to sleep.

In the morning I awoke early, and had been awake about an hour, part of which time had been passed in conversation between Dr. Redman and myself, when suddenly we were startled by the sound of wings, and a white dove flew across the room from the door to the window, and alighted upon the projecting wood-work above. The first question that arose was, how the little intruder could have found access to the chamber. The door was locked, and though the high window was open above and below for the free admission of air, the Venetian blinds were closed; and aside from the door and window, there was no place of entrance. Full of wonder, the thought occurred to me, whether this incident was not connected with the announcement of the day before, and I commenced looking about for some evidence which might afford a solution of the inquiry. On the carpet in front of the bed, was discovered a small piece of paper, folded square, of about the size of a quarter of a dollar, one part being slipped into the other, and a thread of floss, which had originally been tied with a square knot, but now gave full evidence of having been severed by force, passing through it. The missive, on being unfolded, was found to measure about four inches by three, and contained four lines of writing, or rather printing, in pencil, in the character employed by the House's telegraph. The first line was the address to myself, and the fourth was the signature, as follows:

** *** *********:

HAVE I NOT REDEEMED MY PROMISE?

*********.

At a late hour of the morning, I had another conversation with the spirit of my friend, through the same channel, and under the same conditions, as before. It was as follows:

"*********, I thank you from my heart for your present."

This I wrote, and the following was immediately written in reply:

"*******, there is no way in which I could come to thy very face, like that. You wondered, didn't you?"

"Did the dove come into the chamber *this morning*?"

"About *midnight*."

"Through the lattice?"

"YES, I *bade* it, or influenced it by my own spirit, which had embodied it, to contract its form. The spirit-world is even now rejoicing *with me* over it?"

"Where was the note written?"

"I wrote it through an entranced medium."

"Through Redman?"

"No: a lady."

"In this city?"

"Yes."

"Was it attached to the bird's——?"

(Interrupting me,) "Round its darling neck."

"I want to keep the bird, and still I dislike to confine it."

"I but borrowed the bird, to hide my spirit in. It will seek the element of heaven, even though its door be closed."

"I must not try to keep it, then?"

"I *shall ever* be more or *less*, in and *through it:* it is my earth *symbol*. For that you may keep it a day or two."

"And when it takes wing, will you not afterward occasionally bring it back?"

"Indeed, I will come to thy couch, through the dove."

The white-winged messenger is very gentle—evidently a domestic bird—but is restive under restraint; and I see I must very shortly set it free. And so endeth, for the present, this new, romantic and instructive chapter of Modern Spiritual History.

J. R. ORTON.

CHAPTER XIX.

"And behold a shaking, and the bones came together, bone to its bone." EZEKIEL.

My acquaintance with this character, so well known from his remarkable feats with his own skeleton, began in the dissecting room of the Medical College of Philadelphia, in the winter of 1857–58. He was a remarkably well developed muscular subject, hence was desirable for dissection.

As one of the class, I chose the right arm and corresponding parts as my share of the cadaver; in order the better to distinguish my portion from the others, I took my scalpel and leisurely wrote my name on the skin of the negro (which, in the absence of a slate, answers all its purposes, as a slight scratch on the cuticle leaves a white mark) and began figuring up some private accounts on the thorax, when suddenly the table tipped and raps called for the alphabet, the result of which was,

"You needn't make a memorandum book of my hide."

"Who are you?" I asked.

"Cornelius Winne."

"How long since you left this body?"

"I don't know."

"What was your disease—can you tell me?"

"They sade I had the tremens." (delirium tremens.)

In process of dissection, we found undoubted proof that such was the case. From the illness of the janitor and the mildness of the weather the subject was neglected, and for want of neatness, it was anything but desirable to continue our work, and a number of the students abandoned it. I found myself, therefore, often alone with my new acquaintance and we chatted together freely. One evening as I was dissecting off the integuments of the palmar surface of the hand, the hand closed suddenly on the knife, and held it firmly. I was startled not a little, for I had no desire for the prostrate carcass to assume animation in such a dilapidated condition. The flexor muscles of the fore-arm were completely severed, and I was aware that the manifestation was purely spiritual. After this I left the body with the instrument still grasped, and the next morning found it in the same place, except that the fingers were somewhat extended, leaving me to continue my dissections.

With the consent of my late partner, Dr. J. R. Orton, I herewith subjoin the account of the manifestations by the spirit Winne, as communicated by him to the "New York Dispatch," which statement is perfectly correct in all its particulars.

In due time the dissection was completed; and the bones, from their size and perfectness, formed a desirable professional acquisition. Again Cornelius made his presence known to Dr. R., and expressed the desire that he should become the proprietor of his skeleton. Dr. R. replied, that as the five were to cast lots for the possession, it was not at all probable that the wish could be gratified. The spirit then told him to draw first, and the bones should be his. Accordingly at the distribution he drew first, and won the prize.

On graduating, in March, Dr. R. removed the bones to his wife's father's—Mr. Simeon Arnold—at the city of Hartford, where he deposited them in the garret; and leaving his wife there, who was in delicate health, and has since died, came on himself to New York, when we became associated together professionally. Soon after, at my request, in his transits back and forth, he brought on to the city the four bones of the pelvis, and the three long bones of one of the arms, which were deposited in a closet in our office, then at No. 58 West Twelfth street.

It soon became evident that those bones possessed the faculty of motion, or, at least, that they were moved without any visible human agency. I occasionally heard a rattling in the closet, which, though I did not suppose it was made by the bones, I could refer to nothing else. At that time, Dr. R. slept mostly at the office, and sometimes, when detained late, as a matter of convenience, I remained and lodged with him. One night, on retiring, we had scarcely touched the pillows, when a loud blow resounded on the wall above us, and a missive of considerable size, fell on the bed. I arose and lit the gas, and found it to be one of the hip-bones.

"You here, Darkey?" inquired Dr. R.

Three loud raps in affirmation, were at once heard on the floor.

"If we had those bones all here and wired together," said Dr. R., "I believe he could walk them across the room."

This was also affirmed. I replaced the bone in the closet, which we had locked just before getting into bed, and we heard nothing more from them that night."

Not long after this, in the middle of the day, as some company had just passed out of the office, Dr. R. arose from his chair, when I noticed something strike him gently on the back, which looked about the size and color of a stick of pine wood, such as is used in making fires in a grate. It fell on the floor, and proved to be the large bone of the fore-arm. I was looking directly at Dr. R. at the time, and saw no motion by which he could have produced the phenomenon, had he desired. He was not nearer than ten or twelve feet to the closet, and had not been there since the departure of the company. The missile came from that direction, and there was no window or door in that part of the room, through which a third party could have thrown it. The closet door was found closed, but not locked nor latched; and Dr. R. and myself were the only persons present.

Dr. Redman's arm was immediately influenced, and he wrote:

"Well, Doctors, I'm in an odd country, and I kind o' like your place here. Don't be alarmed. I was thinking, as the old preacher used to say, how wonderfully we're made, when I let the old arm drop.

Your sarvent,

CORNELIUS WINNE."

"Cornelius," said I, "could you not bring the rest of those bones from Hartford?"

"I'll play h-- with them yet. They're mine, ain't they?" was his reply in writing, as before.

"Yes; but you are willing we should use them, are you not?"

"Yes. Oh, I wouldn't have them under the sod for a ten spot."

"Well, could you bring them on from Hartford?"

"Yes."

"And not drop and lose any of them by the way?"

"I'm off. Good bye!"

Very shortly after this occurrence, one afternoon—the 6th or 7th of May—the large pelvis bone called the *sacrum*, suddenly flew across the office, and struck heavily against the wall near the door. This happened the moment after two gentlemen—Capt. S. and Mr. G. of the St. Nicholas---had passed out—the very instant that the door was closed after them. Dr. R. and myself were the only persons remaining in the office: we were both near the door where we had bidden our guests good day; and the closet door was found shut.

On the 11th of May, at 3 P.M., as Dr. R. and myself were alone in the office, without any previous warning, a vertebra, or joint of the backbone, dropped down gently into a chair almost directly in front of me. The chair was standing nearly in the centre of the room: Dr. R., at the time, was in full view, a dozen feet or more from the chair at my left; and the bone by its motion seemed to have made a perpendicular descent, and remained lodged in the chair. I could discover no physical means of accounting for the occurrence.

On the following day—May 12th----at about eleven A. M., Dr. R. and myself passed out of the office together into the street, and had proceeded about a rod from the gate, walking abreast, when another vertebra came down with great force, eight or ten feet in front of us, on the walk, bounding twelve or fifteen inches high, as it struck. As I picked it up, I remarked, that I should have supposed it would have been broken by the force of the blow. As near as I could determine, I caught sight of this bone in its descent, while it was yet in the air, some half a dozen feet higher than my head.

Again on the 14th, as I sat in the office writing a letter, and at the close had just ended a paragraph about the singular appearance of these bones, having spoken of them playfully as brought by Cornelius' Express, two or three persons who had been engaged with Dr. Redman, went out; when another vertebra, from the direction apparently of the top of the door, flew by my face and struck on the floor near me. On taking it up I was surprised to see marked on it with a pencil the words, "C. W.'s Express."

Cornelius at once announced himself by loud raps, and I asked him where he got his pencil.

"Don't you think I've got a pocket?" he replied.

"I didn't calculate you'd get the start of me, and give me an express, without I really had one."

"How do you bring these bones?" I inquired.

"Now, you look here," he replied. "We're getting things in this country, so we are sort of independent. I know I'm a green un, but the folks up here show me how to do it, and so I goes ahead, hey! Can't get the start of me! I heard today that one of my babies was sick, and near to die, or to come here; so I've been making arrangements to go and see the darling; and I'm going soon."

I assured Cornelius that we sympathized with him, at which he exhibited much pleasure.

On the next day, the *dentata*, or second vertebra of the neck, was received, and Cornelius again announced himself. I inquired after the condition of his child. He said it was still living, that the doctor said it had got the scarlet fever, and was in a "carious condition." He furthermore informed us he had nine children. I congratulated him, when he replied:

"They are real gold watches to *me;* every one a hunter chock full of diamonds."

I would here remark, that in all my conversations with Cornelius, which extended beyond a simple question, my usual habit was to write the questions, which were not seen by Dr.

Redman, but were replied to by him, in writing, executed from right to left on the paper and bottom side up.

I expressed the hope to Cornelius, that, as his chances for improvement were now better than formerly, he would make a good use of them, and become a better and a happier man; to which he answered as follows:

"I'd do all the Lord says, if I could get only one *horn* a day. I'd work—my gol! I'd—who's that hollerin? (We informed him it was some one crying vegetables in the street.) Well I'd —do *everything*."

A day or two later, I inquired of him again about his child. He answered:

"I is just told that our poor little Minnie is left; and I is going to see her as soon as she be organized."

He accused me of doubting whether he really brought the bones—nine of the vertebræ and one *scapula*, or shoulderblade, having by this time arrived—to which I replied, that in my position I felt bound to avail myself of every means in my power to test the truth of the phenomena; and that to this end I had questioned Dr. Hare, who had assured me that the phenomena were real. With this he seemed satisfied.

It was true that I had consulted what purported to be the spirit of the late Professor Hare, as to the nature of these occurrences. I had, indeed, privately in writing, asked him through Dr. Redman, whether Dr. R. was not himself, by some contrivance which I had not fathomed, performing a strange series of deceptions; to which a denial was at once made through Dr. R's. hand, he, meanwhile, seeming entirely unconscious of the nature of either the question or the answer.

If, on the other hand, the question is asked, whether I believe that, at the time, I was really communicating with the spirit of Dr. Hare, I reply, that I have no belief about it, having no solid evidence on which to found a belief; but that I was conversing with some intelligent being outside of Dr. Redman, I have no doubt whatever.

Dr. Redman, in his frequent visits to Hartford, examined carefully, from time to time, the state of the bones in the attic, where he had deposited them, and reported to me the results. The vertebræ, as he left them, were strung on a cord in their order, the first and the last ones having been secured with a knot. The articulations and parts which made their appearance in New York, were always found to be missing in Hartford, and were evidently the same. On Dr. R's. first visit to the attic, when he brought away the pelvis and arm bones, as he stated to me at the time, there was considerable commotion manifested among the different parts of the skeleton, the pieces he wanted, receding from his grasp; and it was not until they had retreated under the roof, as far as the space would allow, that he was able to secure them.

On Sunday, the 27th of June, Dr. R., in company with another individual, made an examination of the bones in the garret. The correspondence between the missing members, and those received in New York, was found to agree. On this occasion, movements again occurred with the bones. Dr. R. tied the loose ones together, which seemed to give displeasure, and a rib flew some five or six feet and gave him a blow; and as they left the attic and passed down stairs, a heavy pair of men's shoes, one thrust within the other, was thrown forcibly after them, and passing their heads, struck against the wall.

This incident was referred to by Cornelius, in a conversation I had with him very shortly after. I was inquiring of him about his present mode of life; to which he replied, that he did not have to work now, only to "keep the gardens pretty," but that he had to "keep up a devil of a thinking," and each one had his "reg'lar beat to travel on;" that he had "bleached out white," and had taken another woman for his wife.

I asked him if he liked the new one as well as he did the old one, to which he answered:

"Yes; gol, yes—more so. Well, I guess I live as happy as a young kitten, for the old woman used to scold like new beer; but now I'm with the one I first loved. Ah, Doctor, she's just like a honeysuckle, all full and dropping out."

He said further, that he was mad when Dr. R. tied the bones together, which made him throw the shoes at him; but that he could untie them.

I asked him how far away it was to his present home.

"Well, it took me twenty minutes to come here this morning," he replied. "Well, that's because I don't know how to travel; but it takes some only the snap of your finger. I 'spects its 'bout one hundred miles?"

"Is it above, or below the earth, or what?"

"Well, now ye got me. We always come down, and don't know any other way to get here."

"Do you have flowers, trees, ground, rivers, and birds where you are, and other things such as you used to have here?"

"Well, I 'spects they don't have 'em up yonder, but we have 'em; and I tell you it's just like the place we read of, where all was very good. But, Doctor, I'm awful unhappy, for I did so many sinful things on 'arth."

From this time on, at irregular intervals, the bones continued to arrive; sometimes in the office, at other times in the street and elsewhere. One came down in the yard of a house on Horatio street, where Dr. R. and myself had been together to visit a patient. Another fell on the walk beside us as we were walking on Fourteenth street. Two more came within five minutes of each other on Broadway, near Eighth street. At this last occurrence, which, as also the others, happened in broad day, Dr. R. and myself were walking arm in arm, his left arm being passed through my right, while in his right hand he held a cane. I was habitually on the watch, and kept his hands within the range of my eye, and noted all his motions. While thus walking, a vertebra fell by our feet a little in advance of us, among a crowd of people, several of whom noticed me as I picked it up. Immediately after we crossed to the west side of Broadway, and had gone but a few steps, when another fell in like manner.

Another vertebræ came in an eating saloon on Third Avenue, where Dr. R. and myself had been dining. We finished our dinner and departed, but had proceeded but some eight or ten rods, when Dr. R.'s arm began to shake, and on taking a pencil in his hand, Cornelius addressed me, saying, that he had left one of his bones under my chair at the table. I returned and found it. Dr. R. had not been on that side of the table, and it would have been extremely difficult for him to have placed the vertebræ in the position where I found it without notice on my part. Again a vertebræ made its appearance one night at a private residence on Nineteenth street, where Dr. R. had been spending the evening. A lady of veracity informed me that she accompanied Dr. R. as he came down from the parlors above, to depart; and that when near the door, the vertebræ in question fell in the hall, in a direction as though it had come down the stairway after them.

One night when Dr. R. and myself both slept at the office, at somewhat of a late hour, we put out the gas, and got into bed. Immediately loud raps were heard, three or four at a time, following each other in quick succession, in various parts of the room, which terminated in a reveille, almost a crash on the hearth. The noise was about as loud, and not very dissimilar to what would have been, had a shovel, and perhaps a pair of tongs, fallen together by the grate. I arose and relit the gas, when the raps came on the door; and on examining the door I ascertained that we had neglected to lock it. I mentioned this as the probable cause of this demonstration on the part of Cornelius---for I had no doubt it was he --when three gentle raps were given in reply, and we were not again disturbed.

On another occasion, Dr. R. and myself had been invited out to dine in company with Dr. H. and lady of Philadelphia. The dinner was served at the upper Taylor's Saloon. During the meal some inquiries were made about Cornelius, when I remarked that he was doubtless present and enjoying the dinner with us. This was at once affirmed by a shower of raps. I hinted to him that he might, if he chose, give us a slight touch of his quality, when instantly one side of the marble table at which we were sitting, covered with dishes as it was, tilted half a foot in the air. This being received by us with a burst of laughter, he next gave the table a whirl of one or two feet, when I requested him to desist. This occurred in the midst of a swarm of waiters, and the usual crowd frequenting that eating place at the dining hour, who, if they noticed this disturbance at all, it is presumed, were far from divining its cause.

On numerous occasions I have had Cornelius take hold of me sensibly. At one time I wound my hand in a pocket handkerchief, and secured it with pins, when, on holding it under the table, he pulled the handkerchief off with three or four strong tugs. At another time he worked over my shoe for half an hour or more in an attempt to get it off, during which time he handled my leg to the knee. The weather was warm and the foot sweaty, which made the task a difficult one. He succeeded, however, in drawing it completely off at the heel, but failed at the toe, though the force he there laid out must have equalled, I should think, some ten or fifteen pounds, if not more. These occurrences took place at my office in the evening, but with a good light, and there was no one under the table nor other contrivance by which the results named could have been effected. I have had him touch me repeatedly in broad daylight.

During July and August, Dr. Redman was much of the time at Hartford, in attendance on his wife and child, both of whom were ill. When he was absent from the city the phenomena of the bones ceased. In August, I received from Hartford, by mail, a characteristic letter from Cornelius, written through Dr. Redman's hand, and enclosed with one from himself. Hitherto in transcribing Cornelius' language, I have somewhat amended his orthography; in this I will let him *verbatim et literatim* speak for himself. The letter was as follows:

SECOND SPHERE.

My Friend, Doctor Orton, I s'pose the malo will take a leter for me, as well as it will for Doctor Redmond; at any rate, I'se goin to try it. I used to pay three cents pece for carrying letters when I was with the old woman, and I suppose that's what they ask now; but I'll get this in with one of the Doctor's leters, and that'l be rite. Now I s'pose ye want to no what I'se been 'bout since the doctor's wife, or lady, has been so orful sick. Well, don't fret—the baby's living. That's what the old woman used to say. Well, I ain't going to fret, but to rite all I want to. I used to fret when he was in New York, for such an olmitey lot of fellers use to be there, that Winne didn't get more'n a few minutes to tell a whole hour's full. I fret, too, the other day; I don't no the time, fur I left the old Bull's Eye with the folks, and I s'pose that feller as wates on the old woman is got it for this time.

Wall, as I was sayin', I did fret when I visited a medium in Boston,* some days ago. She was a purty good specimen of a lady, and looked as if she'd make one so happy, I kinder took a liken to her, for she dosen't send a poor feller away, if he hain't got his knowledge-box as full as some. Well, I went thar, and I had to shuv and push sideways, and corner ways, and all sorts o' ways, to get in; for there was the orfulest sights of sperets there; sum just like me, and sum knowd mor'n me; and sum didn't no as much as me.

Well, after pushin' through, I got in; and I was goin' to wate for my turn, when a gentleman they calls Hair † took me by the arm, and says:—"Step up, step up, Kornel, you nede this help mor'n the rest of us." And so he pushed me rite in, and I sed a few words. I tell you, didn't I feel as if I was some? Well, I did.

But what in thunder made the old feller call me Kornel? I aint a Kornel. Well, I s'pose he wanted to 'tract my attention. Well, I luv him; I'd had to stay there—well, I don't know how long. I'll talk to her some more yet.

Oh, I went to a nigger meetin' last nite—not in heaven, but on earth

* Mrs. Covant, connected with the "*Banner of Light.*" At about this time a negro Spirit, calling himself Cornelius Winne, presented himself to Mrs. C., and made a short communication through her.

† The late Professor Hare.

Well, I never! The feller took a verse out of the Bible tc speke on. It was in Second Kings. Kings is in the Bible, I believe. The verse was:

But he sed: Then bring mele, and he cast it in the pot; and he sed, pour out for the people, that they may ete. And there was no harm in the pot.

I lafed rite out loud, when he began to say, the mele was the Word, and the pot was the Bible, and the minister was the one to pour it out; and there was no harm in the pot—that's the Bible. And he sed some folks made pots of their own, and them pots would brake; they were klay, and not stone. Then I lafed again; and I'd like to told him that the pot of the hart was worth all the book pots.

I'd like to tell you all he sed, but you'll get tired, I know you will. Then he prade that the mele that filled the Holi Pot of God's word, might be made bred for all; and that bred be broken by faithful servants of God. And they all hollered out, A-men! a-men! a-men!

I left then, and went to luke after *my teacher*, who is learnin' me how to rite and tork.

Now, Doctor, jest rest easy 'bout my bones, fur I tell you I ain't begun yet. If I can't do it up, then I ain't Winne. I's been countin' them over. Why, how many a feller's got! I didn't know as I had mor'n 'bout twenty, but there's mor'n that in the back bone, else I don't count strate. I used to think it was all one. I'm now going to see that Boston woman. I tell you, if I could only drop one of my bones down there, wouldn't that be a sertifficate fur my identity? I'll *see* what's to be *dun*.

Your sarvant and friend, CORNELE WINNE.

CHAPTER XX.

Cornelius Winne. Lightfoot's Communication Letter from Dr. A. B. Child's.

In July, I think it was, Cornelius first announced that he had got a thigh bone under way, as also the skull, and was having difficulty with them in getting them along. At one time, he informed me, that the *os femoris* or thigh-bone, was temporarily deposited in some woods near Berlin; and at another, that it was similarly secured at a place considerably this side of that town. On examination, both of these bones were found to be missing at Hartford.

On the evening of the 21th of September, having been engaged out, I returned to the office---which was now at 108 Fourth Avenue---at about half-past ten o'clock or a little later. I found Dr. R. in his shirt sleeves, preparing for bed; and contrary from my habit, for I rarely solicited any communication from Spirits, I requested him to sit up to the table for a moment. At first, he objected, as he was partially disrobed, but instantly recalling it, with his customary good nature, complied.

Though I had not Cornelius in my mind at the time, he at once announced himself with loud raps and a good deal of clatter. Suddenly, there was a sound of something striking the floor, and he at once made known---writing through Dr. R.'s hand---that he had delivered another bone. There were two gas jets burning brightly immediately over the table; and passing around to the opposite side from where I was sitting---the one farthest from the windows---I picked up from the floor the long small bone of a leg, known technically as the *fibula*. This brought me facing the open window, at some fifteen or eighteen feet distance, which looked out on a wide piazza and backyard, lower than the piazza by the basement story, and surrounded by a close fence twelve or fifteen feet high. So far as the eye could detect, the piazza and yard were empty; and as the piazza was enclosed with Venetian blinds, only open at points opposite the two windows, and as the two windows, were partly drawn down from the top and partly raised from the bottom, and the clear spaces were considerably impeded with painted shades and gauze curtains festooned within them, and coming together at the top, it would seem quite impossible that anything could be thrown from the yard below, with such precision as to clear the curtains, or in such direction as to cause it to travel two-thirds the length of the office without giving notice of its presence until it struck the floor. A missile projected from the yard could not have been sent in through the lower openings of the windows except by accident, nor through the upper openings without the almost certainty of striking the ceiling overhead.

Yet, while there facing the windows, with the *fibula* in my hand, and Dr. R. sitting directly before me, with his arm on the table, and the office boy, a younger brother of Dr. R., the only other person present, sitting on a sofa in front at my right, also fully in my line of vision, suddenly another and much larger bone whistled through the room from the direction of the windows, passed close by the gas-burners, and about on a level with them, went by my head, and with a curve quite too short for its apparent momentum, fell on the floor almost at my feet. It proved to be the large bone of a human arm, and compared perfectly with the parts of the skeleton already received. Cornelius then announced, that that was all for "to-night," but that we might expect another instalment soon.

The next instalment came, as was promised, on Thursday evening, the last day of September, 1858; and was followed by another on the next day, Friday, the first of October, which, taken together, I am disposed to believe, equal in strangeness and mystery any of the strange phenomena which the world has ever witnessed.

On the evening of the first of those days, at twilight, as Dr. Redman and myself were standing in conversation on the piazza at the rear of the office, a small bone, with a smart blow and rebound, struck on the floor at our feet. It could not have been thrown by him, as I stood directly facing him, nor from any point, as would seem, to strike as it did, aside from the vacant air outside and above the piazza, or perhaps, by a strong propulsion, from the naked ceiling over our heads. It was followed by two or three others in quick succession, when I called to several persons, principally ladies, who were sitting in the office, who at once came out on the piazza to witness the phenomenon. All of us then watched to the best of our ability, for about half an hour, during which time the bones continued to fall at intervals, and as we passed into the office through the hall, more came there, striking some of the ladies; and after all of us were in the office, not excepting Dr. Redman, with the bones spread on the table, one or two more were heard to fall on the piazza, which I went out and secured. Sixteen bones came at this time, principally small bones belonging to the hands and feet, including one *patella*, or kneepan, and one small rib.

At the apparent conclusion of this singular exhibition I drew up the following paper, which the persons present subscribed:

"We certify, that on the evening of the 30th of September, 1858, we were present at the office of Drs. Orton and Redman on Fourth Avenue, when a number of small bones, apparently human---sixteen in all---fell in the hall adjoining said office, and on the piazza in the rear; that they came in parcels of two or three at a time, apparently from a direction above; and some of them on the piazza, when all of us, including Dr. Redman, were standing at the table in the office examining those already received.

Mrs. M. R. TUCKER,
Mrs. J. HAYWARD,
Mrs. J. W. DOW,
A. N. REDMAN,
J. R. ORTON,
G. A. REDMAN."

Cornelius made a demonstration by means of raps on the table, expressive of his pleasure at the success of this crowning effort, when our company departed. They were scarcely gone, however, when the fall of bones re-commenced. This time it was in the office itself, instead of the piazza, which was well lighted with gas, presenting every facility for close observation, and the detection of trickery, had there been any.

I immediately placed myself in the rear part of the room, facing the windows, with Dr. Redman and his brother both in front of me, so that I could see every motion they made, and, at the same time, command the windows, which were the only places through which a projectile could come; both of the doors leading into the office from the hall being closed. Singularly enough, a large part of the bones that now came, dropped in perpendicular lines from the white ceiling above, lodging in chairs, and on the carpet in different parts of the room. Some came, however, swiftly, in nearly horizontal lines, from the direction of the windows; but with all my watchfulness, I was unable to detect any one in its passage through the windows, nor was I able to discern the starting point of any of those that dropped from above. Keeping the whole room as near as possible within the circle of my vision, I would fix my eyes on the open spaces above the window sashes, and hold them there for two or three minutes, and the moment I removed them, a bone would come from the direction of the very point I had been guarding. It was the same with the ceiling. Turning my eyes in such position that its whole surface would be reflected upon them, together with any intervening object, and, at the same time, being careful not to lose sight of the lower parts of the room, I would keep watch for several minutes together, without discovering any thing on the wall, or in the air, larger than a fly, when, on turning my eyes away, a bone would instantly drop, perhaps at my very feet. Fourteen bones, similar in size and character to the others, and occupying fifteen or twenty minutes in the delivery, constituted this second instalment; making thirty bones in all, received on that single evening.

Astonishing as were the occurrences of the evening of the 30th of September, those of the following day—October 1st—in broad daylight, were fated to throw them altogether in the shade. During the morning, Dr. R. and myself were occupied. Between eleven and twelve, however, our company having departed, we found ourselves alone; Dr. R., his brother Alexander, who filled the place of office boy, and myself, being the only persons present. At this time the bones again began to fall, and the manifestation, occurring at intervals, was extended over a period of about three hours.

On this occasion, the two office doors, both leading into the same hall, were closed, and the open windows and piazza, as on the evening before. Aside from these two windows, there was no access for a missile to the room. The bones fell all around us—on the floor, in chairs, and on the table—some flying swiftly and forcibly from the direction of the windows, and some falling perpendicularly from the ceiling above. My efforts at watching the window and ceiling, were attended with no better success than on the evening before. I failed entirely in getting a glimpse of even a shadow of one of these projectiles, until it was clearly within the window two or three feet, or in mid air between the ceiling and the floor.

The bones that were now delivered, consisted of the large bones of the heel, another *patella*, another small rib, and a variety of other pieces belonging to the hands and feet. Finally, in an interval, as we had gathered the bones and placed them on the table, near the centre of the room, and were all three of us standing round it, examining them, suddenly there dropped down in our midst, as from the ceiling above, a small muslin bag containing *sixty one* of the smallest bones of the human body. It struck on the table with such force as to indent it, and came down immediately before my face—much nearer me than to either of the others.

At this time I was standing some twelve feet from the windows, with my back toward them. The table, over which I was slightly leaning, spread about five feet in front of me, and on the side at my right hand, stood Dr. Redman, and on the one at my left, Alexander; both, with every motion they could make, directly under my eye, and both stooping over the table and engaged with me in an examination of the bones: and that either of them could have produced this phenomenon, or that a third party could have entered the room through the windows, or otherwise, and dropped this sack among us, in broad daylight, and secured a retreat without detection, I apprehend, is not a supposable case. The bag was about fifteen inches long by seven or eight in width, and not tied; and Dr. R. recognized it as the one in which the small bones were deposited at Hartford.

There was now a pause of an hour or two in the exhibition. After dinner I wrote a couple of brief letters, and stepped out in the street to drop them in a U. S. letter-box. On my return, I passed in at the front door, and along the common hall, a distance of twenty-five or twenty-seven feet, to the door of the office. There was no one in the hall, and no one on the stairs, which were wholly passed by several feet before reaching the door. I placed my hand on the knob, and was in the act of pushing the door open, when there fell across my arms, in a seeming perpendicular descent, the *os femoris* or thigh-bone of a man—the largest bone of the body, and in this instance measuring over eighteen inches in length. It came swiftly, but without hurting me in the least, knocked an apple I was eating out of my hand, pitched forward through the partly open door, and fell on the floor in the office. Redman I found lying on the sofa where I had left him a few minutes before, and his brother at the other end of the room.

Picking up the enormous bone, I proceeded with it to the table, and both the Redmans came forward to examine it. Suddenly we were startled by a prolonged crash in the farther corner of the office—the one farthest from the windows, and farthest from the doors—when on going there to examine into the cause, I found a *tibia*, the second largest bone of the leg, lying there on the carpet; having apparently, in its descent, first struck a clothes-press standing near, and thence fallen on a violin case, and from that passed to the floor. This finished the programme for the day, *one hundred and nine bones* having reached us in this surprising manner, within about eighteen hours of time.

During the occurrences of the day, Cornelius had several times announced himself, and manifested his satisfaction by loud and repeated raps, and a few words spelled out by the alphabet, or written through Dr. R.'s hand. Now I sat down at the table to have a little conversation with him. His first explosion was as follows:

"Ha! ha! ha! No more doubts now! The world will believe by and by. Oh, this is a holiday to me."

In reply to a question he answered:

"I cannot bring any more to-day. I have done the best day's work since I came to the spirit-land. They tell about dry bones—pshaw! they are nothin' to these. Ye see I was mitey keerful not to hurt you."

I asked him if any of the bones had been brought from Hartford that day; to which he replied:

"Ye know I've had the thy (thigh) bone some time. Yes, some of the small ones."

"When did you start with the bag?" inquired I.

"Yesterday morning."

"When did you bring the thigh-bone into the house?"

"I brought the thy-bone in with you."

"What, when I came in from the street?"

"Yes."

"Did any one see it in the street?"

"Yes; but they tho't some one throwed it, it came so quick."

"Did you bring these bones alone?"

"No. There were one hundred and two of us, all interested. Ain't we a happy party now, hey? But only about twenty three of them relly worket."

"Did you bring the bag alone?"

"I'll bet I did. I wanted the creme of the thing."

"Did you bring the thigh-bone alone?"

"Two of us, one on each end—for it's a mitey big thing, and I can't stere it alone. Well, I'll leave now, and let ye think over it. Good-bye—I am going to rest a few days."

"Your sarvent, Cornele."

With this culmination of the extraordinary affair the manifestation substantially ceased. Dr. Redman informs me that two vertebræ have since arrived, when I was not present; but Cornelius says that the matter has set the world so much by the ears, and pointed so many ill-natured suspicions on Dr. Redman, that he is afraid to go on. The skull is yet missing, having disappeared from Hartford, and not having been received in New York.

I have thus given the substantial facts connected with these wonderful manifestations, so far as my memorandums or recollections supply them; and the world must do with them whatever it please. I have never felt at liberty to conceal them in any particular; and, accordingly, from the first, have spoken of them freely to all who have had the curiosity to inquire. One thing, however, I should add. During the first weeks of the occurrence of the phenomena, Dr. Redman visited Hartford, as his family were there, about once a week. His habit was to leave New York on Saturday evening and return on Monday. His baggage, in passing back and forth, consisted simply of a medium-sized traveling bag, of India-rubber cloth, which, as the key was lost, was not locked. With this bag, as also with the pockets of his duster, and other garments, I took liberties, which neither our familiar relation, nor anything else, aside from the necessities of the case in my peculiar position, would have justified, and which are not even yet fully justified to my own mind. I examined his baggage and effects, from time to time, especially on his returns from Hartford, and informed myself of the nature of the freight he carried.

On one occasion I supposed I had discovered a clue to the mystery. I found a vertebra in his traveling bag, inside of the lining, which was ripped or torn. I did not remove it, but kept track of it, and he transported it back to Hartford with him, once, and I think twice, apparently without having noticed it, when, in our change of offices, wishing to pack some things in the bag, I took it out myself. Meanwhile the bones continued to come; and whether this one fell from the shelf in the closet into the bag, which generally lay on the floor beneath, at no very great distance, or found its way there in some other manner, I know not. This much, however, I feel called on to say for Dr. Redman. After a full opportunity of witnessing the various manifestations made through him, extending over a period of months, I have never discovered any indication of trick or deception about them. The raps have come freely at all times, day and night; when he was in bed, as well as when he was sitting at his table. The table itself has tipped and rocked, when he was in contact with it, and when he was not. I have sat twelve feet away from the table when he could have had no suspicion I was watching him, and when I had a full view of his legs, and it is certain that the movements of the table were not produced by any action of his lower extremities. Nor was the table in our office—which was one he commonly used—confined to any particular spot on the floor, so that it might have been moved by concealed machinery, but it would act as well in one place as another. I have seen it rise several inches from the floor, and there sustain itself for a brief time, rocking like a boat on a wave; and I have seen it dance, when no one was touching it, keeping time to a hand-organ in the street, for eight or ten minutes together.

If any one should desire to know whether I really believe that the bones in question were brought from Hartford by Spirits, I reply: I am unable as yet to devise any other theory which will cover the facts. The facts are these, and are to be disposed of in some way, or dropped as inexplicable. On the other hand, as it is impossible to establish a spiritual identity, I do not consider it settled that the Spirit who performs these feats, or is the leader in them, is the veritable Cornelius Winne who once inhabited those bones, although I incline to believe it is he, and see no reason why it should not be, as well as another. J. R. ORTON.

From the Banner of Light, I extract the following, which is one instance of the many, where Cornelius has appeared to circles throughout the country and given indubitable proofs of his spirit presence and progress:

COLLINSVILLE, CONN., June 14, 1858.

MESSRS. EDITORS.—I have noticed with much interest several communications in your paper in regard to the bones of Cornelius Winne; the "antics" cut up by them and their curious migrations, in violation of the commonly-received notions of gravitation, &c.

I will state to you a little circumstance which occurred at

one of our circles in this village. It was on the evening of May 20th, at the house of Mr. P——. While eight or ten of us were sitting at the table, Mrs. P—— became entranced, and appeared to be somewhat frightened, and tried to shrink back from an unpleasant spirit controlling her. In a moment after she exclaimed---" Oh, it is a great negro !" and described him very accurately, (according to the description given in the Banner,) he saying at the same time, " My name is Winne." The medium was made to perform remarkable feats of strength. She would smite the table repeatedly with her fist with sufficient force to break the bones of the hand, in a normal condition. Her arms were then extended, and made so rigid that a strong man was unable to bend them, although several present tried it. The medium is a small woman---only weighing ninety pounds. The spirit described the manner and time of his death, the moving of the bones, &c., and further said, he would allow the doctors to put his bones altogether, and then he would walk his skeleton around the room, and astonish the people with his wonderful movements. He said he should then pull his skeleton in pieces and scatter some of the bones where the doctors could not find them. He then went through the motions---pulling at the finger joints---and showed us how he would scatter the bones in all directions.

The above manifestation seemed more remarkable, when the medium assured us that she never had read anything about " Cornelius Winne," or his antics with his bones.

Yours in the bonds of truth, and hopeful progression,

D. B. Hale.

From time to time, I may say almost daily, I have some message from this spirit. He appears gradually ascending the scale of progress, and it affords me much pleasure and gratification to be enabled to assist him in his efforts to become wiser and better.

The manifestations recorded here, have caused much discussion among different classes, both spiritualists and non-spiritualists, and in no place has it been so thoroughly debated as in the New York Conference. It is only surprising to me, that after the various remarkable exhibitions of spiritual strength, as have been recorded from time to time, this should receive so little welcome. Still the efforts made to discover collusion on my part, have fallen ineffectively: watching my transit back and forth from Hartford during my wife's illness; sending deputies (what honorable espionage!) to my home, there to glean, if possible, from the family some, if even trivial, indications of my personal intervention in the matter; having failed to accomplish the desired end, the subject has been dropped, temporarily perhaps, to be referred to again in the future, when nothing better can be found to feed the vindictive wrath of some splenetic, disappointed individual. During all the contumely, that has been poured forth, I have been perfectly passive; and, although friends, who have been exasperated for me, have thought

> "My blood hath been too cold and temperate,
> Unapt to stir at these indignities,"

I have taken, and shall continue to preserve, as my motto,

Mens conscia rectæ,

and feeling the full force of these words, will not be drawn from my state of quiescence. I was promised by Cornelius, that *all* the bones should be brought, and that after they were wired together, he would *move* them about, that the public might see and know his power; but his reason for not fulfilling this phase of his remarkable feats, is given in his own words, thus:

DERE DOCTOR—

These fokes are makin a terrible fus about my cummin back, and tho' I knowed it wouldn't do you any good at the start, I see I am doin' you more hurt nor good. I have tended the Conference whar they tork of all of us up here; but they don't do no good—they kill themselfs, and the truth, and us sperets and ebry thin that is good; and they do no good at all. Good sperets won't go thar, and I won't: so if I don't do you no good by bringin my old mortal bones here, I'm goin to quit, so I'll bring you a few more and then I'm done, its thar own folt if I don't du mure. Give my luve to the other doctor, and beleve me Your sarvant,

CORNELE.

A few more bones were delivered after this, the last coming Dec. 15th, 1858; since then I have received much from him and continue so to do; but as sufficient space has been given to this account, I withhold his other communications.

In almost every circle of Spiritualists, we find instances of spirits appearing who, while on the earth sphere, were total strangers to all present, who beg the privilege of communicating. I have seen this prayer, (even in my own circles) refused by many: when alone, I am ever ready to afford all intelligences an opportunity of making known their wishes through my hand. For, in several cases, by giving unenlightened spirits a channel, through which to express their feelings, and receive advice and encouragement, their progress is greatly assisted.

Spirits, who while in this sphere, were (to use a church term,) "totally depraved," pass into the higher spheres with scarcely a ray of hope, and almost ignorant of the means of progress; these derive much consolation in returning, and expressing their regrets for ills done in the body; and it is not uncommon to find an inherent determination to persevere in their evil course, even after entering spirit life, until reason arouses a feeling of remorse, and, on receiving our sympathy, a gleam of hope is awakened, an aspiration after a purer life kindled, which bid them strive upward.

A happy instance of this kind was illustrated in the progress of the spirit Lightfoot, who was executed about forty years since, at East Cambridge, Mass., for highway robbery and murder; he was a desperate and determined character, as evinced by his first communications, which were certainly too profane for publication. His ideas of progress were exceedingly limited, but by the kindness and sympathy of Dr. A. B. Child, he afterwards expressed a desire to grow in knowledge and wisdom. Arrangements were made by the Doctor, for regular meetings for his especial benefit, the mediums being Mrs. John S. Adams and myself—it was during these sessions that Lightfoot first met his spirit mother, whose love kindled in his benighted soul a keen desire for a higher life. The following is a portion of the dialogue between them:

Lightfoot—"Where, where is my mother? I want to talk with her."

Mother—"Your mother is here; she has a star that will pierce you."

Lightfoot—"Mother, mother, speak to me."

Mother—"Take away the cloud; I will grow calm; you shall come to me."

Lightfoot—"Oh, how I love to meet thee here; let me hold thee by the hand; there is a sweet perfume, my mother, that rises from thy spirit breath. Oh, give me one word from thy progressive life. Mother, do, dear mother."

Mother—"Sweet and calm as the evening breezes, are the joys I would bring. Live nearer me, child of my heart; lay thy aching head upon my breast; closer, closer come. I am waiting for thee. Look above thee, and see myriad spirits waiting to convey thee home; long lost, long absent one. A mother's heart still clings with fondest emotion, and ever shall my wings of affection fly around my flower, broken from its parent stem. Blossom, hasten to thy bower of happiness. Blighted by sin, come, fly, I call, I beseech—come, come, hopeful, erring one; hasten to these arms. Oh, my God! who can make the parent heart forget!"

Lightfoot—"I advance towards thee, mother; reach down thy hand, and let me kiss the rising virtue that emanates from thy form. Methinks I see thee handing to my thirsty soul the nectar of life eternal.

Oh, come, *come*, COME to me, and let my head rest upon thy bosom, and my hand from thee gather the fruit of progression. Thou hast yet the feelings of a mother; and though low has fallen a leaf from thy stock, yet will there ever remain a silent pulsation of gratitude to thee. I am rising, I am rising."

Mother—(Addressing the circle.) "Turn away the gaze of the curious; let pity come and shed her tears, for the lost one is once more folded to the heart of a fond mother.

Hope, hope has drawn away the dark curtain, and my child is unveiled to my view. We have met as thousands more shall meet. Oh, give me angel flow of words to breathe out gratitude. Think you that I was happy when sorrow wafted her cold breeze around my child in darkness, unfolded in error, and blossomed in sin? Did an angel mother not weep for him? Oh, let him come and anchor on the ocean of hope. By your united efforts you have brought him to me. Oh turn him not away. My lost lamb is called home. He hears these glorious accents. Oh, the gushing, bursting, swelling joy that keeps within my soul! Oh! give him spirit wings of faith to bear it on the brighter forms.

Seest thou the path o'erspread with flowers by angel-hands? and from angel-tread a fragrance shall ascend to fill your souls. We are grasping heaven's joys; we are nearing our heavenly home: we are blended in sympathy, shrouded in one mantle of hope.

I love you all; a mother's joy is full. Oh, let it ring; oh, let angels echo the glad tidings; oh, let it ring on, *on* to eternity."

Lightfoot.—"It was dark; a gloomy sorrow hung over my spirit when I went to a spirit-land. No ray of sunshine lit the darkened portals of my heart. My mother was lost to me. Alone did I wander over the dark prairies of the spirit-world till I came to earth; and here I have met friends; and here I would express my gratitude. Here, while wandering still in darkness, I saw a star; 'twas dim at first; in it I saw a *mother's love.* I saw the sweet smile of recognition, and now the arms of *my* MOTHER twine close around me."

Mother.—"Earth shall yet hear all my gratitude. It shall hear a mother's joy; page after page shall be inscribed. His life, oh, what a blank! These eager arms have caught him; these heart-throbs pillow his head again; and a mother's arms of love now cradle him to repose. Long did he rove, an undiscovered star. Distance, not love, divided us. In shadowy dreams, in phantoms wild, I used to stand beside him. Now no longer hope comes in the dream, but reality has fired my soul and clothed it, and has brought me back my wayward child. Our threads of life are thickly twining now; he grows within my soul; eyes of affection now bathe his soul with the dews of a mother's tenderness, twining around him. Was he once dark? Oh, tell me not that! The fountain-source of love has the shadow and the light. The parent stem will claim the blighted leaf, will own the decaying buds. He is mine, restored to me. If thanks will recompense, my soul would speak in volumes."

Lightfoot.—"Mother, we will place the dew drop within the flower that blooms within the heart of him who first lent to my soul the gushings of progression. Let us hie away, and give him thanks. See, all are pleased with this pure thought. 'Twill tempt his brother to do likewise; to pluck from the dark pit of misery a blighted soul. Let us press our spirit thanks upon his brow; for by his kind hand I now repose upon progression's bosom; by his kind words I gained the smile from thee; by his friendly look I learned that you were near. He taught me, mother dear, that the same motives he had towards me came from my mother.

Then let us go, no longer stay,
We'll put one flower there;
Let's go, let's go, no longer stay,
We'll raise for him a prayer—

That he may learn to aid others as he has aided me; that he may learn to water still the fading flowers upon the shores of life, and cease not to give them drink while there is the least greenness to the stock. Already I see him proffering to another blighted one a friendly hand. The flower openeth its tender leaves, and its petals receive his kindness as the rose receiveth the dews from heaven. O, could I learn the use of words, that I might express with glowing language the gratitude within my soul!"

A spirit purporting to be James Raymond of Bowling Green, Kentucky, was *among* the first, who presented himself to me for development. He came unsolicited, and, I must say, often to my great annoyance, for his uncouth messages and physical manifestations were any thing but agreeable ; when a more developed party was offering words of consolation to a visitor, he would frequently in the very midst of a communication insert his own originalities. For instance :

"The evening prayers, that made our fireside *cheerful*, were not spent in vain, for the sincere desire, whether expressed or unexpressed, is like the ('dried tail of a cod-fish unfit to wag,') fragrance of the *finer flower unperceived*, but rising to the heavens."

The above is an extract from a communication to a lady, in which the undeveloped spirit of Raymond inserted his voluntary contribution, and in many instances did he render ridiculous, what was otherwise soul-stirring and sublime ; until by patient endeavors, I turned his mind toward progress. He stated in his first communication, which is too obscene to be published, that he committed suicide by poison, after being convicted of a crime, that had caused sentence of death to be pronounced upon him. I asked if it were murder, he answered "No." Further than that I could not ascertain.

By daily communication, I introduced him to other spirits, who assisted him upward, and now he rejoices in the prospects of a happy future, and like Lightfoot, is active in aiding his fallen comrades to rise. Ann Merrick, the heroine of many spiritual battles with mortals, is another instance of the development of a spirit through the assistance derived from earthly friends; once we blushed at her utterances, and the written communications from her were destroyed as soon as received; and now to use her own words, "She has wiped the filth of years from her *spirit's* visage, and feels happy that she can look both spirits and mortals in the face." Too little attention is given to this class of our phenomena. I am satisfied, as we progress, we are able to bestow on spirits below us what we have received from those (whether mortal or spirit) in a more advanced state of progression.

LETTER FROM DR. A. B. CHILD.

On the 7th of March, 1855, a spirit came to me through Mrs. J. S. Adams, manifesting great aversion to everything we call good. I read to him the dialogue formerly given by Lightfoot and his mother; after which reading, he manifested great penitence, but did not give his name. Two evenings after, while with a large company of friends, including Dr. Redman, he, without any previous knowledge of the interviews I had with Mrs. Adams, was seized by some influence, and wrote:

"I am the spirit that communicated with you last evening, and the evening before, through Mrs. Adams.

My name is De Soto. I first discovered the Mississippi River. I traversed the western wilds, and trod many fair hearts beneath my sinful feet. The waters of the Mississippi washed away many stains that by me were left upon its peaceful banks. The wild flower hung its head, to see my wicked heart unroll its carnal appetite. The waters murmured as I thrust from the bosom of many a harmless one, the germ of purity that is wont to grow there. The winds heaved a sigh, as, with a wicked heart, I made the widow, and multiplied the orphan children. My ears were dull to hear; my eyes were blind to see; my heart refused entrance to one pure motive. All within was one volcano of impure feelings towards the unwary and innocent.

I have sought for water to quench my thirst, ever since I placed my weary feet upon the sandy desert of the spirit land. Clouds of dust filled my spirit-nostrils, and the burning sands scorched the soles of my feet until I found in thee an oasis where I could cool my parched tongue, and rest my weary body.

The dialogue* you read me, placed the rainbow of hope in the skies to betoken the coming pleasure."

From time to time various messages were received from him, and a gradual and pleasing improvement was obvious. One or two of his last messages may indicate the evident change from the character of his first communications, which were indeed void of all hope or happiness.

Addressing me, he says:

"You twinkle like a star that's seen on earth, as you are seen by angel eyes in heaven.

Each kind deed that you render to those who were once like myself, adds a new blossom to the already gathering wreath, which spreads its fragrance now on the breezes of the spirit-land. While I retrace my past experience, I can see that

* Dialogue between Lightfoot and his mother is here referred to.

while I was writhing in hellish agony you brought the first cooling drop to my parched tongue. When flames of despair writhed around my soul, you first put a blossom of hope within my reach. If the light of progression can reach other souls, if the morning of progressive life can dawn on other darkened spirits, O, stay it not, but make it flow along in mighty waves, in bounding billows, and fill the world with joy and beauty. Your ransom shall be when you pass to the spirit-world. Those you have aided in the ways of eternal life will stand with open arms and bursting hearts of gratitude to receive you. While thou art mortal, receive the thanks of mortality. Nature will thank thee for what thou hast done for me. Each flower that you pass, its fragrance will bless you; the first ray of light that drives darkness from thy chamber at morning will bring thee a blessing; the moon shall smile on thee through thy window when thou art resting on thy pillow, and then she'll whisper words of thankfulness for me. Even the whistling winds shall bring thee echoes of our gratitude. The morning sun, the plaintive notes of nature's songsters, the rippling waves, and the dew that falleth on each humble flower, shall all sing to thee as thou dost pass them by; for as thou dost help one of God's creatures, God through his works will bless you.

I seek now to aid the pilgrim through the darkened valleys of mortality. When I can picture to the erring one my past career, and reflect to him my future, it gives me joy. Like the waters that fall from some lofty point, I throw my sprays upon the noonday sun, and cast a rainbow upon the unprogressed, that they may feast upon its beauteous colors; that they may see that there is an arm outstretched from on high, ever ready to assist in cropping the thorny limbs from the tree of mortal life; that they may see the garden of truth, and walk therein. Many a flower yet blooms unplucked, waiting for some ready hand to convey its fragrance to the soul. O, that I could gather from the fields of spirit-life some blossoms of purity; O, that I could press their leaves within the book of mortal remembrance, and compel the possessor to cast one lingering glance upon the purity thereof.

My wish for the progress of others is growing stronger and stronger. As each throb of my spirit heart is telling to me my destiny, the love for those below seems to be my every wish. I long to throw some cable to those who are struggling in the waters of infamy, that they may grasp thereat, and safely bring their forms to the shores of brotherly love. I seek some ray of penetrating light to enlighten the dark recesses of their spirits. As each ripple of progression's waves echoes on my ear, as each flower in yonder valley speaks to me of its Creator and his designs, it but renews and strengthens my ardor, to give my fellow mortals a taste of the waters from the well-spring of eternal life, love and wisdom. There is a crown of rejoicing for each, whose diamonds sparkle in the sun of truth, and whose surface reflects the smile of Deity. He that hath obtained this crown, obtains the smiles of his God. As I grasp each thought of future happiness, it but brings me nearer to where I can gain that crown, and press to my spirit bosom the smiles of nature's only teacher, Father, God. Each thought, that I express to you, but adds to my hope of becoming the possessor of that gem of gems. Each aspiration, whether given to you or kept within my own sphere of thought but shortens the distance between eternal happiness and me.

Roll on, roll on, thou mighty river! Let the dashing spray from thy banks moisten the hearts of mortality. I saw thee once in all thy glory, when nought but craggy cliffs and bending trees hung o'er thy shores; when the hungry wolves prowled round our fragile tents; and when burning thirst for blood, preyed upon my sinful form.

Roll on, thou mighty prince of rivers! Methinks I see upon thy banks Progression: how sweet, O! how sweet, it is to me. When first I knew Progression's features, she told me, she had conversed with a darkened brother, whose evil ways were but a shadow of mine. Should thy clear waters have reflected upon their surface another image like mine, O! give you him a lesson; ope thy book of nature, and let each rippling wave speak forth in accents of purity its mission, to teach the benighted heart to live. Let there come a smile from thy countenance, O, Mississippi wave! and when the moon lendeth to thee her shining features, cast thou a reflection therefrom into the soul of the wanderer. Wash, O waters! from thy banks the stain that I have left thereon. Frown not for ever, for I have been broken. Let me clasp within my spirit hand thy forgiveness, and blot out from thy memory the hellish evils, that were perpetrated upon thy banks a few centuries ago.

DE SOTO.

I trust should he present himself at other circles, everything will be done to aid him in the desire, which he now evinces, for Progression.

And here, dear reader, we part—ere doing so, may I express the wish, that in the foregoing pages you have found some encouragement (if a Spiritualist) to continue faithful, if an inquirer, to investigate.